Praise for
Social Media ROI

"Blanchard is demanding. He won't allow you to flip through this book, nod your head, and leave. If you're in, you're going to have to invest to get your rewards."

—**Chris Brogan**, president of Human Business Works

"Social media isn't inexpensive; it's different expensive. The human effort required to do it right is significant, and not knowing precisely how social media helps your business and how to gauge that progress is a dereliction of duty. In *Social Media ROI*, Blanchard provides the missing playbook for sensible, sustainable, profitable social communication. It's about time."

—**Jay Baer**, coauthor of *The NOW Revolution: 7 Shifts to Make Your Business Faster, Smarter, and More Social*

"*Social Media ROI* gets down to the heart of the matter: How will social communications positively impact my organizational goals? Olivier takes us through a journey starting from the start, creating a strategy to achieve objectives, and in turn, the means to measure return on investment. If you want to get serious about online communications, you can't go wrong with *Social Media ROI*."

—**Geoff Livingston**, author of *Welcome to the Fifth Estate* and *Now Is Gone*

"Olivier explains the intricacies of building a social media–influenced company for every layman to understand. It is important to understand reach, attention, and influence for social media ROI. This is the book to help with that understanding."

—**Kyle Lacy**, principal at MindFrame (yourmindframe.com) and author of *Branding Yourself*

"Ladies and gentlemen, the social media code has officially been cracked. In *Social Media ROI*, Blanchard reveals how companies can apply the massive power of social media to achieve equally massive results. Incredibly practical, yet supremely enjoyable, this book offers a clear roadmap to growing your revenue in the dizzying world of tweets and retweets, likes and shares, connections and comments."

—**Sally Hogshead**, author of *Fascinate: Your 7 Triggers to Persuasion and Captivation*

"If you know Olivier, you know he goes beyond the bullshit. He 'gets it.' This book will put you in the mindset to successfully plan and achieve real business objectives with social media. It's a hard fact that good business decisions depend on real results. Olivier avoids the fluff with clear-cut ideas that will help you produce results."

—**Brandon Prebynski**, social media strategist

SOCIAL MEDIA ROI

Managing and Measuring
Social Media Efforts
in Your Organization

Olivier Blanchard

800 East 96th Street,
Indianapolis, Indiana 46240 USA

Library of Congress Cataloging-in-Publication Data is on file.

Copyright © 2011 Pearson Education, Inc.

ISBN-13: 978-0-7897-4741-9
ISBN-10: 0-7897-4741-3
Fourth Printing September 2011

Editor-in-Chief
Greg Wiegand

Senior Acquisitions Editor
Katherine Bull

Development Editor
Leslie T. O'Neill

Managing Editor
Kristy Hart

Project Editor
Betsy Harris

Copy Editor
Bart Reed

Indexer
Erika Millen

Proofreader
Language Logistics

Publishing Coordinator
Cindy Teeters

Book Designer
Anne Jones

Compositor
Nonie Ratcliff

CONTENTS AT A GLANCE

I SOCIAL MEDIA PROGRAM DEVELOPMENT 1

1 Creating the Social Company 3
2 Aligning Social Media to Business Goals 13
3 Planning for Performance Measurement 29
4 Establishing Clarity of Vision, Purpose, and Execution 41

II SOCIAL MEDIA PROGRAM INTEGRATION 55

5 Understanding How Social Media Plugs into
   the Organization 57
6 The People Principle 71
7 Establishing Social Media Guidelines for the Organization 83
8 Laying the Operational Groundwork for Effective
   Social Media Management 95
9 The New Rules of Brand Communications in the
   Age of Social Media 113

III SOCIAL MEDIA PROGRAM MANAGEMENT 125

10 Listening Before Talking 127
11 Social Media and Digital Brand Management 135
12 Real-Time Digital Support: Fixing Customer Service
   Once and for All 157
13 Social Media Program Management—Putting It
   All Together 173

IV SOCIAL MEDIA PROGRAM MEASUREMENT 191

14 Creating a Measurement Practice for Social Media
   Programs 193
15 ROI and Other Social Media Outcomes 207
16 F.R.Y. (Frequency, Reach, and Yield) and Social Media 239
17 Social Media Program Analysis and Reporting 257
   Afterword 277
   Index 281

TABLE OF CONTENTS

I   SOCIAL MEDIA PROGRAM DEVELOPMENT 1

1   Creating the Social Company 3
    Evolution, Human Nature, and the Inevitable
        Socialization of Business 4
    Moving Beyond Channels: Social Media vs. Social
        Communications 7
    Why Social Media Matters to Business .7
    Influence and Media: Lateral vs. Vertical Forces 9

2   Aligning Social Media to Business Goals 13
    Social Media's Value to the Organization 14
    Differentiating Between Strategy and Tactics 15
    Differentiating Between Goals and Targets 15
    Tying a Social Media Program to Business Objectives 16
    How to Create a Roadmap by Turning Goals into Targets . . .17
    The Top Five Business Functions That Can Be Easily
        Enhanced by a Social Media Program 18
    Sales 18
    Customer Support 20
    Human Resources 22
    Public Relations 23
    Business Intelligence 24
    Social Media for Nonprofits 24
    Outcomes 24
    Member Support 25
    Human Resources 25
    Public Relations 26
    Member Loyalty 26

3   Planning for Performance Measurement .29
    Tools, Methodologies, and Purpose 30
    Selecting Adequate Social Media Measurement Software
        for Your Program 30
    Key Performance Indicator (KPI) 32
    Social Media and Sales Measurement: F.R.Y. 35

4   Establishing Clarity of Vision, Purpose, and Execution 41
    Getting Top-Down and Bottom-Up Buy-In Throughout
        the Organization 42

    Change Management, Social Media Style 48

        Myth Number 1: Social Media Is a Waste of Time 49

        Myth Number 2: Social Media Is Complicated 49

        Myth Number 3: Anyone Can Do That Job 50

        Myth Number 4: Social Media Is the Shiny New Thing.
            Two Years from Now, That Bubble Will Burst 50

        Myth Number 5: I Am Going to Have to Change the
            Way I Work 51

    Laying the Groundwork for Integrationand Management . . .52

II   SOCIAL MEDIA PROGRAM INTEGRATION 55

5   Understanding How Social Media Plugs into the
    Organization 57
    Creating Structure: Your First Social Media Process
        Mapping Draft 58

    Understanding the Four Phases of Social Media Adoption . .59

        Phase One: Test Adoption 59

        Phase Two: Focused Adoption 60

        Phase Three: Operational Adoption 60

        Phase Four: Operational Integration 61

    Genesis vs. Pirate Ships: Social Media Integration Models . . .62

    From Skunkworks to Full Deployment of a Social Media
        Structure 64

    Centralized vs. Decentralized Social Media Management
        Models 67

6   The People Principle 71
    Hiring, Training, and Certifying for Social
        Media Activity 72

    Hiring a Social Media Director (Strategic Role) 72

    Hiring for Tactical Social Media Roles 76

        HR and Social Media: The Need for Social Media
            Policies, Guidelines, and Training 78

        The Value of Internal Certifications 81

7   Establishing Social Media Guidelines for the Organization 83
    Guidelines, Policies, and Purpose 84

        1. The Employee Social Media Bill of Rights 85

        2. Internal Social Media Usage Guidelines 86

3. External Social Media Usage Guidelines 87

4. Employment Disclosure Guidelines 89

5. Anti-Defamation Guidelines 90

6. Social Media Confidentiality and Nondisclosure
(NDA) Guidelines 91

7. Official vs. Personal Communications Guidelines 91

8. The Employee Digital Citizenship Contract 92

9. Training Resources 93

10. Social Media Guidelines for Agency Partners,
Contractors, and External Representatives 94

8   Laying the Operational Groundwork for Effective
Social Media Management 95
Establishing a Social Media Program's Organizational
Structure: Leadership and Reporting 96

Establishing a Social Media Program's Organizational
Structure: Cross-Functional Collaboration 100

Basic Technical Requirements 103

9   The New Rules of Brand Communications in the Age of
Social Media 113
Social Media's General Impact on Brand
Communications 114

Transparency, Opacity, Confidentiality, and Disclosure 119

Confidentiality and Data Protection in the Age of
Social Media 122

III   SOCIAL MEDIA PROGRAM MANAGEMENT 125

10   Listening Before Talking 127
Business Intelligence and Search 128

The Power of Real-Time Situational Awareness 130

New Avenues of Market Research: From "I Don't Know" to
"Let's Find Out" 133

11   Social Media and Digital Brand Management 135
Introduction to the New Paradigm in Digital Brand
Management 136

Community Management 137

Marketing 140

Advertising 143

Product Management 144

Digital 145

Corporate Communications and PR 146

Online Reputation Management 151

Crisis Management 152

Putting It All Together 156

12 Real-Time Digital Support: Fixing Customer Service Once and
for All 157

The Superhero Principle 160

The Basic Social Media Customer Service Model 162

The New Digital Concierge Service and Customer
Service 3.0 166

Digital Conflict Resolution 168

From Risk to Opportunity: Turning Anger on Its Head and
Other Considerations 171

13 Social Media Program Management—Putting It
All Together 173

Social Media Management: In-House, Outsourced,
or Somewhere in Between? 174

Monitoring and Measurement 176

Campaign Management 176

Eleven Key Best Practices for Social Media Program
Management 179

Staying Focused on Business Objectives: How Marketing
Campaigns Should Fit into Your Social Media
Program 183

Final Thoughts on Social Media Program Management ...188

IV SOCIAL MEDIA PROGRAM MEASUREMENT 191

14 Creating a Measurement Practice for Social
Media Programs 193

Before the *How*, the *Why*: Keeping an Eye on
Objectives and Targets 194

A Word of Caution Regarding Measurement in the Social
Media Space 195

The Cornerstones of Your Measurement Practice:
Monitoring, Measurement, Analysis, and Reporting 195

Monitoring 196

Measurement 196

Analysis 196

Reporting 197

Best Practices for Performance Measurement 197

Maintain a List of Everything You *Can* Measure 198

Maintain a List of Everything You *Must* Measure 200

Stay Current on the Best Measurement Tools 202

Ensure the Neutrality of the Employee(s) Tasked with
the Measurement of Your Social Media Program 203

Tie Everything You Measure to Business Objectives 203

Test, Measure, Learn, Adapt, Repeat 203

Building Velocity and Specificity into Your Social Media
Measurement Practice 204

15 ROI and Other Social Media Outcomes 207

ROI and Business Justification 208

Financial Outcomes vs. Nonfinancial Outcomes and a
Word About Conversions 210

What ROI Is and Isn't 215

Tying Social Media to the P&L 220

Tying Nonfinancial Outcomes to Social Media
Performance 223

Step 1: Establish a Baseline 227

Step 2: Create Activity Timelines 227

Step 3: Monitor the Volume of Mentions 228

Step 4: Measure Transactional Precursors 230

Step 5: Look at Transactional Data 231

Step 6: Overlay All Your Data (Steps 1–5) onto a
Single Timeline 233

Step 7: Look for Patterns 233

Step 8: Prove and Disprove Relationships 235

16 F.R.Y. (Frequency, Reach, and Yield) and Social Media 239

The Importance of Finding the Right Words in the
Language of Business 240

Financial vs. Nonfinancial Aspects of Frequency 243

Financial vs. Nonfinancial Aspects of Reach 248

The Financial Value of Yield 253

17 Social Media Program Analysis and Reporting 257

Shattering the Vacuum: The Need for Collaborative
Analysis 258

Best Practices in Data Reporting for Social Media 260

Lateral Reporting 260

Vertical Reporting 262

Program Validation by the Numbers 268
Looking at Performance Data as Actionable Intelligence ...271
Afterword 277
Index 281

Foreword

ROI Doesn't Stand for Return on Ignorance

I'm often asked, what's the ROI of social media? To which I answer, you can't measure what it is you do not value or know to value.

Sounds simple enough. But, the truth is, determining value is not an easy process. But then again, whoever said using social media effectively in business was easy...is wrong.

As in anything in business, the ability to tie activity to the business values is critical. If we are to commit time, resources, and budget to social networks, our investments must be justified. Indeed, social media strategies must prove long-term value and contribution to the bottom line in order to evolve into a pillar of business success. But how do you measure something when best practices, case studies, and answers in general are elusive? We are struggling to prove the merit of an important ingredient in the future success of business because precedents have yet to be written or tested.

While many companies are already investing in social media, the reality is that most are done without the ability to demonstrate any return on investment. The truth is that you succeed in anything if success is never defined. The good news is that success is definable and attainable. It just takes a little work...well, honestly, a lot of work to tie intended outcomes to the "R" (return) in ROI. And, even though social media, as a platform and series of channels, is inexpensive or free to host a presence, time and resources still carry fixed costs. To that end, if we enhance our presences or apply greater resources, the investment goes up exponentially. It comes down to the old adage, "time is money."

Everything starts with the end in mind.

Success is not a prescription. There isn't one way to excel or measure progress. But that's the point. We must first design outcomes into the equation. What do we want to accomplish? What's the return we seek? Are we trying to sell, change, drive, cause, or inspire something specific? Are we reducing customer problems as measured by inbound volume, open tickets, public discourse? Are we trying to shift sentiment to a more positive state that increases referrals as a result?

Success requires definition based on intentions, goals, and mutual value...across the organization from the top down, bottom up, inside out, and outside in. Success is defined departmentally and also at the brand level. And success is tied to desirable actions and outcomes. As we've already established, it's impossible to measure the

ROI for something if we haven't first established the R (return) or the I (invest-ment). No amount of new acronyms will change this, yet we see new terms intro-duced as if we've already given up on defining ROI: return on engagement (ROE), return on participation (ROP), return on listening (ROL), return on fluid listening (ROFL), return on ignorance (the new ROI). In the end, everything carries cost and effect.

The debate over ROI is only going to gain in importance. But that's where we need to go in order to gain the support we need to expand our investment in social media. You're in good hands though. Olivier Blanchard is indeed one of the few who can help. Here, he has written a comprehensive guide that will help you at every step, from planning to program integration to management to measurement.

Thanks to Olivier, you'll find the answers to your questions and also answers to the questions that you didn't know to ask.

As they say, failing to plan is planning to fail. The success of all things social media is up to you to define, quite literally.

—Brian Solis
Principal, Future Works
Author of *Engage: The Complete Guide for Brands and Businesses to Build, Cultivate, and Measure Success in the New Web*

About the Author

Olivier Blanchard is a brand strategist with 15 years of B-to-B and B-to-C marketing management experience ranging from manufacturing and distribution to new media and consumer goods. He manages BrandBuilder Marketing, a brand consulting and marketing management firm that helps companies combine traditional and new/social media, and the Red Chair Group, which delivers executive social media training worldwide. When he isn't writing, speaking, or consulting, he can be found on his blog at www.thebrandbuilder.wordpress.com or on Twitter at www.twitter.com/thebrandbuilder. An avid triathlete, photographer, and travel junkie, Olivier lives in South Carolina with his wife, two children, and their roving pack of wild Chihuahuas.

Dedication

For Lisa, Ethan, and Rowan, who help change the world every day— and for everyone with a mind to do the same.

Acknowledgments

A lot more goes into a book like this than people realize, and I need to thank a few folks who contributed to this one in their own particular way.

First, because without them, this book would not be what it is, I want to thank my team of editors and reviewers: Greg Wiegand, Leslie O'Neill, Kristy Hart, Betsy Harris, Maddie Grant, Bart Reed, Erika Millen, Cindy Teeters, Kristi Colvin, and Scott Gould. Had it not been for their tireless work, this book would still read like a choppy first draft. Thanks also to Pearson Publishing and the Que team for being wonderful human beings. I also want to send a particularly warm thank-you to my acquisitions editor, Katherine Bull, for fighting for this project, taking a chance on an unpublished author, and patiently seeing me through to the finish while chasing me around the globe for the better part of six months. Her diligence, professionalism, and particularly her patience are a credit to her profession.

A very special thanks to Brian Solis, one of the smartest people I know, for agreeing to write such an elegant foreword for what is essentially a *meat and potatoes* business book.

Kudos to Rob Moyer and Microsoft's channel distribution team for introducing me to F.R.Y. Without them, a lot of this book would make very little sense.

From the bottom of my heart, thank you to Dr. Judith Bainbridge, who many years ago in a small classroom at Furman University inspired me to write more than term papers—and more recently to Steven Pressfield (though he may not know it) for picking up where she left off.

I cannot thank enough my courageous clients, the faithful readers of the BrandBuilder blog, and my Twitter tribe for pushing me to be smarter and more focused on solving business problems than I would ever have been on my own. This book is in no small part the result of our many exchanges over the years and would not have ever seen the light of day without you.

I also need to thank a few key people without whose support, sense of humor, and encouragement, doing what I do wouldn't be nearly as fun: Kamran Popkin, Trey Pennington, Kristi Colvin, Jim O'Donnell, Alicia Kahn, Bobby Rettew, Drew Ellis, Phil Yanov, Adam Gautsch, Evan Tishuk, Geoff Livingston, Kim Brater, Gabrielle Laine Peters, Jacqueline Collier, Michael Kristof, Debbie Morello, Roby DiGiovine, Scott Gould, Cd, Andy Sernovitz, Guy Kawasaki, the Clogenson clan, Ben Schowe, Misty McLelland, Ellen McGirt, Michael Duffield, Kelly Olexa, Clay Hebert, Seth

"Click on my head" Godin, Jim Mitchem, Amy Wood, Gemma Went, Gavin Heaton, Isaac Pigott, Amber Osborne, Keith Privette, Joseph Gier, Peter Shankman, Hajj Flemings, Jeffrey Jacobs, Geno Church, Beth Harte, Yann Gourvennec, Keith Burtis, Valeria Maltoni, Scott Gould, Chris Brogan, Daniel "Raptor" Agee, Karima Catherine, Andrew Davies, Matt Ridings, Peter Kim, Tom Asacker, Mike Wagner, Scott Monty, Christopher Barger, Francois Gossieaux, Jon Evans, David Armano, Tom Fishburne, Ken Sparks, Hugh MacLeod, Raul Colon, Steven Matsumoto, Frank Roth, Steve Woodruff, Tom Peters, Jay Baer, Robert Lavigne, Owen Greaves, John Heaney, Jeffrey Summers, the SmartBrief team, the PVSM Social Media Punks, the LikeMinds, WOMMA, Ungeeked, and SMC Greenville communities, my co-pilot Chico, and of course Instigator #149. I routinely learn something valuable from all of you.

To my parents—Alain and Francine Blanchard—*merci* for teaching me to question everything and draw clear ethical lines in the sand. I suspect that you have been watching in complete horror the degree to which I have applied your advice from day one. You can stop worrying now.

Finally, a deep word of gratitude to Lisa, Ethan, and Rowan for the love, patience, and support with which you showered me in the long months it took to put this book together.

We Want to Hear from You!

As the reader of this book, you are our most important critic and commentator. We value your opinion and want to know what we're doing right, what we could do better, what areas you'd like to see us publish in, and any other words of wisdom you're willing to pass our way.

As an associate publisher for Que Publishing, I welcome your comments. You can email or write me directly to let me know what you did or didn't like about this book—as well as what we can do to make our books better.

Please note that I cannot help you with technical problems related to the topic of this book. We do have a User Services group, however, where I will forward specific technical questions related to the book.

When you write, please be sure to include this book's title and author as well as your name, email address, and phone number. I will carefully review your comments and share them with the author and editors who worked on the book.

Email: feedback@quepublishing.com

Mail: Greg Wiegand
Associate Publisher
Que Publishing
800 East 96th Street
Indianapolis, IN 46240 USA

Reader Services

Visit our website and register this book at quepublishing.com/register for convenient access to any updates, downloads, or errata that might be available for this book.

Social Media Program Development

1 Creating the Social Company 3

2 Aligning Social Media to Business Goals 13

3 Planning for Performance Measurement 29

4 Establishing Clarity of Vision, Purpose, and Execution 41

Creating the Social Company

Building a social media program for an organization is hard. I won't try to convince you otherwise. The truth of it is that it takes patience, long hours of intricate planning, and a razor-sharp focus on getting things right. When you look at the companies that first started to successfully integrate the social web into their business models—companies such as Ford, Starbucks, Virgin Airlines, Dell, IBM, and Best Buy—what you often don't see is the mountain of diligent planning it took for them to get there: the research, the team work, the block-by-block building that went on behind the scenes. What those friendly Twitter interactions and expertly managed Facebook walls don't tell you is that behind every corporate success story in this space is a basic operational framework that places all the right elements in the right way and at the right time. Social media success doesn't happen by accident. It is engineered.

It is also important to note that success in social media doesn't happen overnight: Reach, attention, and influence cannot effectively be bought in this space. They have to be earned and developed, much like friendships are earned and developed. In this way, social media is different from other forms of media already employed by the business world. The "spend and reach" campaign mentality of "traditional" media does not produce long-term results here. The social web requires more subtlety and commitment, which is why terms such as relationships, trust, and conversations are such popular buzzwords in professional social media circles: These three words describe the social web's lifeblood, especially as it relates to business.

Evolution, Human Nature, and the Inevitable Socialization of Business

One of the fundamental reasons why social media has been so readily embraced by the general public is that it helps connect people with each other in ways that are valuable, meaningful, and convenient, on their own terms, and on an unprecedented scale. Bear in mind that Facebook isn't "Brandbook," Twitter isn't "Promotweets," and YouTube isn't "CorpTube." After decades spent enduring thousands of daily marketing messages being shoved at them across every communications channel known to man, the public found in the social web a means of turning the messaging *off* and turning instead to what mattered to them more: relationships, trust, and conversations. Businesses planning to develop a presence in social media therefore need to tread lightly and pay attention to the unspoken rules governing interactions in this space.

The secret to how social media works won't be found in marketing or business books. It doesn't live in data about digital influence or the purchasing habits of web users. In order to understand the true power of the social web, you have to look into the nature of humanity itself: We are social creatures. We crave social interactions. We love to belong to social groups, listen to stories, share experiences, and contribute something of value to the groups to which we belong. Thirty thousand years ago, we gathered with our tribe around the campfire. Today, separated by thousands of miles, complicated schedules, and busy lives, we instead gather around our social networks to fulfill the same needs. The technology and the world around us may have changed, but we haven't. We still crave those interactions, that dialogue, that need to participate in social dynamics, and social media has given us a means to do just that.

What smart businesses have always known is that tapping into this need for group validation and social connections is the foundation upon which brands and customer loyalty are built. As far back as the first days of commerce, the more businesses treated their customers like friends, the more those customers preferred to do business there. The more businesses made their customers feel welcome, the more these customers recommended the experience to family and friends. The more businesses built an engaged community of customers around them, the less likely they were to ever have to discount products and services to attract business. This type of mentality created the business cultures that made brands such as Apple, BMW, Coca-Cola, Starbucks, and more recently Zappos so successful.

What these companies managed to do was reject the notion that customers were mere "numbers" in an elaborate game of marketing and sales. More to the point: These companies made sure that no customer was ever made to *feel* like they were a "number." Their success, and the success of companies like them, depended on this critical point: connecting with customers on a deeper level in order to develop them into outspokenly loyal repeat customers.

Over the last few decades, however, scale, automation, and modern marketing techniques have conspired to make the special relationship between customers and the companies they do business with difficult to maintain. Fifty years ago, a regular customer might have been greeted by name when she entered the store. Nowadays, only when she produces her rewards card might a part-time clerk be prompted to address her as a valued patron. In a cruel twist of irony, efficiency and growth made companies forget the value of being social, got in the way of building lasting bonds between frontline employees and their customers, and made the "social company" the exception rather than the rule—that is, until social media came along to potentially make things right again.

Sometime in 2008, when businesses started noticing the almost exponential growth of activity on social networks, the term *social business* began to make its way into business development conversations, and the opportunity for organizations to leverage the social web to improve their business became an increasingly common topic of discussion among business managers. Could a small engineering firm in Portland, for example, benefit from a presence in social media the way that a major global brand might benefit from it? Did social media offer the same opportunities to B2B industries as it clearly does to B2C industries? These joined hundreds of equally pertinent questions being asked daily in conference rooms around the U.S. and the world, but the fundamental truth of it was that they could all be answered in the same way: If you want to take the time to build relationships with customers the way businesses used to, then yes, social media is worth a closer look.

In and of itself, social media is not particularly complicated: It is a set of easy-to-use platforms and technologies that allow people to talk with other people. Social media is the new campfire, the new market square, the new water cooler, only it lives on our computers, smart phones, game consoles, and other networked devices. It can be accessed from virtually anywhere and pretty much at any time. As applied to the business world, social media recalibrates the question of B2B or B2C into a concept as old as human commerce: All businesses, regardless of industry, vertical, or sector, are fundamentally "P2P"—*people to people.* Understanding that businesses rely first and foremost on connecting people with one another (buyers and sellers, managers and employees, and so on), then building relationships based on value, preference, trust, and convenience is the first challenge facing executives trying to grasp how social media fits into their business models. It is this emphasis on human interaction that constitutes both the essence and the elusive "secret sauce" of the *social company.*

What does the social company look like? One way to put it would be to say that it is business, *evolved.* The signature characteristics of the social company are essentially the antithesis of most corporate entities today: The social model is more human, less burdened by departmental silos, fluid with its communications (both internal and external), and with a much flatter operational structure. You see some of its cultural qualities emerging in companies such as Zappos and Best Buy, albeit not yet fully deployed. In a bizarre twist of irony given that modern technology is responsible for making this model possible, it is very much a return to basics. It is how business was done hundreds of years ago: face to face, one handshake at a time. The difference is that now, scale is no longer a hurdle. Companies can, if they want, build loyalty 140 characters at a time, shake hands from hundreds of miles away, and have "face-to-face" interactions with tens of thousands of customers per day.

Just as a radical evolution in human communications was spawned by both the Internet and mobility, social media is now bringing about its own evolution, not only in communications, but in the very nature of the competitive business model. There is simply no stopping this. People will not put the ability to share stories and stay in touch with each other back into a box. They will not turn away from the ability to be connected to the world anytime they want and in the way they choose. Companies that both understand and embrace this socio-technical evolution will likely enjoy a decisive strategic advantage over companies that choose to ignore or reject it.

Organizations are already moving toward this model because it works. Some will get there faster than others, and some will only make it some of the way, but the reality of the next decade is this: Social media will change business at its core. It is already radically transforming the way companies do business, forcing shifts in methodology, procedure, culture, and operational structure.

Moving Beyond Channels: Social Media vs. Social Communications

What do people *do* on social media all day? They talk to each other and share thoughts, opinions, information, photos, videos, podcasts, blog posts, articles, data, resources, and whatever they can get their hands on. The social web also gives people the ability to play games, invite each other to events, send birthday reminders, and let their friends know where they are at any given time. At its core, what people do on the social web is *communicate* and *interact*.

It stands to reason then, that if the term *social media* describes the pipes, *social communications* and *social interactions* would describe what people *do* with them. The difference between social media and social communications—or my preferred terminology: *socialized digital communications*—is that the former indicates the *infrastructure*, whereas the latter indicates the *activity* within and across it.

Now that we are bringing some specificity between the machinery and the skills, which of these two titles conveys purpose better to, say, a Public Relations department:

- Social Media Director

- Social Communications Director

Which one conveys a sense of purpose? Which one is most closely aligned with a role that everyone in an organization—from the CEO on down to the most junior intern—can understand without needing an explanation?

Now that we have established the difference between media and communications, we can begin to have a conversation, in earnest, about the role social media can play in an organization, about its purpose, and the structure it will require to exist and flourish. It is crucial to understand that these two discussions—that of the infrastructure and that of the activity itself—while joined at the hip, are very different. They each require their own focus, as we see later in this book.

Why Social Media Matters to Business

A social media program is not a mere marketing add-on. Neither is it a blogging experiment whose purpose remains forever unclear. It is not a justification for conversations, engagement, and whatever buzzwords generally find their way into a discussion about social media. More than anything, a social media program is neither simple nor easy. It is not what most people think.

A fully deployed social media program is a completely integrated communications mechanism that amplifies the impact of every function within an organization by leveraging the power of human networks via social networking platforms. It is a complement to all other forms of tactical communications (from advertising to PR), not a replacement for any of them. In military terms, social media is what is known as a *force-multiplier*—a tactical element that makes a given force significantly more effective than it would be without it.

Now that we have touched on what a social media program *is*, let's discuss what a social media program *does*.

A social media program can provide organizations with detailed, virtually instant feedback from customers and valuable market intelligence. Used in conjunction with specialized monitoring, measurement, and analysis tools, it can amplify not only activities, but the acquisition and analysis of valuable data, from consumer insights to the calculation of ROI. A social media program also brings into heavily compartmentalized companies the potential for enhanced collaboration, increased departmental efficiency, cost reductions, and of course business growth.

Forget about blogs, Facebook, Twitter, and all the social media channels and platforms for a moment, and focus instead on what matters to your organization: Is lead generation an area of your business that could use some help? You can create a social media program that will help you acquire new leads. Are you losing customers to competitors? You can develop a social media program whose focus will be to help you enhance your customer retention activities. A social media program can plug into every type of business function you need it to and help you make it work better, smarter, and faster.

A fully developed social media program can, for example, protect a brand in times of crisis, alert an organization's decision makers to new trends in consumer interests and sentiment, influence hundreds of thousands of consumers to prefer one brand or product over another, and help tens of millions of consumers discover a company, organization, or product at a fraction of the cost of other forms of "traditional" media.

Because mobile devices such as cellular telephones increasingly incorporate social media capabilities that go beyond simple texting, voice, and email, digital social networks now live on mobile devices, not just personal computers. This matters because portability means both increased use and lower barriers of adoption. Because of this, the acceleration in global social media use is rewriting the way humans communicate, share ideas, recommend products, and connect with each other. Not being a part of this means not being a part of the world. Just as the telephone, email, and mobility could not be held at bay by companies reluctant to accept change, social media cannot be ignored either. The company that chooses to resist this latest step in the inexorable evolution of business will find itself having to work increasingly hard just to stay afloat. Conversely, the company that chooses to adapt and implements a business-focused social media program will have the opportunity to gain an advantage over its competition at very little cost and improve its position in the market.

Influence and Media: Lateral vs. Vertical Forces

To understand the way influence is applied across various channels when it comes to brand communications, especially as this relates to the inclusion of social media, we need to take a quick look at the dual concept of *vertical* and *lateral* forces.

Once upon a time (ten years ago), B2C corporate communications were basically one-dimensional: The organization crafted a message, packaged it, and pushed it out to its audience. The audience then either accepted it or didn't, and that was that. Back then, the audience didn't have an effective way of communicating with the organization aside from using comment cards, speaking with a customer service representative, or maybe participating in the odd protest or two. When the organization decided it wanted to know how its customers felt about something, it hired a marketing firm to conduct market research. Influence wasn't only vertical between the organization and the customer, but mostly one-directional as well: from the organization to the customer. This model is shown in Figure 1.1.

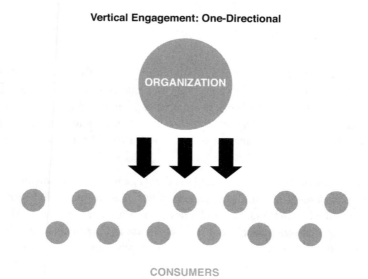

Figure 1.1   Vertical engagement: one-directional.

Then in the early days of Web 2.0, the online experience became more collaborative and user-centric, spawning the birth of social networking sites, free blogs, and applications that allowed customers to leave comments on digital content. Suddenly, customers found that they had a voice. Communications were still mostly vertical, but they had evolved from what was essentially a monologue to a rudimentary dialogue (see Figure 1.2).

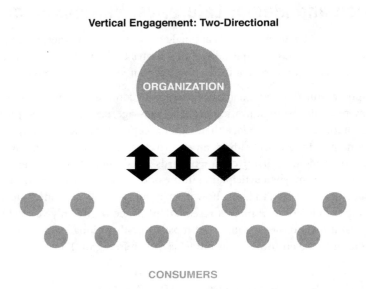

Figure 1.2   Vertical engagement: two-directional.

Driven by the vision of a more collaborative Internet promised by proponents of Web 2.0, digital social networks came along and changed everything again by adding a new dimension to the evolution of engagement and influence: the advent of true peer-to-peer networks in which users could create and share content at will. This time, the forces of engagement were *lateral* instead of being strictly vertical (see Figure 1.3).

The significance of this change is that lateral engagement is word-of-mouth. Until social media, word-of mouth didn't scale very well. Recommendations came piecemeal. If you liked something, you told a few friends, maybe some co-workers and neighbors, but that was the extent of it. Chances are that because of your busy schedule, by the time you got around to having lunch with someone you might recommend something to, it was no longer on your mind. This has changed.

Consider that the average Facebook user is connected to between 100 and 200 friends on that service alone and spends an average of about 55 minutes per day posting updates and recommendations, sharing links, and endorsing products and

Lateral Engagement

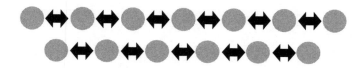

CONSUMERS

Figure 1.3   Lateral engagement.

brands by clicking the service's ubiquitous "Like" button. To this, add personal blogs, Twitter, location-based applications, and hundreds of other community platforms. What social media does is this: It takes your basic word-of-mouth process and multiplies both its velocity and its reach.

Because of the lateral engagement forces of social networks, word-of-mouth now knows no geographic barriers. It cuts through time zones like a warm knife through butter. With the click of a button, a recommendation can be shared with hundreds, in some cases thousands, of people in an instant. Depending on the context, these hundreds and thousands of people may choose to share that recommendation laterally with their connections, who in turn may do the same.

Social media creates both influence and scale in a way that traditional media cannot. Better yet, it does so at a fraction of the cost of traditional media. How is this possible? Word-of-mouth, in order to be effective, must be relationship-based: Influence and trust, within lateral channels, are earned, not bought. The chief currencies of lateral channels, of social media, are trust and relevance. Compare the cost of reaching one million people just once through traditional (bought) media channels to the cost of touching one million people once through social media (earned) channels, where the public spreads your content and message for free because they *want* to and because they *can*. Now you can understand why every major brand in the world is busy integrating social media into its business model.

2

Aligning Social Media to Business Goals

First things first: Having a "presence" in social media is worthless unless you do something with it. It isn't enough to merely have a blog, a YouTube channel, and accounts on Facebook, Twitter, and half a dozen other platforms. Is it a good start? Sure. Is it better than not having a presence at all? To an extent. However, what is the value of any of this to your organization? Let's be realistic: Having a social media program without attaching it to some sort of goal just creates more work for your staff. That's about it. Someone has to write blog posts. Someone has to push out content to social networking sites. Someone has to read and respond to comments. And while that someone is doing this, he or she isn't doing something else.

To a certain extent, the issue here is opportunity cost. In case you aren't familiar with the term, opportunity cost refers to the cost of doing one activity instead of another. Economists usually explain it as the best alternative forgone because a particular course of action is pursued.

In other words, the question is this: Of all the activities your employees could be focusing on, is social media the best choice? The answer hinges on one thing—whether or not activity in social media creates the most value for the company at that given moment.

Social Media's Value to the Organization

Social media can be used in two very different ways: for personal entertainment and for building a community around your company. It all depends on how your employees use the social media sites and tools. An employee catching up with his friends on a social network doesn't create a whole lot of value. Watching YouTube videos of talking kittens doesn't do a whole lot for the company either. The value to that employee may be clear (combating boredom), but for the company, it amounts to wasted productivity. This is the kind of at-work social media usage that gives the space a bad name in the corporate world and sometimes obscures its strategic value to an organization.

Now let's talk about how social media activity at work might bring a little more value to the organization: an employee monitoring social media channels for positive and negative mentions of the product he is responsible for, managing customer service requests in real time on micro-blogging platforms, or engaging in reputation management activity, for example.

In the first scenario, the employee is wasting time. In the second scenario, he is focused on activities that support specific business objectives. Same employee, same desk, same tools, same channels, yet we see a completely different picture now that the employee has specific goals: business intelligence, customer support, and online reputation management.

With purpose comes value, which brings us back to this: Having a "presence" in social media is worthless unless you do something with it.

So the question is, what do you do with social media? Before that question can be successfully answered, you must clearly understand your organization's overall business strategy, tactics, goals, and targets.

Differentiating Between Strategy and Tactics

Whereas the difference between strategy and tactics is crystal clear in the military world, it often seems nebulous to business managers. As a result, I often find myself having to quickly go over this topic to eliminate any hint of confusion.

A *strategy* is a plan of action designed to achieve a particular goal or objective. Strategies are often complex and made up of many moving parts. Strategy tends to be the realm of executives who can manage a high level of operational complexity.

Tactics are the means by which a strategy may be carried out. Typically, tactics are the *methods* used on the ground to execute a strategy.

> **Example:** The current strategy to acquire net new customers (the goal) is to use Facebook to increase both our reach and our prospect-to-customer conversions. Two of the tactics that will be used are a) discount coupons for new connections on Facebook on their first online purchase and b) $5 off his or her next online purchase to anyone who shares one of our Facebook offers this week.

Differentiating Between Goals and Targets

Another area of confusion I often run into with business managers is the difference between goals and targets. I'll quickly shed some light on the difference because we will be talking about both subjects a lot throughout this book.

- A *goal* is an organization's desired end point, also known as an *objective*.
- A *target* is the specific value assigned to an objective within a finite timeframe.

Goals set the direction and focus of an activity, whereas targets establish specific parameters of success for accomplishing the goals.

> **Example:** If the company's goal is to increase net new transacting customers, the target would be expressed as 100 net new customers in Q1.
>
> If the company's goal is to improve a brand's overall image, the target could be expressed as a shift from the current 1:4 ratio of positive-to-negative sentiment across social web channels to a 1:1 ratio of positive-to-negative sentiment across the same channel by year end.

Tying a Social Media Program to Business Objectives

A common misconception in the business world is that social media stands somehow apart from the rest of the company—that it is its own silo, its own little "engagement" and "conversation" engine with no clear connection to other business functions. This is false. Organizations that treat social media as a fifth wheel don't usually get very far in the space. The reality of social media is that it isn't an add-on. It is 100% an integration piece (which is why Part II, "Social Media Program Integration," focuses on social media integration).

Here is a simple way to look at it: Your business doesn't plug into social media. Social media plugs into your business.

What does that mean? It means that social media is not its own function. Social media is a communications tool, like the telephone and email, that serves the purposes of critical business functions, including public relations, marketing, lead generation, customer service, and market research. Some of the best uses for social media activity are *in support* of these particular business functions, and here is the best part: Each one of these business functions already has its very own objectives and targets, which you can plug your social media activities into.

That's right. You don't need to come up with a social media strategy, other than figuring out where it fits and how to make it work for you.

Whenever I hear people say that their company either has or sells a "social media strategy," I cringe. There is no such thing as a "social media strategy." It is kind of like having a "telephone strategy" or an "email strategy." It's a meaningless buzzword. What you *do* have, however, are business objectives and strategies to achieve these objectives. Start with those and incorporate *social* into them.

Let me give you an example. I was having lunch with the head of a fairly large marketing department not long ago, and started talking about social media. It didn't take long for him to bring up the difficulty of developing a social media strategy for his CEO. As he explained it, it came down to acquiring 25,000 followers on Twitter in the first year and 50,000 fans ("Likes") on Facebook. I asked him why. His answer: Reach. He wanted to increase reach. A few buzzwords popped up as well, such as "engagement" and "conversations," for good measure.

Then I asked him, "What is the value of having 25,000 followers on Twitter? To your company, I mean."

He hesitated and finally answered, "More reach. More impressions."

Then I explained to him, "Does a company want a million followers on Twitter or a million net new customers acquired through Twitter?"

Something seemed to click. His face lit up, and he nodded, finally understanding why it had been so difficult to come up with a social media strategy: He was looking at the problem from the wrong end. Trying to come up with a social media strategy to somehow justify the need for a social media program in the first place was pointless. But using social media as a vehicle to support existing business objectives, now *that* made a lot more sense.

Here is a simple rule that may find its roots in the military world but applies to the business world equally: *Objectives dictate tactics.* Never, ever, ever do tactics dictate objectives.

Social media activity, in and of itself, is not an objective. Acquiring net new customers, increasing reach, building loyalty, capturing more market share, even increasing net new revenue—*these* are objectives.

The *tactics* might include creating content for a blog, driving online discussions, measuring changes in online mentions of the company or customer perceptions, sharing company news, and leveraging social web channels to amplify campaigns, for example.

A social media program, in order to deliver results, must have a purpose rooted in business objectives. Understanding this will get you started on the right foot.

How to Create a Roadmap by Turning Goals into Targets

Now that we understand how to align social media with business objectives, let's briefly talk about setting targets. The golden rule of establishing targets is this: Stating goals and objectives is not enough. In order to drive toward a specific result (a *desired* result), an organization must set targets. It is not enough to state "winning a world championship" as a goal. You also have to know what targets you need to hit in order to accomplish that goal, including training targets, performance targets, and scheduling targets.

I often find myself in meetings with organizations whose goals are legitimate but vague: increasing social participation, growing a pool of followers, improving the ratio of positive-to-negative sentiment for the brand, increasing awareness for a product, growing market share, increasing sales, continuing to earn more mentions of the company name across social media channels, and so on. This is a good start, but you need to take it up a notch. What these goals lack is *specificity*. How do you measure success when your goals are this vague? As an organization, you must set targets.

Think about reframing "increasing social participation" as "generating 300 comments and mentions per day." Instead of "growing a pool of followers," consider "acquiring 6,000 net new Twitter followers per month." "Improving the ratio of positive-to-negative sentiment about the brand" should see a number attached to it and a due date. If your organization wants to see more traffic to a web page, then set a target. If actual traffic this month is 2,500 visits per day, then aim for 3,000 daily visits next month. Be specific.

Why? Two reasons: The first is that it forces your staff to think about ways to accomplish the goal, which is to say, it forces the organization to shift from a *maintenance* mode to a *problem-solving* and *business-building* mode. This is how organizations grow—by thinking through challenges and finding ways to make things work better. The second reason is that setting targets creates accountability. It is one thing to do just enough to get by and show vague "growth" or an "increase" in performance. It is another to make someone accountable for hitting (or failing to hit) a predetermined target. This forces the organization to focus on specific outcomes and make sure they happen.

The specificity of targets drives accomplishment. The more specific, the more likely the desired outcome will be reached. The less specific the goal, the less likely it will be met. Always set targets.

The Top Five Business Functions That Can Be Easily Enhanced by a Social Media Program

Now let's talk about some of the ways a social media program can help a business. Most organizations share certain needs: They depend on some kind of funding or revenue, they have to keep customers or stakeholders happy, and they have to support their employees. Social media can be used by both for-profit businesses and nonprofit organizations to help satisfy these needs. We start with for-profit organizations and then discuss how social media can help nonprofits and associations.

Sales

Most businesses depend first and foremost on revenue. No need to pretend that social media isn't about ultimately generating sales or driving business. If it weren't, this book would be irrelevant. Social media, like all other communications channels, can and does help drive sales revenue. The first thing we need to do here is shed the notion that "being social" and making money are incompatible. That would be like saying that being friends with a customer or client precludes you from doing business with them. It's absurd. Likewise, bunk is the notion that bringing sales or money into the social media space is somehow dirty. How you do it and in what context is what separates good taste from bad taste, but social media and sales should not exist at opposite ends of the business spectrum. We discuss this further in Chapter 3, "Planning for Performance Measurement," when we discuss ROI.

So how can social media help you drive sales? For starters, social media can help you acquire new customers—first through its reach, then through influence. We saw in Chapter 1, "Creating the Social Company," how vertical and lateral engagement work together to create both depth and breadth of engagement. One of the end results of this type of activity is a conversion funnel that begins with awareness of the brand, leads to regular online participation with the brand via social platforms, and converts social participants into customers.

When it comes to leveraging social media to increase sales for an organization, *acquiring net new customers* via social networks and *developing* them via social engagement are two basic ways of driving toward that objective. Furthermore, social media can be leveraged to increase the frequency of customer transactions (buy rate) and the yield of certain transactions (average $ value per transaction), as we discuss in more detail in Chapter 3.

Another way to increase sales using social media channels is by amplifying the reach (both in breadth and depth) of marketing campaigns. Here's a quick example: Say you want to increase sales of your new sedan. You create an ad campaign for it, with PR and other marketing and promotional components. Ten years ago, this would have meant TV, radio, print, billboards, events, dealer incentives, point of purchase displays, and trade reviews. That is still true today, except now the media environment is much richer. Television spots and other videos can also find an audience on YouTube. Blogs can enhance the relevance and depth of content around the new sedan. Branded Facebook pages can be leveraged to promote discussions, publish videos and articles, schedule events, launch contests, distribute special offers, and so on. Those are just a few examples of how social media not only can scale a campaign's reach, but make your message stickier by virtue of being digested as more than mere "marketing."

Finally, as long as a company doesn't go overboard, it can promote special sales and offers directly through social networks without coming across as being pushy. A 20%-off discount code with a hyperlink to an e-site can generate sales on the spot. Dell started doing this in 2007. Whereas most companies were not yet aware of Twitter or its future business implications, the computer manufacturer had already begun the process of building a network of customers on the micro-blogging platform. It soon began testing the public's response to special offers published there. Two years later, the @DellOutlet account had generated $2 million in sales using this technique. Why such a small amount of business? Simple: Back then, not many people used Twitter yet. Still, $2 million in two years, when virtually no other companies had made one dime off their Twitter activity, was an impressive proof of concept. By December of 2009, that amount had grown to $6.5 million in sales, just from Twitter alone. This, from about 1.5 million followers acquired over less than three years.

Using what we have learned about objectives, targets, strategy, and tactics, one simple way of organizing your thoughts and clarifying your plan of action is to simply write it down as a tiered process. Here is an example:

> **Objective:** Increase sales.
>
> **Target:** (Fill this in with the financial or unit amount you want to drive toward.)
>
> **Strategy:** Acquire net new followers by developing followers into transacting customers, further developing existing transacting customers into repeat/loyal customers, and leveraging followers to increase reach through lateral engagement (word-of-mouth, retweets, and so on).
>
> **Tactics:** Publish special offers on Twitter via our various accounts. Answer questions from customers and prospective customers on Twitter. Be a resource to our customer community.

Customer Support

The beauty of social media channels is that most conversations and mentions of your company and brand are out in the open, where your customer support department can easily keep an eye on what is being said and join in when necessary. Companies now have the power to respond to their customers (and potential customers) in real time. The ability to spot trouble, help customers in need, and answer questions within seconds (and without having to force customers to jump through procedural hoops simply to get your attention) offers an opportunity for companies looking to better support their customers that simply did not exist five years ago. Social media now allows companies to increase the efficiency of their customer support practices and improve customer satisfaction—without necessarily adding cost to the model.

When it comes to monitoring social media channels to improve customer support, you will need two elements: The first is qualified staff. Rather than focusing on hiring social media "experts," consider hiring (or training) experienced customer support professionals with a good grasp of the social web. Remember that it is easier to train a good customer support representative to use social media than to train an experienced social media user to be a good customer support professional. The second element is tools. You are going to need technology to do this. What kind of technology? That will depend on your budget, your organization's need, and your preference. There are three basic routes you can take when it comes to adopting monitoring tools: One is to invest in an advanced social web monitoring tool and dashboards like the ones used by very large enterprises. These types of tools have an amazing degree of functionality but can be difficult to master and usually require a serious financial commitment. The second method, favored by many small businesses, is to use an assortment of free tools and build a patchwork-style dashboard. A quick search on the Web will identify several dozen such tools, and I recommend that you try them out. Trial and error is the best way to identify what works best for your particular organization. The third option is to do a little bit of both: Combine an assortment of free tools with more professional-level tools. Just remember that tools are just tools. The real focus of a customer support department here is to make sure that if someone mentions your company or product anywhere on the Web, you will be notified immediately and be in a position to respond quickly and appropriately.

The value of being able to respond in real time to a problem or a negative mention is that a bad situation can be turned around before the customer's frustration escalates into anger. Perhaps this person had a bad experience, and you make things right. Perhaps the customer thinks her product is broken, when in fact, she needs help turning it on. Perhaps she needs help with something and doesn't know where to turn. Monitoring mentions of your company or product on the Web gives you visibility to these types of conversations. The faster the response, the faster a crisis can be averted.

Overall, here are the advantages of adopting this new mode of digital customer support:

- Constant real-time feedback from customers, users, and the general public.

- The ability to respond to customers in real time rather than making them wait.

- Faster resolution times than through other types of media (such as phone and email).

- Because of the faster resolution times that come with providing support on social media channels, even a 10% shift from toll-free phone support to social media may result in a significant cost reduction for many customer support departments.

- Don't forget the most important outcome of all: happier customers. Not having to spend the better part of an hour on the phone to have a problem fixed is just one more way you can set yourself apart from your competitors.

Giving visibility to your customer support process and the proactive way in which you focus on helping your customers will improve your company's image.

Human Resources

You have a choice when it comes to recruiting talent: You can either sift through piles of resumes or hire through trusted networks of peers, colleagues, and friends. You can either take your chances on strangers or trust someone you know has your best interest in mind to recommend only qualified applicants they think will be a good fit. Which one sounds like a better model?

Because so many of our professional and personal relationships are increasingly intertwined with our use of social media channels, and because a hefty percentage of our professional information is searchable on the Web, it isn't difficult to see how Human Resources can leverage social media to identify, recruit, and even monitor employees.

Let's begin by talking about the popular social network for professionals: LinkedIn. By now, most white-collar workers, at least in North America, manage a LinkedIn account. The original premise behind LinkedIn was twofold: One, it allowed users to post their resume and contact information to their online profile so that these could be easily accessible to peers, potential employers, and even prospective clients. Second, it allowed users to connect with peers and colleagues in such a way that they could keep track of their contact information and their latest career changes. But that wasn't all. LinkedIn also allowed recruiters to search its database for specific types of skills and experience, when trying to proactively identify a key hire. More importantly, because each user's network was clearly mapped by the site, a recruiter could browse through a potential hire's network and identify common "connections" who might provide valuable insight into that individual.

LinkedIn has evolved a lot since its early days. Users can now opt to have their blog's content feed directly into their LinkedIn profile page, along with their activity on Twitter, travel schedules, favorite books, presentations, and more. More importantly, as more and more professionals began using LinkedIn, the average user's network grew as well. This growth was also fed by an increase in the size of personal and professional networks on other social networks such as Facebook and Twitter. How? Simple...say that you engage in a conversation about marketing with fellow marketing professionals on Twitter. During the course of the conversation, you meet several industry peers unknown to you until now. Understanding the value of building a professional network, two or three of these individuals ask you if it would be all right for them to connect with you on LinkedIn. You say yes. Your professional network on LinkedIn has now increased in size due to an interaction you had on a completely separate network.

This mechanism is the engine that drives social and professional connections in the social media space: The result of increased interactions between people online is the growth of their personal and professional networks. That growth, in turn, creates more opportunities for individual A to be connected to individual B. It is that increase in connectivity that gives recruiters the ability to better identify and pre-qualify candidates by using social media than a stack of resumes from strangers. A recruiting manager with an extensive network can now either search for a qualified candidate using specific keywords on LinkedIn and reach out to common connections to obtain more information about them or simply ask her network (on any social media channel) if anyone can recommend an individual for a particular position.

The process in and of itself is simple, but it was impossible to scale until now. Social media significantly increases a recruiter's ability to recruit through trusted networks and validate candidates through recommendations from people he actually knows. The integration of social media into Human Resources is covered in greater detail in Chapter 6, "The People Principle."

Public Relations

Public relations is one area where social media can have an immediate impact on the way your business is perceived and interacted with by the public.

The ability to monitor online mentions of a company name or particular product gives companies the opportunity to respond to negative attitudes, clarify a position on an issue, invalidate false rumors, and separate myth from fact. Public Relations departments managing social media practices have stumbled onto a new type of service for the companies they serve, called *online reputation management* (also known as *digital reputation management*). An early example of online reputation management at work in social media came from Ford in early 2009, when Scott Monty (who heads Ford's social media practice) found himself having to set the record straight about the auto giant having accepted government "bailouts" during early months the global financial crisis. Ford had, in fact, turned down financial aid from the government, explaining that the company could emerge from the crisis without government assistance. This fact was lost on a significant portion of the population, and Ford's name became erroneously tied to the unpopular "auto industry bailout." Nowhere was this confusion clearer than on social media channels, including blogs, Facebook, and Twitter. Monty spent weeks helping set the record straight, and Ford's image improved as a result.

Whether a company finds itself battling false rumors or battling deliberate attacks on its good name, an online reputation management program can help the company or brand hold on to its good name. When not under attack, a PR team can leverage social media to improve a company's reputation and standing through more frequent and relevant engagement with the public. By helping customers and potential customers develop deeper relationships with a brand through social media channels, a PR team can also help increase both trust and mindshare for the company, as well as foster an alignment of values between companies and their would-be customers that will result in a higher degree of positive sentiment and even loyalty.

Business Intelligence

Wouldn't it be nice to know what your customers are saying about you? About your competitors? How many people are saying it? Where they are having these discussions? How mentions and perceptions may be changing over time, or how a campaign, program, review, or release might have affected company mentions and sentiment across the Web? Because everything in social media is both easy to monitor and searchable, access to business intelligence is now cheaper, faster, and richer than it has ever been. The same monitoring techniques we discussed in regard to customer support and public relations can be applied here. From keyword searches to analysis encompassing share of voice, sentiment, and volume of mentions, the amount of actionable information a company can capture on the social web is astounding. Though often understated as a social media practice because it is unseen by the public, business intelligence is in my opinion one of the most important areas of focus when it comes to social media integration for organizations and the first area they should tackle.

Social Media for Nonprofits

Social media can be equally valuable to the nonprofit world, although the list of functions changes somewhat.

Outcomes

Because not-for-profit organizations do not usually rely on sales to generate revenue, we can replace "sales" with "outcomes." *Outcomes* are essentially an organization's desired end result. This end result could be financial or not. Here are some examples: Raising $30 million for a charity program, rescuing 500 pelicans from a major oil spill, getting 10,000 voters to sign a petition, increasing plastic bottle recycling in a major urban area by 10% YoY (year over year), and increasing revenue from memberships by 30% over the next 18 months.

For associations, one of the ways to drive outcomes is to recruit new members. These members may be called upon to contribute financial donations, donate their time, spread information, write letters, attend demonstrations, and perform whatever task the organization requires in order to reach its desired outcomes. Members, in this case, take the place of the for-profit organization's *customers*. You can imagine how leveraging social media to both recruit new members and activate existing ones might be more effective than relying on more traditional methods of communications and engagement.

Social networks are the perfect environment in which to ignite movements, organize people around a cause, and drive participation for associations and nonprofits. In terms of effective reach, you could do worse. Facebook pages, Twitter chats, blog posts, photo albums, audio podcasts, and videos posted to sites such as YouTube can amplify an organization's web presence quickly and at very little cost. Regardless of its size, whether an organization's objective is to increase awareness for a cause, raise money, trigger a boycott, recruit members, or educate or increase the public's participation in an event, the social web is a powerful medium. In 2010, CitizenGulf.org, a small not-for-profit organization whose objective was to provide financial aid to fishing families affected by BP's catastrophic oil spill in the Gulf of Mexico, raised about $11,000 in just a few short months with no budget, using the social web as its primary mode of communication. The same year, but on a larger scale, environmental action juggernaut Greenpeace pressured global food production giant Nestle to reconsider its palm oil cultivation practices by simultaneously launching an aggressive information campaign via YouTube and flooding Nestlé's own Facebook wall with protests.

The combination of low-cost, global reach and potentially high impact makes social media an ideal set of channels for nonprofit organizations with ambitious goals to see them through.

Member Support

In this case, *customer support* becomes *member support*. The focus is a bit different, but the outcome is the same: Enjoy immediate feedback, respond to queries faster, increase positive impact in public forums, enjoy potential cost reductions (from reducing call center headcount), increase interactions with the public and members, engineer more *varied* interactions (not just push and messaging), not to mention making your resources portable by extending your social web presence to the mobile universe.

Human Resources

This is basically the same function as before, except that with associations and nonprofits, many members tend to also work for the organization the way employees might, even if they do so as volunteers. By adding volunteers to the mix, then, social media can help associations and nonprofits smoothly identify, develop, and recruit volunteers and leverage online communities to streamline the process. In terms of risk management, you can also monitor employees and volunteers' online communications and catch potentially damaging activity early enough to be able to fix whatever problems might arise out of it.

Public Relations

The role of public relations doesn't change from for-profit to the not-for-profit world, so all the points we covered in the previous section apply here as well: Online reputation management, improved brand image via the social web, clarification of the organization's purpose and value, and direct communication with the public all benefit organizations exactly as if they were operating in the for-profit world. The added bonus of using social media for nonprofits when it comes to PR is that campaigns of education and awareness—which are the subject of greater focus in the nonprofit sector—tend to be better received in the social media space than campaigns focused on selling products. Education helps grow membership and participation in a cause, and a PR team well-versed in social media can see its efforts well rewarded there.

Member Loyalty

Traditional forms of media, such as television, radio, and print, provide an excellent means of reaching vast amounts of people quickly, but their downside is that these touches are both brief and scarce. This works if the objective is to create awareness, but it falls short of creating loyalty for an organization or a cause. Loyalty, unlike awareness, takes time to develop. It finds its roots in the trust, familiarity and respect that stem from frequent interactions with an organization, and the repetitive validation of a value alignment without which these interactions are meaningless. Through the use of social media, organizations can breed loyalty in their members by interacting regularly with them, befriending them, and empowering them to make a difference. The magic stems from the fact that social media can help humanize communications to such a degree that genuine friendships can begin to form between an organization's staff and the members they interact with online, even if they have never met in the real world. The depth of these interactions, combined with their potential frequency, can accelerate this process to such an extent that a new member can begin to feel loyal to an organization in a matter of days rather than in a matter of months.

One of the most common mistakes made by organizations when they first contemplate experimenting with social media is that they focus too much on social media tools and platforms and not enough on their business objectives. The reality of success in the social web for businesses is that creating a social media program begins not with insight into the latest social media tools and channels but with a thorough understanding of the organization's own goals and objectives. A social media program is not merely the fulfillment of a vague need to manage a "presence" on popular social networks such as Facebook and Twitter because "everyone else is doing it." "Being in social media" serves no purpose unto itself. In order to serve any purpose at all, a social media presence must either solve a problem for the organization and its customers or result in an improvement of some sort (preferably a measurable one). In all things, purpose drives success. The world of social media is no different. Define your purpose first, then identify your business goals, set specific targets, see how social media fits in, and start developing your program from that point. Approach social media program development in this way, and you will be well on your way to creating something of tremendous value for your organization.

3

Planning for Performance Measurement

Most of your social media program's effectiveness will rest on your ability to establish measurement methodologies that are aligned with your organization's goals, objectives and targets. Without a clear means of gauging success and shortcomings every step of the way once your program is launched, you will not be able to determine the extent of its impact on these objectives. Even the most carefully crafted and executed social media program in the world can crash and burn if both success and areas of improvement cannot be properly identified and measured. You could wait until the program is launched to think about measurement, but because this measurement methodology is directly tied to your program's goals and targets, it is better to develop it now before you begin assigning resources to the program.

Tools, Methodologies, and Purpose

Because measurement methodology is driven by the needs of the organization and shaped by its capabilities, before planning for performance measurement, you need to remember to do the following:

- Align your program's goals with existing business goals.

- Set realistic targets.

- Determine what metrics will help you gauge progress and the ultimate success of your program in regard to accomplishing its goals and hitting its targets.

- Develop best practices to ensure that measurement is handled ethically, accurately, and consistently.

- Find ways to improve the model. Turn everything into a learning experience.

Performance measurement is pointless without first establishing purpose, so determine the purpose of your program first. Second, determine the purpose of your activities within the program. Third, determine the purpose of your measurement practice in regard to the program's activities.

Remember that purpose can refer to more than one outcome: From measuring the progress of a campaign to holding employees accountable, from calculating ROI, to determining the impact the program has on a breadth of business functions, each program can bring its own unique set of measurement opportunities. Just make sure your measurement practice serves specific purposes (not just monthly reporting for the sake of it), and you will be off to a good start.

Selecting Adequate Social Media Measurement Software for Your Program

It is futile for me to recommend specific social media measurement software in this book because it changes so quickly, and new players enter the market almost weekly—but take solace in the knowledge that such software is in no short supply. Some are free. Others are extremely expensive. Some fall somewhere in the middle. Some focus on one type of metric only, whereas others provide their users with elaborate dashboards that incorporate a plethora of data, insights, and measurement capabilities. If you elect to go with enterprise-class software, chances are that most of your social media measurement (that is to say, measurement specific to social

media channels) will be taken care of. If you elect to use free or inexpensive software, look for specificity of purpose. In selecting measurement software for social
media, err on the side of tools that offer a high degree of precision when it comes
to measuring one specific thing rather than selecting software that measures ten
things poorly. Better to use ten reliable tools to measure ten types of data than to
use two that may leave you wondering if your data is reliable. Doing your homework when it comes to selecting the best measurement software will pay off in
the end.

A word of caution in the selection of monitoring and measurement software for
social media: Start by thinking about what the company wants to measure. Don't
just invest in measurement software because it is the one used by big companies or
because it seems to be getting a lot of positive press. Start with what metrics matter
most to you and find a tool that measures those well. If one piece of software does
it all, that's great. If you must combine several tools, that works, too. Most companies use a combination of measurement tools, so don't be afraid to experiment.
Every company is different. Find out what works for you.

Here is a simple way to do it:

1.   Write down everything you want to be able to measure online that
     directly impacts your program or campaign.

2.   Look for software that measures this type of data.

3.   Test the software.

4.   Organize the software from best to worst—in terms of accuracy,
     flexibility, reliability, and ease of use. (Don't underestimate user-
     friendliness.)

5.   Select the best software your budget allows for.

Choose the tool that best meets your organization's needs, whether it is a simple
open-source tool that you download for free or the most expensive, sophisticated
application on the market. One of the central themes of this book is that one-size-
fits-all solutions rarely work in the world of social media program management.
Measurement software falls into that category. What may work well for one company may not suit the needs of another. Moreover, one set of measurement tools
used for one campaign may not work at all to measure the effectiveness of another,
even within the same company. Chances are that your mix of tools will change
often in order to keep up with the ever-growing needs of your social media program. Do your research, ask for live demos, test the tools that strike your fancy, and
go with what works for you.

Key Performance Indicator (KPI)

We cannot talk about performance measurement without bringing up the term *key performance indicator*, or KPI. Key performance indicators illustrate the effectiveness of a campaign or program as it relates to hitting a specific target. What constitutes a key performance indicator depends on what you want to measure. Anything can be a KPI—from website visits and clicks on a banner advertisement, to RSS subscriptions, foot traffic at a retail location, registrations for a webinar, and sales revenue. The list is virtually infinite.

A word of caution: Though most web measurement professionals may try to sell you on the notion that key performance indicators are the same in social media as they are in other digital disciplines, remember that what you are measuring is not limited to the Web. In the world of social media program measurement, what makes a particular metric a key performance indicator is both its relationship to the program's purpose and its value in evaluating the program's effectiveness.

What is vital to remember is that the breadth of measurable data available today should not cloud the water. Countless companies spend an inordinate amount of time measuring things that were neither critical nor relevant to diagnosing the effectiveness of their programs and campaigns. If the golden rule of business measurement is "measure what matters," the golden rule of social media measurement is "just because you can measure it doesn't mean that it matters."

The challenge that many business managers run into when they begin working with measurement in the social media space is that the abundance of data can be overwhelming. Many fall prey to the temptation to measure everything. The problem with trying to measure so much is that data overload is the enemy of focus. Knowing ahead of time what metrics matter and what metrics don't will help program managers avoid falling into this trap. In order to create an effective measurement practice for your social media program, you must be diligent when it comes to separating critical data (KPI) from noncritical data.

For more advanced measurement professionals, layering metrics in tiers (basically levels) with an eye to both the importance and relevance to the program and its desired outcomes can help broaden the range of performance indicators without causing data overload or confusion. A simple structure to help organize performance indicators in tiers might look like this:

Top tier: Key performance indicators

Second tier: Secondary performance indicators

Third tier: Other data

Let me give you an example:

Objective: Increase sales of red tires

Target: 25,000 additional red tires sold in Canada in Q3

Key performance indicators (KPIs): Sales of red tires sold in Canada in Q3

- Positive online mentions of red tires leading into Q3
- Net new "Likes" of red tire content on Facebook page from Canadian locations
- Net new click-throughs of links leading to red tire web content from Canadian accounts
- Redeemed coupons and discount codes for red tires in Canada in Q3

Secondary performance indicators: Sales of red tires outside of Canada in Q3

- Net new "Likes" of red tire content on Facebook page (global)
- Net new click-throughs of links leading to red tire web content (outside of Canada)
- Net change in global online sentiment for red tires in Q3

Other data: Sales of black tires sold in Canada in Q3

- Visits to company home page
- Comments on the company blog
- New followers on Twitter
- Bounce rate
- Brand mentions (global)

What is the difference between these three tiers? Simple: The KPI tier focused on metrics that directly illustrate the connection between your activity and the outcome, starting with the outcome: "Sales of red tires in Canada in Q3." The target in this example is 25,000 net new red tires sold. The first KPI is simply: Are we hitting our target? The other key performance indicators in the group are directly linked to this target. They focus on activities aimed to drive purchases of red tires in Canada leading to and during Q3.

"Positive online mentions of red tires leading into Q3" shows whether or not the company's campaign is having an effect on the perception of red tires. More mentions means a win. More positive mentions means a win. Net new nods of approval for red tires from Canadians on the company's Facebook page means a win. It simply means that the company's activities are driving its audience from awareness to preference, bringing them closer to a purchasing preference.

Secondary performance indicators help illustrate the impact that a program may be having on other parts of the business that were not included in the program's objectives. These collateral outcomes can be helpful in identifying new opportunities and understanding the broader impact of a program.

Here, the secondary performance tier measures red tire sales and the drive to grow that part of the business, but these performance indicators do not directly touch the target of 25,000 net new red tires sold in Canada in Q3. It is, however, important to measure changes/deltas in sales of red tires outside of Canada during Q3, if only to baseline Canadian sales. Likewise, online activity relating to red tires that isn't specific to Canadian consumers is secondary. Why? Because the campaign's target, in this particular case, is specific to Canadian sales. Online activity from consumers in Europe and Japan, for example, although important, is not a key performance indicator when it comes to this very specific target. Because it has no direct bearing on the desired outcome, it falls to the second tier.

The value in identifying and monitoring secondary performance indicators is that they can help business analysts identify critical correlations that would have otherwise remained undetected. Let me give you an example: What if a clever data analyst realizes, over time, a link between positive activity about red tires in France, Switzerland, and the Benelux and red tire sales in Quebec (Canada's French-speaking region)? What if a clear correlation exists between the volume of positive mentions in Francophone Europe and sales in Quebec? In such an instance, this data would have to be considered for an upgrade to the KPI tier. Sometimes, key performance indicators aren't obvious. You might uncover them by accident or by process. Make no assumptions about cause and effect, but if you spot a pattern, test its validity. If you can prove this type of correlation exists, that is one more data point you can add to your list of KPIs.

The third performance tier shows data that is too *vague* and unfocused to relate directly to the campaign and its specific target. This brings me to a word of caution about KPI measurement, especially in the digital world. I am not limiting my comments to social media here, but the Web as a whole: Beware of cookie-cutter web measurement methodologies that treat key performance indicators as a nonvariable group. For many digital measurement analysts, visits to your website, bounce rates, click-throughs, and other general metrics constitute the bulwark of KPI reporting. This is wrong. Web measurement professionals don't get to tell you what your KPIs are. You tell them. The typical cookie-cutter approach to web measurement rarely assigns KPI nomenclature to program/campaign-appropriate metrics.

Case in point: If your campaign's objective is to increase positive mentions of your brand across the Web by 30% in Q3, your key performance indicators will not be the same as if your goal were to shift 10% of your customer service "tickets" from toll-free call centers to a micro-blogging platform over the next six months. Different objectives mean different sets of KPIs.

Key performance indicators are media-agnostic. They are based on the target you have set for a program or campaign. When developing a measurement methodology with your team, get together with them and go through the process of separating KPIs from secondary performance indicators and secondary performance indicators from all other metrics. Creating a tiered system like the one I have just described will help give your measurement order, clarity, and purpose. Map it out.

Social Media and Sales Measurement: F.R.Y.

F.R.Y. stands for *frequency, reach*, and *yield*. I first came in contact with it while developing SMB (small and medium-sized business) reseller communities with Microsoft. The software giant was trying to help its distributors identify specific areas they could target to increase sales. "Sell more stuff" wasn't good enough. Microsoft wanted to be able to teach its distributors how to peel back the layers of their sales process and understand the various ways in which sales behavior could be influenced. What it came up with was F.R.Y.

The beauty of F.R.Y. is that it breaks down transactional mechanisms into three distinct and easy-to-understand elements. Here is how it works:

Let's assume that 100% of your company's revenue comes from sales. No royalties or anything of the sort. The sales department's general objective is to increase sales. Now, what are the three basic ways you can increase sales?

1. Get existing customers to buy from you more often.

2. Acquire new customers.

3. Get existing customers to spend more with you every time they buy something.

Boiled down to the core, what you are looking at is buy rate, net new transacting customers, and average amount per transaction—or frequency, reach, and yield.

With these three elements now clearly defined, you can get under the hood of your revenue model.

One principal objective of most businesses is to generates revenue, probably through its sales process. Using our previous example, we can start to map out our goals, objectives, and targets:

Goal:	Increase revenue
Objective for small tire group:	Increase sales of red tires
Target for red tire product team:	25,000 net new red tires sold in Canada in Q3

Now let's plug-in frequency, reach, and yield: If increasing sales revenue from red tires in Canada in Q3 comes from increasing the customer buy rate, acquiring net new customers, or increasing the amount of each purchase specific to red tires, how do we achieve these objectives? How does social media fit in, and how should we measure success? The social web provides opportunities not only to generate new customers, influence buy rate, and impact yield, but to determine the extent to which each contributes to the increase in revenue you are looking for.

Because we know that the objectives dictate the strategies and tactics, we know that the objectives also dictate program measurement. At this point in our program's development, frequency, reach, and yield exist as both a means to reach a desired outcome and the heart of what types of metrics will constitute the core of our measurement practice. Our list of key performance indicators as it relates to sales will be directly derived from frequency, reach, and yield data.

The company's frequency strategy can be summed up in one simple question: How do you get existing customers to buy red tires more often than they do now? Let's assume that most red tire users buy a new pair of tires every three months. The idea is now to change their behavior in such a way that the interval between purchases of red tires will be reduced. In the short term, you can push a special sales campaign in which customers are incentivized to buy their tires now rather than when they normally would, some weeks or months from today. You could use social media channels to amplify your campaign, and that would be that. For many companies, this is what social media boils down to: another set of channels through which to cram promotions. But let's look at this a bit closer because short-term thinking, although effective, falls short in a space that rewards long-term vision.

The problem with short-term thinking is that its impact is limited to the here and now. In our example, a promotion would satisfy the aims of the Q3 target (selling more red tires in Q3) but perhaps at the cost of Q4 sales. A key point to understand is that accelerating a one-time purchase is not the same thing as shortening buy rate. The overall aim of increasing transactional frequency is to shorten the purchase intervals over time, not just once. So let's put this option on the back burner for now and consider smarter ways of meeting this objective.

Instead, what if the company created an awareness campaign that focuses on tire wear? Content could be produced that shows how after two months of normal use, small tires start to wear out. Their roundness edges down to a flatter surface, which creates more resistance against the road. The impact of more resistance: It takes more energy to go fast than when the tires are new. In other words, three-month-old tires slow you down and new tires make you faster. For cyclists, for example, such a revelation would surely strike a nerve.

This content could come in the form of reports, fact sheets, videos, podcasts, and tutorials. The company could embed sales information about their tires within the content and plant the seed of their audience's next transaction: Don't wait three months before buying a new set. Buy it now or soon.

In terms of social media, the method is simple: Create the content. Post it to your website and blog. Push it out through social networks and online communities. Make it easy to share. If you have reports or fact sheets, make them available in a format that's easy to attach to a social network update. (PDF still works fairly well.) Post videos to YouTube. Make your podcasts available on iTunes. Whatever works. Seed every relevant social web channel with your content. Engage in discussions. Answer questions. Drive attention to the campaign, to tire wear, to tire performance and value. Inform people and keep their minds on your point. Use social media channels to amplify your campaign and drive to the desired outcome: a change in behavior leading to an increase in buy rate for your product.

You can also take a safety approach to the frequency strategy: Old tires are less safe than new ones. Don't risk getting a flat or crashing to save a few bucks. Change your tires often. Two months between sets is safer than three...and so on. Whatever the angle you choose for your campaign, the social communications mechanism is the same.

Now, how do you *measure* changes/deltas in frequency? Well, because of the nature of the bike tire business, you may not be able to measure it at the cash register because your resellers are independent of your company. They are an external layer. Although you influence their customers (the end users), you don't have visibility to what is happening at the point of sale. Problem? Not really. This only adds a layer of complexity to the measurement, nothing more.

If you cannot measure transactional frequency directly, bypass the obstacle: Your resellers react to demand. When their customers start buying tires more often, your resellers have to start increasing their stock faster. This data, you have access to. Whereas a reseller may normally order four sets of red tires per month, he may now start placing orders for eight sets for that month.

Twice the amount of tires for the same time period? Something is happening. Call up your reseller and ask him: Why the change? He'll know. If he doesn't, see if he will ask his customers for you. Better yet, create a survey on one of your sites (or a social network) for tire buyers. In fact, create a painless mechanism to drive buyers of your tires to that survey. A prompt and web address on a sales receipt perhaps, or a decal on the packaging, a point of purchase display with tear-off cards, an insert, a daily prompt across social networks? Whatever works. The data is there. Sometimes it comes to you. Sometimes you have to go hunt for it.

The point is, if frequency of transactions is one aspect of transactional behavior you aim to influence, you must find a way to measure it.

Now let's talk about reach. Here's a question for you: Where do new customers come from?

Let me ask you another question: If your message currently reaches 10,000 people and 1,000 of them are transacting customers, what would be the impact of reaching 100,000 people? By growing your audience to ten times its current size, is it possible that you might acquire net new transacting customers from the additional 90,000 people you are reaching?

Without making any assumptions about conversion rates from prospect to customer, and also without making assumptions about the quality of your interactions, can we assume that the bigger the audience, the greater the chance of attracting more customers? Generally, yes. This is the premise behind *reach*: Increasing reach should in turn increase the number of net new transacting customers. Think of it as building a pipeline, using social media as the funnel.

Why did Dell's @DellOutlet Twitter account take two years to reach its first $2M in sales yet reached $6.5M in its third year? Why the sudden acceleration? Simple: reach. The numbers tell the story. When Dell started experimenting with Twitter, it was still a relatively unknown micro-blogging platform. As the number of Twitter users grew, so did Dell's reach. Reach determines the potential size of your pipeline. This is true for sales, for information, for feedback, and for influence.

Measuring the impact of reach on sales performance begins with measuring changes in the size of various key communities managed by your social media program. Examples might be your number of new followers on Twitter, your number of new connections on Facebook, net new group members on LinkedIn, and new subscribers to your RSS feeds or your YouTube channel.

The next step in the process is to measure the impact that these increases in reach have on your number of new transacting customers. The secret to a company's reach strategy lies in the program's ability not only to acquire fans, followers, subscribers and connections, but to convert them through its use of social media into transacting customers.

The final step in the conversion is to develop these customers not only into loyal customers but into brand advocates and ambassadors as well. When customers begin to help you recruit new customers through lateral engagement, your ability to increase your reach can be scaled beyond your own limited resources. One community manager can only interact directly with so many people on any given day, but thousands of enthusiastic customers can cover a lot of ground for you. Their networks become your networks. This is the secret to building an ever-growing pipeline across social media channels.

From sales to online reputation management and everything in between, measuring reach is possibly the single most important aspect of your program's methodology.

If you measure nothing else, at least measure reach. If growth is an objective for your organization, increasing reach is at the core of its execution. Track it.

Finally, we come to third element of F.R.Y.: yield. In both sales and social media terms, yield is simply the average dollar value of a transaction. If you cannot acquire any new customers and you cannot increase buy rate, then you are left with convincing your existing customers to spend more money with you when they transact.

There are two ways of increasing yield. Your first option is to raise your prices: If you were selling red tires for $35 each in Q2, selling for $35.50 each in Q3 might do the trick. Caution: If prices tend to be inelastic in your industry or for that product category, you might do more harm than good by raising prices.

Your second option is to develop your customers in such a way that they will *want* to spend more money with you. Go to any coffee shop in the United States and order a small cup of coffee at the counter. What is the barista trained to do? Suggest a bigger size. "Are you sure you don't want a medium? It's only 35 cents more." (Insert smile.) "Would you like a croissant with that? Or a cranberry muffin? They're really good today."

What may have started out as a $2 transaction has just become a $6 transaction. By inserting dialog into the process, then additional options, and then creating value for those options, the seller has convinced the buyer that it was in best his interest to spend a little more money than he intended to.

Airlines do the same thing by offering seat upgrades, for example, or the option to move up to Business Class. Giving you the option to upgrade is not a means to increase yield just one time. It is also a discovery mechanism that aims to convert you into a premium services customer. Increasing yield isn't easy, but it can be done by making the value of an upgrade difficult to resist. Build value, reduce the upgrade barrier, give customers a little push, and voilá.

How this relates to social media is twofold. First, social media is a means of creating awareness for upgrades or bundle packages (anything that will incentivize customers to spend more per transaction) directly from the company. This is vertical engagement. Second, it uses the power of lateral engagement to reinforce the value and increase the message's reach. By encouraging customers who have just been wowed by their first upgrade experience to share their enthusiasm with other people via social media channels, more customers may be moved to upgrade as well.

As Virgin America's Porter Gale explains: "The community closes the sale." She's right. Leverage your *social capital*. Use social media to create awareness for the value of a premium service and encourage your community to be a part of the process.

Measuring performance in regard to changes in yield can either be straightforward or pretty difficult to pinpoint, depending on your business. In the straightforward category, companies with CRM (customer relationship management) systems that track individual customer behavior will have no problem spotting changes in yield from specific customers. Most hotels, airlines, and an increasing number of retailers (especially e-retailers) are able to track these types of changes. For companies whose products fall into distinct categories (bronze, silver, and gold levels, or basic vs. premium, for example) it also isn't too hard to figure out changes/deltas in yield by looking at changes in those ratios.

Sometimes, though, it isn't that simple. You may have to look into your transaction data (your receipts) and look for changes in product sales. In the instance of the coffee shop mentioned earlier, assuming that the number of transactions remains the same (say, 500 coffee drinks per day), you would want to look at changes/deltas in the percentage of large, medium, and small coffees sold.

Say that before you launch your next social media marketing campaign (this one focusing on increasing yield), your mix of coffee sales looks like 30% small, 40% medium, and 30% large coffees. Within a week of the start of your campaign, you start to see a shift. Your numbers now look like this: 20% small, 45% medium, and 35% large coffees. That is the basis of your measurement for this project. The main KPI to track in this instance would be the net number of small, medium, and large coffees sold, relative to each other. This would most clearly illustrate the trend toward a change in purchasing behavior favoring larger sizes.

What you can then do is look at social activity and determine whether or not your social media program and campaign played a part in supporting that objective and perhaps even determine how much of a role it played. The number of online mentions promoting the value of upgrading to a larger size coffee for this particular chain of coffee shops, as well as where and when these mentions occurred, would be obvious key performance indicators to consider.

What else could *yield* stand for besides sales? Any type of outcome that shows a quantifiable increase in zeal from your community. You could measure yield in terms of engagement: A particular subgroup of Twitter followers could go from lightly sharing some of your content to sharing and discussing it in greater depth. This increase in participation would mark a positive change in their level of involvement. If you are a charity organization, existing members may escalate the level of their volunteerism from just showing up at events to help out, to volunteering to help manage them for you. These are examples of nonfinancial yield.

Now that we have properly discussed the role that measurement will play in your social media practice, we can start exploring the need for structure, talent, organizational buy-in, and commonsense change management.

4

Establishing Clarity of Vision, Purpose, and Execution

It would be easy to assume that most companies' first reflex when the topic of social media comes up is to resist the notion that it has a legitimate role to play in the business world. This couldn't be further from the truth. Most companies I have spoken with so far are excited about the potential that social media brings to the table. The problem is that they generally have a tough time understanding how to make social media work for them. The disconnect that often exists between the business world and social media is the result of a simple lack of clarity on the part of social media evangelists. It is one thing to articulate the value of social media as a whole to a business manager or CEO. It is yet another to articulate what specific value social media can bring to his organization.

To get buy-in for your program, you must understand the business enough to see where social media fits. Social media finds its value in supporting, enhancing, or amplifying business functions focused on achieving specific business objectives. In order to get buy-in from an organization, you must be able to clearly outline social media's value not to only the organization as a whole, but to key decision makers who will endorse, support, and benefit directly from your program.

Getting Top-Down and Bottom-Up Buy-In Throughout the Organization

Start with what matters—the CEO's principal objectives for the business. If your program can help solve a critical business problem or help the organization accomplish its goals faster, better, and more cost effectively, you will find an eager audience in the chief executive. If, however, your social media program's value to the CEO remains unclear, you may not get the buy-in you need to move forward with your social media program.

One way to illustrate the value of your idea to a CEO is by demonstrating some of the clear and tangible benefits of your social media program. Here are examples of effective ways of discussing the value of a social media program:

- "I want to cut 20% out of our current customer service costs by shifting some of our resources out of our call center and into social media channels. Aside from making us more effective, chances are that it will improve people's perception of our company as well."

- "I want to use social media to increase our reach. We should be able to leverage our engagement with the public on Facebook and Twitter to double our customer acquisition rates over the course of the next year."

- "Social media seems like a great way for us to turn our loyalty program into stronger repeat business. I want to start by focusing on frequency and yield campaigns so we can get our sales numbers back on track before the end of the quarter."

- "Right now, we have no idea what kind of impact our marketing campaigns are having on the public. The kind of data we can pull from the social web would give us a glimpse of what is working and what isn't and how to get the most out of our market budget next year."

- "One of the reasons why our business isn't doing as well these days is that we have become disconnected from our customers. I want to use social media to reconnect with them, find out how we can improve our products and services, rebuild trust and loyalty, and become the company they want us to be."

Clarity and purpose create value. It is that simple. Here are examples of how *not* to approach the subject with a CEO:

- "Our competitors have a Facebook page. We probably need one, too."

- "Blogs are good for search engine optimization (SEO). Our website could use the traffic."

- "I don't know what social media will do for us yet, but let's test the waters and see what opportunities materialize."

- "We want to *engage* with our customers and have *conversations* with them."

Note how these arguments are vague and convey neither clear purpose nor tangible value. In the best of worlds, they might get buy-in for a social media program, but odds are that the outcome of such a program will not yield tangible results for the organization. If your program doesn't seem to have a point, if it doesn't appear to benefit the organization in specific, tangible ways, then it will have little value to the CEO.

The CEO isn't the only person you need to convince. In order to get buy-in from the entire organization (and you do), department managers whose staff will be involved in the program need to buy in to it as well. Remember that launching a new program will mean more work for somebody, not just you. This means that some departments will feel additional strain on already stretched resources. New responsibilities also bring the risk of failure and exposure to potentially negative feedback.

Last, a new program means change, which as we all know is never easy to sell in any organization. Everything in business boils down to a risk-versus-reward equation: Ask peers to take a risk without a clear indication of reward, and you may not receive the support you need. Conversely, if you can articulate the value of your new program to key decision makers across the organization, and the reward outweighs the risk, you will have a much better chance of getting the widespread buy-in you need to move forward.

Speaking of risk, getting buy-in from your organization for your social media program isn't as simple as articulating its value to the business. Part of the process focuses on managing objections. The "why we should do it" argument is half of the battle. Now, you must address the "why we should not do it" part of the discussion.

Here are some of the most common questions about risk that new social media program proposals typically encounter in the business world:

- "What if people start saying really bad things about us?"

- "What if we say or write something embarrassing?"

- "What if we accidentally leak confidential information on one of these social networks?"

- "What if we are criticized?"

- "It seems like a lot of work. We don't have the manpower to manage something like this right now."

- "How do we know our customers even use social media? I don't use it."

- "Does all this social media stuff open us up to lawsuits? Has anyone even considered that?"

- "How will you tie your 'Facebooking' to business performance?"

Before you stiffen up and start feeling defensive, understand that these are all valid questions. This part of the process is healthy. It provides you with an opportunity to educate your peers, to demonstrate that your program already covers all these "unknown factors," and gives you a chance to speak to "how" the program will be managed. More often than not, the answer to a "what if" question is best answered by a "how this fits into our execution" reply. If you find yourself unable to answer many of these questions, take that as a sign that your game plan needs a little bit more work before you can truly move forward. *Purpose* may get you in the door, but having a solid plan gets you the *go-ahead*.

Let's take a closer look at how you may want to answer these types of questions:

Q: "What if people start saying negative things about us?"

A: Some already are. We just aren't there to hear about it. Look at it this way: Not being able to hear what is being said about us is a liability. Instead, by having a social media program in place, we will be able see negative comments and complaints as they happen. That degree of visibility will provide us with the opportunity to respond to whatever criticism, complaints, and attacks we are not paying attention to now. Negative sentiment is one of the things this program aims to minimize. We will be measuring our impact on it and reporting regularly on our progress.

Q: "What if we say or write something embarrassing?"

A: Well, let's make sure that doesn't happen. First things first: We are working on social media guidelines and policies for the company. Second, once the policies are put in effect, we will *train* our employees—even the ones not involved with our social media program—to avoid getting in trouble on social networks. Third, employees who represent us officially online will be carefully selected and will go through more advanced training to ensure that *faux pas* don't happen. This program will be managed by professionals, not amateurs.

Q: "What if we accidentally leak confidential information on one of these social networks?"

A: Our social media guidelines and policies will address that clearly, reinforced by employee training. Also, official company accounts will be managed by professionals. All employees will know that whatever guidelines apply to other forms of communications—verbal, email, telephone, fax, and so on—also apply to social media.

Q: "It seems like a lot of work. We don't have the manpower to manage something like this right now."

A: It is, and we don't. We are going to have to invest in some headcount and some software. Note that my proposal outlines companywide cost savings and business development objectives, complete with goals and targets to justify the investment. It isn't much, and we want to start small, but we have to be serious about this if we want it to work. And it *will* work. If it doesn't, cut the program's funding and try something else.

Q: How do we know our customers even use social media? I don't use it.

A: Some may not, and for them, this won't have much of an impact. Many of them do, however, and for them, our activity in social media will be a benefit. Having an active social media presence will make us more accessible, for example. Remember that one of our objectives is also to acquire *new* customers, many of whom will hopefully discover us because of our presence in social media. This will not take the place of anything that already works for us.

Q: "Does all this social media stuff open us up to lawsuits? Has anyone even considered that?"

A: The section of the proposal on legal considerations, exposure, and defamation addresses all of that. We will need to work pretty closely with our legal team as we develop the program. They need to be a big part of it, starting with our social media guidelines and policies. Great point. I'm glad you brought it up.

Q: "How will you tie your 'Facebooking' to business performance?"

A: Measurement is so easy in the social space that the kind of data and reporting we will be able plug in to our business performance will help us connect the dots better than we can now—and in real time. All of our measurement will focus on key performance indicators *specific* to the business objectives the program directly supports. We will also be looking at both nonfinancial impact to the business and financial impact—in other words, return on investment. I want to make sure this program drives business. That's the whole point.

Answering these types of questions is crucial to getting buy-in from decision makers across the organization. Understand that fear of change, fear of the unknown, and fear of what might happen can be appeased by the clarity of a plan that turns what *might* happen into what *will* happen. Understanding the objectives, clarifying the value, and demonstrating that you understand the risks, hurdles, and challenges ahead will go a long way toward deflating fear and instilling confidence in your endeavor.

When pitching an idea to a CEO, you must think like a CEO. Likewise, when pitching an idea to a marketing manager and a customer service supervisor, you must be able to put yourself in their situation. You must be able to objectively balance the pros and cons of the program and investment in that program, and you must be willing to address every possible reason why your idea might fail. Simply willing it to succeed isn't enough. You must also be honest with yourself about all the ways in which things might go wrong and have a plan to address each of these scenarios.

I cannot stress enough how important it is for a program of this type to receive buy-in from the entire organization. Simply getting the go-ahead from the CEO is not enough. Without buy-in from IT, you will have no chance at implementing the elements of your program dealing with software and bandwidth. Without buy-in from the Sales department, good luck tying social media activity to F.R.Y. (frequency, reach, yield) or ROI. Without HR and Legal in your corner, your social media policies and guidelines will never be properly drafted, and employee training may never happen. Without the web designers at your side, seamless integration of social networks with your other digital properties will be forever on hold. You can walk to every desk in your organization and find either a roadblock or an ally. The choice is yours. The more allies you have, the better chance your social media program has of being approved and being smoothly deployed. You have to know how to sell it, and you have to know the importance of doing so. You cannot be the sole champion in the early days of this endeavor.

Here is something else you should know: Organizations are composed of factions and cliques. Few decisions are made by one person alone. More often than not, decisions are made following a number of unseen interactions, often behind closed doors. A CEO, even inclined to grant you *carte blanche*, will seek the opinion of her trusted advisors. She will gauge the mood and inclination of the company as a whole, probing for dissent and uncertainty. Fail to convince the majority of the organization to rally behind your cause, and you may find yourself outgunned not by flat-out opposition, but by the specter of uncertainty.

If after having gone through this entire grueling process, you receive the answer, "I like what you have in mind, but we aren't ready yet," it simply means that you have failed to get sufficient buy-in. "Let's talk about it again in six months. We have too much on our plate right now," is the same thing. Don't lose hope. Find out what the real objections are, what the real unanswered questions are, and start working on them. Eventually, through diligence, patience, and with enough support, your social media program will get the go-ahead.

I close this section with an uncomfortable question, but one that must be asked if your program is turned down. It has nothing to do with having clarified the value your program brings or having outlined the ways in which you have addressed fears about the program's risk. Ask yourself this: Is it possible that the CEO and her executive team, while aware of the opportunity presented by a social media program and impressed with the depth of preparation you have put into the proposal, are not 100% confident in *your* ability to manage it? In other words, is it possible that they see you as a smart, able person with great ideas but not the person to turn your idea into a reality?

This is a very difficult question to ask oneself, but it cannot be skirted. Worse yet, you may have to ask your CEO directly and remove your ego and feelings from the equation should the answer be what you fear most. In such an instance, you have to find out what matters most: your wounded pride or getting the job done?

If pride wins the day, then look for another place to work. If getting the job done seems like a better option, then do this: Build a team and find someone to build and manage the program, someone the leadership will trust implicitly. In other words, lead from the middle instead of leading from the top. Delegate the politics to someone else. You can be the brains of the operation without wearing the crown. It happens all the time, and more often than not, such arrangements yield wonderful results. There is no shame in accepting that being chief strategist instead of program director might work best for the program, the organization, and even you.

Keeping ego out of social media as much as possible isn't a bad rule to follow, even in these early stages of program development. Do what needs to be done to get the program approved and an adequate budget assigned. If that means having to share the glory and delegating some of the work, so be it. Chances are, you will be glad for it later, when division of labor and responsibilities will actually make execution possible. Just make it happen and adapt to whatever gets thrown your way.

Change Management, Social Media Style

Okay, let's not beat around the bush: Change is unpredictable. Change is dangerous. Change is scary. Change is the enemy of security, which is a big deal when you have spent years, if not decades, working your way up to the title of Director or VP or Manager, and one false move could jeopardize everything you have worked so hard for.

Risk is not good career sport for most business executives. Because of this, change is rarely easy to sell to an organization, and integrating social media into an organization *is* change.

This is important because when it comes to building a social media program from scratch, hiring the right people, choosing the right tools, creating content, and measuring ROI will not be all that difficult in comparison to the *change management* aspect of this endeavor. That is why Part II, "Social Media Program Integration," is entirely devoted to the process of properly and painlessly *integrating* social media into an organization.

You have communicated the value of your social media program to the entire organization, addressed fears, appeased doubt, and secured buy-in from every level of the organization. You have also recruited key departments to your cause and begun the process of creating a team that will not only champion the use of social media but manage the program as well. That was a good start, but the work isn't over.

The next step is to begin demystifying social media across the organization.

Your company is made up of two categories of people: The first is familiar with social media. Individuals belonging to this category play there, read blogs, share photos, watch videos, and chat with friends and peers. Some may even already be using social media for semi-professional uses, such as connecting with industry contacts on LinkedIn and perhaps even managing an industry blog. The second category is made up of people who are not at all familiar or comfortable with social media.

To the second category, an announcement through company channels that your organization is now going to engage in social media activity means precisely squat. What they may be hearing is, "We are going to start using Facebook and Twitter," to which the only reasonable reaction may be a well-deserved "So what?" or a perfectly executed rolling of the eyes to the amusement of their cubicle-mates. Who can blame them, really. Social media? Isn't that what people do at their desks when they get bored with computer solitaire?

Myth Number 1: Social Media Is a Waste of Time

This is the first myth you need to dispel in your organization. Start with this: If indeed the organization is going to talk about the development of a social media program, be clear about its purpose, value, and the business functions it will support. Remember how you sold the CEO and the rest of management on your idea? Guess what? The rest of the organization needs the same level of clarity from you on the subject. Explain it:

> **Wrong:** "We are happy to announce that John Smith has been promoted to the role of Social Media Director. In his new duties, John will be exploring ways in which social media may benefit the company."
>
> **Right:** "We are happy to announce that John Smith has been promoted to the role of Social Media Director. In his new duties, John will be working with key departments across the entire organization to help generate leads, drive new business, gather business intelligence, and bring us closer to our customers."

Additionally, the difference between employees commenting on their friends' Facebook photo galleries every ten minutes and the company's business-focused use of social media must be established early and reinforced regularly. If the organization is large enough, internal newsletters can be used to feature interviews with employees managing social media–related roles. When HR conducts training for employees, the distinction between personal use and official use should be made clear to all. The company's new social media guidelines and policies should also clearly delineate the two types of use.

When asked, "So your job is to talk to people on Facebook and Twitter all day?" by colleagues, employees in social media roles should be prepared to explain how their job is a little more complex than that. There is content curation as well as research, customer support, reputation management, keyword monitoring, the building of relationships, overlapping communities to manage, and a lot of detailed reporting. Moreover, it directly supports key departments such as Marketing, Sales, Human Resources, and Public Relations. The job is social, sure, but it is all business.

Myth Number 2: Social Media Is Complicated

When we talk about social media in terms of function or activity, we are really talking about social communications—what we *do* on social media channels, not the social media channels themselves.

What seems complicated to most people not yet comfortable with the social web is the technology, the ocean of tools, and the endless stream of oddly named platforms and networks. What actually happens in social media is simply this: People talking with people. Don't be afraid to bring the conversation back to the basics.

If someone doesn't seem to understand how social media works, explain it to them like this: "You talk with people on the phone, right?" (Yes.) "You talk with people via email as well?" (Yes.) "You chat with them at industry events, and parties and other social gatherings?" (Yes.) "Okay, well, this is exactly the same thing. It just happens via digital spaces instead of face to face or through a telephone line."

It takes a little bit of getting used to, sure, but if my 76-year-old mother can learn to post pictures to Facebook and chat with her grandchildren there, surely, so can anyone with a desk, a computer, and a telephone. The reality of social media is that the technologies that make it all work, while seemingly complex to an outsider, are for the most part remarkably accessible and user friendly. Focusing too much on the technology can be intimidating. Instead, make sure to focus on the business objectives, which are much easier for everyone inside the organization to understand.

Myth Number 3: Anyone Can Do That Job

It depends on the job, but no. Not everyone can. First of all, let's be clear about social media "jobs": Eventually, as social communications become embedded in an organization, those jobs will begin to be absorbed within departments until social media is just another tool like email and telephones. Second, every social media function in an organization requires training and mission-specific skills. Just because someone spends a lot of time chatting with friends on Facebook and watching videos on YouTube doesn't mean he is qualified to be a community manager for your organization.

Managing a social media account for a company is not as simple as managing a personal social media account. Not everyone is qualified to be a professional in this space, and so it is important for companies to create internal training programs and criteria of competency for their employees. This should be done not only to ensure that social media roles fall to qualified professionals inside the organization, but also to send the right kind of message to every employee: This is a serious, legitimate type of activity. In spite of the fact that it may first appear to be "what kids do in their free time," its application in the business world is not haphazard.

Myth Number 4: Social Media Is the Shiny New Thing. Two Years from Now, That Bubble Will Burst

Yes, it is the shiny new thing. No, two years from now, that bubble will not burst. There is no bubble. What social media represents is an evolution in the field of communications, just as the Internet and mobility before it. The tools will change, the platforms will evolve, but the way in which people communicate with other people through digital networks and electronic devices has been fundamentally transformed through the development of social media.

We did not grow tired of the telephone, of the television, of the Internet, or of our ever-evolving portable devices. We will not grow tired of the social web either. Its value to us is simply too great to give up, as is its value to organizations. Social media is here to stay.

Myth Number 5: I Am Going to Have to Change the Way I Work

Yes, you might have to change the way you work a little, but not any more than when the IT department upgrades your computer, operating system, or smart phone. The shift will be easy to manage and not particularly disruptive.

At the heart of this myth is fear of change. For many, change is abrupt. Change is violent. Change is revolution. These things are scary. But to some, change is a welcome event. For them, no worries. They will adapt easily and eagerly to whatever you throw their way. With others, fear and uncertainty can be an obstacle. For them, change needs to come with less violence. *Revolution* must downshift to *evolution*. Be sensitive to this group. Shift the conversation from *change* to *improvement*. Better yet, don't spend so much time talking about the change itself, but instead focus on results.

Objectives are everything. New technology, new tools, new procedures, all of these things are just part of life in the business world. Adaptation is necessary for survival. This is no different. That said, there's no need to push. Ease into changes.

Listen to employees' fears and address them. Ask them what they would like to see. If they ask for training, provide it for them. If they need resources they can consult at will, create them. Everyone within the organization will adapt at a different rate. Be prepared for that.

Change management, particularly as it relates to the integration of social media into an organization, boils down to this: inserting new tools, methods, and activities into the existing environment as smoothly and painlessly as possible. How well you manage that piece of the puzzle will determine how quickly your program will be up and running and how effective it will be in its first year.

Remember never to sell "change," but to instead sell results. Few people look forward to the first, but everyone can rally around the latter.

Laying the Groundwork for Integration and Management

Because social media will at first be at odds with some departments or teams within the organization—obstacles may be cultural, political, or procedural—you may start to feel that you have to "fight" for your program, that inserting it into the organization is at its core a battle for supremacy: old ways versus new ways.

Don't.

Resist the urge to see it as a fight. Resist the urge to impose your will on anyone. Push, and someone will invariably push back. Instead, take the path of least resistance.

In the beginning, you are going to have your hands full. Integrating social media across the organization is going to take time and patience. You are going to have to focus on one project at a time. That means one objective at a time until you score some wins and individual project teams start to take ownership of their own social media activities.

The obvious course of action, then, is to start with the most obvious opportunities, and among these, the ones that will pose the least amount of political resistance. The more you demonstrate results over time, the more you will validate the worth of your program, and the more likely you will be asked to help with other teams and projects.

The path of least resistance is simply this: Be helpful. Reach out to a project team or a department, and tell them what you can do. Ask them how you can help them meet their goals. Start building strategic alliances with business development teams, with HR, with Marketing and PR, with product managers and sales teams. Share insights with them. Call them every few days—or better yet, walk over to their desks—and ask them what they have going on. Is there a new promotion launching this week? Great! Why not post it on the company's Facebook wall? Is there a fire sale scheduled later in the month? Why not tweet the link to the web page when the time comes? What if a new press release is looking for an audience, or there's a search for a second-shift press operator, or a new product is hitting the shelves next quarter? You can help with all that.

You can't expect the rest of the organization to come to you, the social media program manager, asking for help. It just isn't going to happen. Not right away. It will take months for habits to change, for your new social media–friendly structure and integration process to take hold and gain momentum on its own. Before things start to click and become habit for everyone, you are going to have to reach out daily and serve the needs of everyone you can afford to help.

One final thing: In your dealings with other departments and project teams, don't lead with processes or long discussions about what you are doing and how. Focus on identifying their needs and reporting results. Here is an example:

> **Wrong:** "So, what we can do is post links to your special promo on Facebook, Twitter, and the blog, for starters. We could update those three or four times per day, maybe change the copy a bit every time. Blah, blah, blah...."

> **Right:** "Cool. Send me the info, and we'll push it out." Later: "Here's a recap of what we did: We tracked the click-throughs, and it looks like we added 1,235 net visits to your promo page. The report shows you where they came from. The graph shows you changes in mentions for the last two weeks. The increase in the middle is from our activity. Want to meet tomorrow and talk about how we can make this work even better for you?"

Focus on objectives, targets, and results. Don't bore anyone with the process unless they ask or until you report on your success. Also putting activities in context with what worked needs to be outlined.

Last, reinforce successes. Put them in perspective. Link results and outcomes to your activity: "Here, we had a win because we did *this* instead of *that*. Do you see?"

Explain it. Show it. Build value every day.

II

Social Media Program Integration

5 Understanding How Social Media Plugs into the Organization 57

6 The People Principle 71

7 Establishing Social Media Guidelines for the Organization 83

8 Laying the Operational Groundwork for Effective Social Media Management 95

9 The New Rules of Brand Communications in the Age of Social Media 113

Understanding How Social Media Plugs into the Organization

A social media program does not live in a vacuum. It reaches out across the organization to include every business function, from marketing and business development to Human Resources and IT. In this chapter, we discuss the various phases of social media adoption some common integration models, how to create a skunkworks program from scratch, and how to get started with social media process mapping.

Creating Structure: Your First Social Media Process Mapping Draft

First things first: Grab a sheet of paper and sharpen your pencil because you are going to draw something.

Think about every business function in your company: Marketing, Public Relations, Human Resources, Customer Support, and so on. Visualize them and then lay them out on your blank sheet. Feel free to use the diagram shown in Figure 5.1 for inspiration.

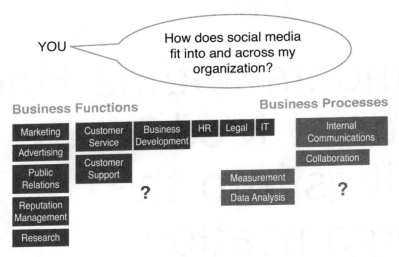

Figure 5.1   Planning for social media integration.

It doesn't have to be perfect or complete. Right now, it only needs to be a draft. You aren't going to be doing complex process mapping yet. You want to start the process by organizing your social media program in terms of the business functions it will serve and the processes (both internal and external) it will support. You will see why this exercise is important to do at this stage of the development process when we use this draft as the basis for your social media program's operational structure in Chapter 8, "Laying the Operational Groundwork for Effective Social Media Management."

Let's now discuss how to begin preparing your organization for the development of its new social media practice.

Understanding the Four Phases of Social Media Adoption

Typically, social media adoption—or integration—happens in four distinct phases. With some companies, these phases can happen within a few weeks, whereas in others, they could take a few years. In many instances, organizations may never quite get to the fourth and final phase. It happens. There is nothing wrong with that. Every organization is different.

The following sections outline how the process usually goes.

Phase One: Test Adoption

In the initial phase, shown in Figure 5.2, the organization decides to test the waters, or to "dip its toe" in the social media waters—a common euphemism at this uncertain stage.

Figure 5.2   Phase One: Test Adoption.

In this phase, an organization cautiously begins the process of creating a presence on social media channels. An official company account is created. Appropriate URLs and account IDs are claimed, hopefully without too much interference from cyber-squatters (individuals who quickly claim online accounts that large brands will want to use as their own). One person is assigned to the project. In many cases, an intern or junior team member with personal experience in the space gets to be the social media person for a while. This person operates under the supervision of a marketing manager of some kind.

At this stage, the program either stalls or grows. If it grows, the role may evolve into an official position along the lines of "social media manager" or some such title. This individual is typically responsible for producing content as well as posting updates and other materials across social media platforms (typically the company blog, its Facebook page, and perhaps its Twitter account as well, for starters).

In the Test Adoption phase, social media is disconnected from the rest of the organization. It is a standalone function with virtually no integration within the organization. This is commonly the result of a program that was not, from the start, tasked to support key business objectives.

Phase Two: Focused Adoption

In the next phase, shown in Figure 5.3, certain key functions within the organization begin to use social media to support their individual objectives. In many instances, because social media involves communications and enhances an organization's reach, functions such as Marketing and Public Relations tend to be the first to pick up on the opportunity. In other cases, Customer Support may jump into the fray faster, as has been the case in the airline industry, for example.

Figure 5.3   Phase Two: Focused Adoption.

What we see in Phase Two is the beginning of adoption driven by the specific needs of individual departments. This implies that managers inside the organization are beginning to understand that social media can enhance their current activities and perhaps help them reach their goals faster. The implication being that social media, when leveraged with focus and purpose, can yield positive outcomes.

In this phase, the framework of cross-departmental collaboration begins to emerge, and the once-lone social media manager now finds himself training, advising, and providing support to departments seeking to apply his knowledge to their needs. The social media management role grows in breadth and operational complexity as coordinating activities between departments, managing multiple accounts, and curating content become part of the daily mix of activities. In some instances, the original social media manager will grow into the role; in others, someone with more operational experience will have to be brought in to take over.

Phase Three: Operational Adoption

Upon seeing the success of the first departments to leverage social media channels to accomplish their objectives, other departments start following suit (see Figure 5.4). First, they can watch a working program live, as opposed to a program initially built on theory and conjecture. The "plan" is now a reality. Second, they have proof of concept: Not only is the program real and tangible, but it is delivering results. Not to be outdone by their rivals, departments start to fall in line. The conversation shifts from "Should we try this?" to "How exactly can we use this to help our team accomplish its goals?"

Figure 5.4   Phase Three: Operational Adoption.

Due to the growing complexity of this evolution, the organization begins to upgrade its internal collaboration tools and channels. Best-practices documents begin to emerge, as do process and methodology guidelines. Coordination between Public Relations, Marketing, Legal, and media partners becomes crucial.

The social media manager's job grows into a director-level role. The nomenclature may also begin to change to reflect the nature of the work rather than that of the channels. This is typically where a social media director becomes a social communications director or a digital communications director. As before, someone with a higher degree of skill and experience may be brought in to perform this type of function if the original manager is not ready for this level of responsibility.

New, more specialized social media roles begin to emerge: online community manager, digital customer relations manager, and digital insights manager, for example. The term *social media* begins to disappear from job titles. Little by little, the use of social media as a set of channels becomes normalized. No longer the shiny new object, no longer the mysterious new frontier of digital communications, social media is embedding itself in every department, and every department leverages it in its own particular way.

Phase Four: Operational Integration

In the final phase, shown in Figure 5.5, social media has been incorporated into the entire organization. Every department uses it in some way. Senior executives may be blogging now and participating in conversations with industry leaders and enthusiasts on key social networks. Human Resources may be leveraging employee networks to recruit top talent and working with recruiters around the globe via social platforms to share information about opportunities and applicants. Business Development may be monitoring the Web to identify trends and working to increase its reach. I could go on and on, but you get the picture: In Phase Four, what we see is a complete operational integration of social media across the entire organization.

Figure 5.5   Phase Four: Operational Integration.

By this point, what was once the sole "social media manager" role is now one of two things: either a VP or executive-level position, or no longer needed. Here is how that works:

For some companies, the central social media management role's requirements and complexity keep increasing to the point where the individual, in order to have oversight and authority over the use of social media across the organization, must be elevated to the same level as senior departmental decision makers across the company.

This individual may have no direct reports of his own. He may simply be a VP or executive-level subject matter expert, strategist, and company-wide coordinator of social web activity. He may be tasked with high-level enablement and interdepartmental coordination, as well as reporting to the CEO—a sort of social media czar, if you will.

For other companies, the need for such a central social media "oversight" role may become completely obsolete. In a way, this may actually mark a fifth phase, beyond even Operational Integration. In this fifth phase, senior executives might become so well versed in the subject of social media program management and the organization's collaborative culture might become so smooth that companywide coordination no longer requires a chaperon.

There is a way to accelerate this process—to go from Phase One to Phase Three in a matter of weeks. It requires a lot of research and due diligence, patience and hard work, but in terms of launching a program across the organization, sometimes the right kind of preparation up front can speed up the implementation of the program when the time finally comes to get it rolling. We return to this in the skunkworks section of this chapter.

But first...

Genesis vs. Pirate Ships: Social Media Integration Models

There are two ways for an organization to formalize its social media practice. The first is to start from zero. This is what is called a *genesis* model. Most organizations start here and with a question: *Should we start using social media?* We focus on this model in the next section when we discuss the introduction of a cross-functional social media program research and development team.

The second is the *pirate ship* model (a term coined by social media author Chris Brogan). This is the situation an organization finds itself in when, upon considering the need for a social media program, it discovers that employees have already taken the initiative to get something started.

Consider the case of a global consumer brand with groups and divisions scattered around the world. Groups in the U.S., Canada, Mexico, Brazil, South Africa, France, England, Spain, Germany, Italy, Switzerland, Belgium, Australia, Russia, China,

India, and Japan. Imagine now that the corporate office, several weeks into doing research into social media usage in its industry, unaware that anyone working for the brand is using social web channels officially, learns that groups in the U.S., Brazil, Japan, and the UK have already created blogs, Facebook pages, and Twitter accounts. What happens next? How would the corporate office handle these "pirate ships"?

One reaction is to panic, call up the legal department, and order the pirate ships to cease and desist, if only for a little while, so that everyone at HQ can wrap their minds around what to do next.

This is absolutely the wrong thing to do. First, this type of reaction will interrupt the way these groups do business. You don't want to do that. Second, it will distract them from getting their work done, and you don't want that either. Third, you will instantaneously create tension and resentment where none existed. Shattering morale is never good, especially when caused by a knee-jerk reaction. Chances are, if you hadn't heard about your pirate ship social media programs until now, they were doing just fine. The best strategy is instead to look into them but let them be.

The other possible reaction, then, is to "keep calm and carry on," as the British would say. In case you hadn't guessed, this is the right approach.

The first thing you should do is start finding out just how many pirate ships exist in your organization and what they are doing. I am not suggesting that you go dig up every Facebook profile of every employee. That isn't it. But if anyone is blogging, tweeting, or using Facebook in an "official" capacity, find them and reach out to them. Tell them that the company as a whole has started building a social media program, and you would love for them to help you with it.

You see, the thing about working with pirates is that they know what they are doing. They already know more than you do because they are sailing and raiding. They are the experts in your organization, and you need to get them on your side, not turn them against you.

Here is how to deal with a pirate ship model in ten simple steps:

1. Respect the pirates. (They know how to execute.)

2. Invite the pirates to the table. Recognize their wins.

3. Ask the pirates to report on what they see and hear.

4. Ask the pirates to report on their wins and losses.

5. Ask the pirates how you can help them win more.

6. Fund the pirates and send them on missions.

7. Ask the pirates to help you build up your fleet.

8. Ask the pirates to play a leadership role.

9. Ask the pirates to write the playbook for you.

10. Turn the pirates into *privateers.*

You can either waste your time fighting them (which serves no one's interest), or you can incorporate them into your program by inviting them to the table and focusing on what they have already accomplished on their own. Be sure to ask them what you can do to help them before you ask them to help you. Find out from them what works and what doesn't work and what some of their biggest hurdles have been so far. From there, you can start to develop formal reporting processes and clear lines of communications between you and them. Bring all the pirate ships together and give them a space where they can share ideas, resources, even coordinate campaigns and research. Find out what they need and fund them. Become their champions and their guardians.

Then and only then, ask them to help you build the kind of companywide program that will help them get more done. Recruit them into your enterprise and let them guide you. Don't bully them or tell them how to run their ships. Not yet, anyway.

The alternative, of course, is to shut them down for a few weeks, send them their new procedures, rules, and regulations, and watch your social media program flop and lose any chance of ever getting buy-in from the field.

Turn your pirates into privateers.

From Skunkworks to Full Deployment of a Social Media Structure

Whether you find yourself starting with a genesis model or a pirate ship model, you are going to need to build a coalition of motivated, curious, and cross-functional advisors to help you get things rolling—a task force of sorts. We have already seen how one person alone proposing a social media program to the CEO probably won't cut it. One person building the program won't work either. Here too, the more, the merrier. If your cross-functional task force involves managers from Sales, Marketing, HR, IT, PR, and Legal, the chances that your program will be successful will be far greater. The process-mapping draft you sketched earlier can be helpful here because it lists the departments and key functions in the organization that should be invited to be part of this team.

I cannot stress enough how important creating this task force is to the well-being of your program.

The objective of the skunkworks program, beyond casting political hurdles aside and not taking chances with the due diligence stage of your integration phase, is really this: creating a framework of purpose and value, driving adoption across the organization, ensuring proper integration and management of each facet of the program, and planning for the adequate measurement of its success.

Early in the game, this task force will essentially become a sort of think tank for your program. The team will meet regularly, fact-find, identify opportunities, seek subject matter experts within the organization and without, answer the C-Suite's questions, and pave the way for the program's inception.

The benefit of building a skunkworks team like this is three-fold. First, as I just mentioned, the group as a whole brings more political clout to the bargaining table. When the time finally comes to seek approval from the CEO and apply for funding, having a diverse group of respected managers to vouch for the program and give it purpose will give you a lot of mileage. Once you read the third reason, you will also understand how by that point, the other members of your team may even be more excited about the potential impact of social media on the organization than you.

Second, the more diverse and capable the group, the better odds you will have of asking most of the right (and sometimes difficult) questions early on. You've built a think tank: Use it. Leave no stone unturned. Speak with every social media professional you can get your hands on. Test every tool you hear about. The beauty of it is that you can spread the load. Having a team means you don't have to do everything yourself.

The task force's job during its first few months will be as follows:

- **Identifying key assets within the organization (aside from those present)**—This includes bloggers, digitally savvy executives, techies, leaders, champions, influencers, and so on.

- **Cataloging all social media activity currently going on (if applicable)**—Is the company working in the social web already? Who is involved? How? Where?

- **Assessing the strengths of the organization**—Strong communications team? Swift IT department? Flat management culture?

- **Assessing the weaknesses of the organization**—Poor internal communications? No Public Relations department? No mobile strategy?

Here are some questions the task force should attempt to answer:

- What channels should we be looking into and why?

- What platforms should we begin experimenting with?

- What monitoring, measurement, management, and collaboration tools should we be testing?
- How does all this plug into CRM?
- How should we start budgeting for headcount and tools?
- How will our agencies fit into all of this?
- How should we divide the work this is going to create?

Third, each department representative will identify the angles that most benefit them. If a customer service manager is part of the group, she will certainly see how Twitter, Facebook, forums, and blogs might be the perfect platforms with which to increase her department's reach and provide assistance to troubled customers. YouTube might be a terrific place to post short "how-to" videos that can then be pushed to other digital media outlets and made available to anyone doing a search on that particular topic. The sales manager will see the opportunities for *his* side of the business. So will the PR manager and the HR manager and everyone else on the team. As the team as a whole familiarizes itself with the pros and cons of social media and social communications, the opportunities for each of their individual business functions will become clear. The focus of their research will shift to their objectives and specific needs. The best practices, methodologies, and processes they begin to research will move ever closer to their own. Before long, they will have mapped out the why, the what, and the how of their own social communications programs—the building blocks of your broader idea.

As a bonus, because your cross-functional team of soon-to-be social media program champions has spent weeks and months working on the project together, its members will have formed personal bonds and developed organic modes of collaboration that will both facilitate and accelerate the integration process once you move into the management (execution) phase of your program.

Think back to the four phases of adoption we covered at the beginning of this chapter. How tedious and slow they seemed: First, one lonely social media person "testing the waters." Imagine trying to do this on your own: doing all the research, conducting interviews, scheduling platform and software demos, meeting with the IT managers, trying to convince one department after another to play a part in your program, and then watching them all fall in line, one at a time over the next year or two or three.

By building a skunkworks program up front, you can speed up that process. Phase One, the Test Adoption phase, can essentially be bypassed. The test phase can be applied to five or six departments at the same time, cohesively, much like raising a barn by connecting preassembled elements rather than by felling trees, sawing them into boards, and building the barn one board at a time all by yourself.

Centralized vs. Decentralized Social Media Management Models

Pirate ship models and genesis models lend themselves to two types of social media program structures: The first, grown out of a genesis model, is centralized. The other, adapting to previously autonomous pirate ships, is decentralized.

A centralized model essentially begins with a central command entity that controls all content and activity for the program. Think of it as a brand communications headquarters. It creates the message, the content, the strategy and makes all the decisions for the entire social media program. Everything outside of this central hub is essentially an execution arm: Community Management, Corporate Blogging, Monitoring, Measurement, Digital Reputation Management, and so on. Procedurally, this is a traditional corporate, even military hierarchy designed to support a command-and-execution model: With this type of model, decisions are made at the top of a vertical chain of command. All communications pass through the central hub.

A basic centralized model is shown in Figure 5.6.

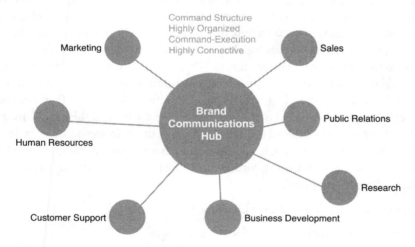

Figure 5.6   Centralized social media management model.

The advantages of a centralized model are clear:

- The organization has complete control over the message.
- The organization has complete control over information.
- The organization has complete control over the execution of the program.

- The organization has complete control over the content.

- The organization has complete control over its social web data.

- Collaboration is simple.

Centralized models also come with their own set of disadvantages:

- You usually have to build it from scratch, whereas a decentralized model allows you to build a structure over existing programs.

- It doesn't scale very well.

- When programs rely too much on centralized approval, they tend to become bureaucratic and slow to respond. Velocity and initiative are vital to the success of a customer-facing social media program.

- Centralized models tend to favor corporate styles of communication, where the tone and message are carefully controlled. This lack of spontaneity and genuine human engagement can backfire in a space where people seek human connections rather than messaging.

The decentralized model, on the other hand, is a little more complex and allows for satellites to act autonomously from one another while remaining connected to a central, less command-focused hub. In this scenario, the central command hub may still create messaging and content, but the satellites may also create their own, specific to their markets and communities. What you have in a model like this is a varying degree of tactical overlap whose management may be more art than science. The military equivalent of this type of structure can often be found in Special Operations groups, which, given the unconventional nature of their missions, are given more operational flexibility than traditional units. To some extent, social media practitioners working inside companies that still have not fully adopted social media across all their departments are the business world's version of a Special Operations group.

A decentralized model is shown in Figure 5.7.

Decentralized models have a number of advantages:

- When programs are managed "locally," not remotely, they tend to be driven by initiative, velocity, and deep insight into a specific market or community. The team that is there, with eyes on the field, knows better than a manager sitting in a corporate office what the best tactical decisions are for its program.

- If the structure was built upon existing programs (pirate ships), it has probably already gained traction.

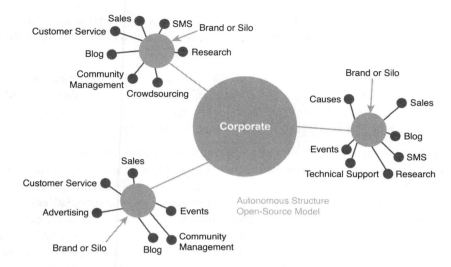

Figure 5.7   Decentralized social media management model.

- Decentralized models tend to breed competency in the field, where they can have the most impact. That is a good thing.

Decentralized models also come with their own set of disadvantages:

- Surrendering control of a program can be risky. Autonomy and initiative equal risk.

- The personality type usually comfortable with autonomy and initiative can sometimes be unpredictable and difficult to control. (It is important not to place this type of individual under the supervision of someone with micro-managing tendencies.)

- Communications and collaboration can begin to fade if central management is not vigilant.

You may have already drawn your own conclusions about what type of organization might be best served by one model or the other. Let me say this: Neither model is better than the other. Each has its strengths. What is important is that when developing the structure and framework of your social media program, you consider which type of model will work best with your corporate culture and operational needs.

A small company, for example, may fare better with a centralized model, whereas a global brand with dozens of groups and divisions might find a decentralized model more effective.

Likewise, a company with risk-averse leadership may prefer a centralized model regardless of its size because it feels more comfortable with a command and control structure.

Pose the question to your think tank/skunkworks team. Get a whiteboard and sketch out your company's structure. Plot all of your brands, groups, divisions, and silos on a map with the corporate headquarters at the center and then connect the dots. What do you see? A centralized or decentralized model?

Understanding how social media fits into your organization is a crucial step in forming the foundation upon which a fully integrated, companywide program can be built. Without clearly defining and mapping the company's functions and building a cross-functional task force to lead the program's fact-finding initiatives and ultimate development, the program could find itself disconnected from the core functions of the organization. Without understanding the four phases of adoption, a manager may not have a clear idea of how to grow his social media program across the organization. Last, without understanding which situation your organization finds itself in (a *genesis* or a *pirate ship* model) and without understanding social media programs' two basic types of structure (*centralized* and *decentralized*), the future program could find itself without a proper framework from which to derive adequate direction. These concepts may seem trivial compared to some of the more operational topics we have discussed so far, but they are among the most important in the process of building a successful companywide social media program.

6

The People Principle

Hiring for social media roles isn't easy. Don't kid yourself for even a second. Recruiting managers agonize over this on a regular basis. Here's why: Qualifications for social media roles are still difficult to pin down. What should an applicant's skill set be? What about work experience? How do you separate the posers and hacks from the genuine article? With thousands of people suddenly selling themselves as "social media experts" on the Internet, finding truly capable, qualified, trustworthy, social media–savvy applicants can be a bear. This section will hopefully help simplify the process of hiring staff for social media–related positions.

Hiring, Training, and Certifying for Social Media Activity

First things first: There is no such thing as a generic social media role. Before you begin to create your requisition, determine what this person's job will be and what he or she will actually do with social media on a daily basis. Qualifications speak to specific business functions and activity in support of that function, not solely "activity" in a medium.

Remember that the social web is a medium, like the telephone and email. You don't hire employees because of their skill with telephones or email, right? You hire them because they are the best at what they do, which happens to include fluency with whatever forms of media their jobs call upon them to use. For example, a customer service representative is a customer service expert first and a telephone conversation expert second. Social media works the same way: When listing ideal qualifications for a position, focus on the activity and function first and the medium second.

Second: Are you hiring for a strategic role or a tactical role? A strategic role would be, say, Director of Social Communications or Chief Social Officer—someone whose responsibilities will involve the development and administration of a companywide social media program. A tactical role, on the other hand, is trench work: a community manager, digital customer service agent, corporate blogger, or new media insights analyst. This is important because strategic roles require a breadth of qualifications touching on strategic planning and operational program management, whereas tactical roles require a narrow depth of qualifications along a specific bandwidth of skills and experience. Think of a strategic role as one requiring an executive type of skill set, whereas the tactical role can range from worker bee to mid-level management and supervisory type of skill sets.

The first lesson to learn here is that because not all social media roles are the same, not all qualifications for social media-related roles are the same.

Hiring a Social Media Director (Strategic Role)

Because the social media director role is still so new, finding an experienced social media director with a proven track record of excellence can be a challenging task. Most social media directors today were not managing social media programs three years ago, and among those few whose resumes may indicate a social media management role in the past, little evidence may exist that they were effective in the role. This puts recruiting managers in the difficult situation of having to select candidates based on a broader and more indirect set of skills and experience than they may normally be accustomed to.

First things first: The exact requirements of the role should be defined and out-lined. Not every social media director role requires the same set of skills. Some may manage existing programs, whereas others may need to build a social media pro-gram from scratch. On its own, the distinction between these two types of skill sets warrants individuals with vastly different degrees of ability. Furthermore, some social media programs may touch mostly on PR and marketing, whereas others might focus almost exclusively on community management and customer service. In this type of scenario, the first program would likely favor a social media director with a PR and marketing background, whereas the latter would favor one with community management and customer service experience. In the same vein, a B2B company looking for a social media director will tend to favor someone with exten-sive B2B experience over an applicant with mostly B2C experience. In the end, the specifics of the role will play as much of a part in determining what skills the ideal applicant should have than the "social media director" title itself. Just as no two social media roles are alike, no two social media director roles are exactly the same either.

With that in mind, let us look at a list of qualifications that might help an organiza-tion prequalify an applicant for a strategic social media role:

- Applicant has developed and managed marketing programs—not just campaigns but *programs*. This demonstrates an ability to think, plan, and manage in the long term, as well as a capacity for complex strategic thinking essential to a social media director position.

- Applicant has at least five years of experience managing projects and working across organizational silos.

- Applicant has spent at least one year in a project management role *outside* of an ad agency, PR firm, or other marketing firm. This is important because a social media director must be able to manage communications and projects from *inside* a "client" company, which is a very different environment from that of an agency or marketing firm. An individual in a social media director role cannot afford to be learn-ing how to deal with internal politics, operational silos, and how mar-keting, sales, product management, and customer service work with each other while at the same time trying to build or manage a social media program. This type of management experience should already be in a candidate's background so he can hit the ground running.

- Applicant has managed a brand or product line for more than two years.

- Applicant has managed national market research projects.

- Applicant is comfortable enough with business measurement methods to know the difference between financial impact (ROI) and nonfinancial impact. He also knows why the difference between the two is relevant.

- Applicant has managed a project team for more than one year. He was responsible for the training and development of that team.

- Applicant has been responsible for managing a budget/P&L.

None of these items are mandatory, but the quality of a candidate applying for a social media director position will increase every time one is checked off as a yes.

Next, shift to the basic social media experience. Every organization should decide for itself which items are mandatory and which are optional, but for a large company or brand, a social media director should be able to answer yes to all six of the following items:

- Applicant has had a continuous *professional* presence in the social media space via blogs, Twitter, Facebook, Ning, or other platforms for at least two years (preferably five or more years).

- Applicant has managed a business blog and/or business community for a minimum of one year.

- Applicant has either built an online community or managed one for longer than one year.

- Applicant has demonstrated a strong ability to forge lasting relationships across a variety of media platforms over the course of his career.

- Applicant's influence across social media circles and platforms is high, as demonstrated by tools such as Klout and Hubspot (although reaching out to trusted professionals and asking them their opinion of an applicant is never a bad idea).

- Applicant has been active on major social media platforms such as Facebook, Twitter, and YouTube for a minimum of two years.

After you have gotten past the basics of an applicant's qualifications, the time has come to dig deeper into his abilities. Here, you want to dig a little deeper than bullet points on a resume. Consider each item on this list to be pass/fail: Lots of check marks mean your applicant is pretty solid. A preponderance of question marks or red x's might be a sign that your applicant, although decent on paper, might not be as capable as his resume implies.

Start the interview or dialogue with some qualifying questions. Try to determine whether the applicant has a strong foundation of social media knowledge before jumping into high-level discussions about the social space. Here are some points to consider:

- Applicant understands the difference between *vertical* and *lateral* forces when it comes to customer/community engagement and has a working knowledge of how to leverage both.

- Applicant demonstrates a high level of proficiency working with several popular social media platforms.

- Applicant is capable of mapping out a basic social media monitoring plan on a cocktail napkin.

- Applicant demonstrates a thorough knowledge of the social media space, including general usage and demographic statistics for the most popular/relevant platforms as well as a few niche platforms of his choice.

- Applicant understands the breadth of tools and methods at his disposal to set goals and measure success in the social media space. (Applicant's toolkit is not limited to Google Analytics.)

- Applicant demonstrates a thorough understanding of the nuances between social media platforms and the communities they serve (for example, MySpace versus Facebook).

Now that you have established that the applicant knows what he is talking about, it is time to demonstrate his fluency, starting with critical thinking about best practices, social business philosophies, change management, and effective social media program management:

- Applicant can cite examples of companies with successful social media programs (other than programs he has worked with himself) and companies with ineffective social media programs. He can also argue comfortably why each was either successful or unsuccessful.

- Applicant can speak intelligently about any number of scenarios you bring up, from crisis management to the process by which a company can leverage its community to achieve a particular business objective.

- Applicant can explain how to build and manage a social media practice that works seamlessly with PR, product marketing, event management, and customer support teams within the organization.

- Applicant demonstrates a firm understanding of the difference between media measurement (social and otherwise) and business measurement and is obviously comfortable working simultaneously with both.

- Applicant can explain in detail what type of data his monthly and quarterly reporting will contain and how it will be presented.

- Applicant is more excited about engagement, building an internal practice, and finding out about your business's pain points than he is about firebombing you with the full scope of his social media expertise.

A note on experience: Remember that social media is still very new to the world of business. Although many qualified professionals have been involved with blogs, Facebook, and Twitter for years—both professionally and personally—very few have yet held high-level social media management positions in Fortune 500 environments. This is not for lack of skill or ability, but rather because executive social media positions simply did not exist before 2007, and were still rare going into 2010. Do not assume that because someone has not yet held a social media director position for a major consumer brand that he will not excel in that role if given the chance. Be diligent with your interview process. Learn to read between the lines and identify in a candidate the types of skills, abilities, and experience that will transfer well into a social media management role. Conversely, do not assume that because a candidate has held such a position before, he is qualified to take on a social media director role in *your* organization and meet its unique demands. The hiring process for this type of role is neither short nor simple. It requires work, patience, and a high degree of clarity as to what an ideal candidate should bring to the table.

Hiring for Tactical Social Media Roles

Social media-related tactical roles tend to encompass roles that are primarily customer-facing or directly in contact with the public through social media. These are your digital customer service representatives, community managers, consumer insights managers, bloggers, content creators, and channel monitoring specialists. These roles tend to be highly specialized and are typically characterized by a specific and narrow focus: listening to customers, creating content, monitoring activity, answering questions.

It stands to reason then, that when hiring for a social media role whose focus is specific, a recruiting manager would have to *begin* the process of evaluating candidates by looking not for broad social media experience, but rather for as narrow and relevant a field of expertise as possible. What you want in this type of role is depth before breadth: From an operational standpoint, experience in the job function being adapted to social media trumps experience in the use of media channels. If the role you are hiring for focuses on digital customer service, the candidate's skill as a customer service professional is far more important than her skill at using social media. The latter is secondary to the first and can be learned more easily with adequate support from the organization. The same principle applies to most tactical roles, from market research to crisis management.

What you are looking for in a tactical role dealing with social media is therefore not so much an *emphasis* on professional social media experience as much as a balance between operational experience in a professional role *and* a certain degree of social media fluency. The ideal applicant for a digital customer service role, for example, would combine several years of experience as a CSR with a high degree of comfort with popular social media platforms such as Facebook and Twitter as well as forums and other community-based platforms. The applicant would have to understand how to set up and manage keyword searches, deal with difficult customers with kindness and a cool head, and have a vested interest in not damaging her own reputation online.

To identify the ideal candidate for a specific tactical position, begin by creating your list of skill/experience requirements based on the function you are hiring for. Outline what the role is responsible for and establish the desired experience levels for each specific skill. To make sure that the social media aspect of the position doesn't interfere with the focus on the business function itself, consider writing the requisition first as if it were a traditional, nonsocial media role. Once that is done, add the social media fluency component, which might look something like this:

- Applicant demonstrates a high level of proficiency working with (insert relevant social media platforms and apps here).

- Applicant has demonstrated the ability to maintain a positive personal and professional presence across a breadth of social media environments.

- Applicant demonstrates a high level of care for her reputation across social media platforms and digital communities.

An applicant's ability to function as a good, respectful social media denizen is crucial, yet often overlooked in favor of presence (years and volume of activity on social networks) and network size (number of followers, fans, or connections). Although the latter can be pretty telling, the quality of an applicant's interactions is far more important with the length of time she has spent online or how many connections she has collected over time.

A common trap that recruiters fall into is to look at an applicant's social media statistics without considering the *quality* of their applicants' engagement. Word to the wise: Connections, fans, and followers can be bought (even on eBay, believe it or not). The size of a network can be faked. The quality of one's interactions, however, cannot. Being conscious of local, state, and federal laws, and without being intrusive, if you have the opportunity to browse through an applicant's public interactions (including the way she responds to comments on her blog), do so. Go as far back as you can. This takes time but it is well worth it.

If you uncover troublesome behavior that—of course—had not come up during initial interviews, you can now choose to bring it up. Don't be too quick to judge but use this opportunity to find out more about your candidate's ability to deal with stressful situations online, what she has learned from past confrontations she might not have handled well, and so on. Personalities can be radically different as they jump from the analog world and the digital world. Get to know promising applicants through the medium you are hiring them to work with. This is the medium your customers will get to know them through. It doesn't hurt to look at your applicants through the eyes of your customers, so to speak.

Hiring for tactical roles is much easier than hiring for strategic roles, for obvious reasons: The specificity of tactical roles narrows the field. Tactical roles are more common and less likely to hide posers and charlatans. Lastly, tactical roles can be built around a promising applicant even if she lacks experience. With the right combination of aptitudes, training, and supervision, even the most inexperienced hire can be honed into a formidable social media professional assigned to a specific business function.

HR and Social Media: The Need for Social Media Policies, Guidelines, and Training

Recruiting is only one of several functions handled by Human Resources when it comes to supporting an organization's social media efforts. Internal development is another.

Once a social media program begins to look like a possibility for an organization, it is HR's responsibility to assist the social media program director in drafting rules and expectations in regard to social media usage for company employees. The main focus of this exercise is not to create a legal framework through which employees can be disciplined or let go if they commit infractions, but rather to help employees stay out of trouble (and by doing so, help them keep their organization out of trouble as well). A well-drafted set of social media guidelines and policies should provide the best possible resource for employees when it comes to social media usage. This document should not be a three-paragraph addendum to the employee handbook that only discusses access to social networks from company computers during business hours. It should instead be a living document that also outlines expectations of behavior, emphasizes personal responsibility, and helps employees understand how their choices can impact their work environment.

All employees should be invited to not only read these guidelines but discuss them at will with HR representatives, who ideally would be trained to answer their questions.

More importantly, once social media guidelines and policies have been established, HR must follow up with a training program for employees. Back in the 1980s, HR departments, upon seeing the need for increased awareness and clarity in matters of sexual harassment and sensitivity training, created training programs for their organizations' employees. This training aimed to improve the work environment, help bring to light some hidden workplace discrimination issues, minimize the risk of lawsuits, and avoid bad press. Consider social media training to be the next step in HR's efforts to educate and equip employees with knowledge that will help them both improve their work performance and minimize the risk of legal exposure for their employers.

Training should begin with an overview of the organization's social media policies and guidelines, starting with usage from work and from company-owned machines and networks and continuing with personal usage away from work. Second, basic security protocols for popular social media platforms should be covered. This module might, for example, help employees understand Facebook privacy settings and warn them about common phishing scams. Third, this training program might outline common traps that social media users fall into and how to avoid them. Examples might include talking negatively about a boss or co-worker online, digital sexual harassment, revealing confidential company information, and so on.

The first portion of the training establishes a baseline for social media awareness and the boundaries it occupies within the framework of employment with the company.

The second portion of the training arms employees with basic knowledge as to how to own and protect their online presence. It establishes them as custodians of their own accounts, teaches them to be responsible for these accounts, and trains them to be the first line of defense against hacker attacks seeking to exploit weak spots in a company's IT infrastructure.

The third portion of the training moves employees into situational awareness and behavioral protocols. Though more advanced than the two previous phases of training, this is often the one which yields the most participation and the best results. Here, employees learn not to get themselves and their employers in trouble. This type of training can easily present hypothetical situations in which employees are asked to select the most appropriate course of action. These situations should not limit themselves to purely professional or job-function-based scenarios. Social media training must take into account the 24/7 "always-on" reality of the space and the impact that every employee decision can have on his or her organization, even when "off the clock."

Situation: Your supervisor just did something that made you angry. You feel like talking about it online. What do you do?

a. Vent your frustration on Twitter and/or Facebook.

b. Write a blog post about it and publish it.

c. Unfollow and/or unfriend your supervisor.

d. Calm down. Social media channels are not the best place to vent your frustrations.

Situation: You are a marketing vice president for a global B2C brand currently under attack by an environmental protection group. Some of the language being used by members of this group in their blog posts and some of the comments being left on your company's Facebook wall is purposely inflammatory, and some of the activities they claim your company indulges in are inaccurate. The level of vitriol and sheer volume of angry comments has escalated to a point where you feel you must intervene. What option seems the most appropriate?

a. Say nothing. Your company doesn't answer to the public. Instead, unleash the legal department on your enemies and let them threaten anyone partaking in libel, slander, or the illegal use of a trademark with legal action.

b. Fight fire with fire: If the environmental group wants a fight on social media channels, give it to them.

c. Ask your PR department to craft a press release and publish it on your blog a few days after the crisis has begun. Make sure it is pushed out via Facebook and Twitter as well. It's always worked before, and it will again.

d. Begin to identify who the most influential commenters are, the most vocal, and the most aggressive. Get your facts straight and calmly join the discussion. Introduce yourself, acknowledge the crowd's frustration, and ask if you can help clarify some of the issues they are so angry about. Keeping a cool head, shift the conversation away from conjecture and state the facts. Point the public to proof that what you say is true. Be respectful, kind, helpful, and patient until the crisis dies down.

You get the idea: Present employees with a breadth of situations they may encounter—situations they might not have considered—then help them work out the best solution together. Use real cases whenever you can: situations in which someone actually lost his job or cost his employer a major contract. Some scenarios may require guidance because your company's social media guidelines might be specific about what to do in such an instance, whereas others may be an exercise in thinking through the problem: What would be the consequences of doing X versus doing Y? This type of training is not intended to cover every possible type of situation your employees might encounter, but rather to help them think on their feet when such situations do arise.

The Value of Internal Certifications

Every once in a while, the subject of social media certification comes up: Should social media professionals be certified in the space? If so, who should be allowed to certify them? How should it be done? What should social certifications even cover or look like? Until these questions can be answered, here is a different approach to the subject of social media certification: Instead of looking at certs as an *external* validation of expertise, look at it first as an *internal* one. Ultimately, the purpose of a certification is to establish a particular level of proficiency in a discipline. Unfortunately, "social media" in and of itself, is not a discipline. Digital crisis management, on the other hand, is. So are digital customer service and online community management. This means that a certification program that focuses on social media *without* addressing each specific business function adapted to social media won't end up certifying anyone in much of anything.

Currently, and for the foreseeable future, the best way for an organization to ensure that an employee has received a minimum level of instruction in social media usage as prescribed by your guidelines and policies is to craft your own *internal* certification program.

This type of program can serve a number of roles and levels of fluency. Aside from the operational benefits of providing employees with some form of training in social media best practices, also consider the legal advantage of certifying every employee in basic social media awareness and usage to a *common standard* within your organization: increased effectiveness in their social media jobs, minimized risk of incidents involving poor judgment by employees on social media channels, and the assurance of a minimum level of proficiency in social media use before an employee takes on his new role. Compare this proactive approach to employee certification in organizations that neither train nor certify their staff and rely instead on the *hope* that their previous social media positions at other companies have prepared them for their new jobs, and that furthermore, everyone on staff knows enough not to say anything stupid on Facebook or Twitter.

What we have at the onset are two distinct types of internal social media certifications: One is a form of basic internal training and ensures that *every* employee is familiar with the company's social media policies and guidelines, for example. The second, more advanced form of training should be offered to all employees with access to official social media account responsibilities. This type of training, building on the basic training program, should touch on PR, customer experience management, crisis management, and how to react to negative comments and attacks in a public forum. It should also incorporate the organization's internal communications structure and social media org chart, along with procedures under which a subject matter expert might be brought into a conversation when needed. In the case of a publicly traded company or an organization in regulated industries, the training may involve modules touching on disclosure and regulatory rules, from the Federal Trade Commission (FTC) to the Securities and Exchange Commission (SEC), for example.

A third level of certification may yet exist, and it should focus on certifying individuals for social media use relating to specific business functions: online reputation management, customer support, community management, crisis management, and so on. Even if a new hire comes with a depth of experience that far exceeds her predecessor's and the training seems more of a formality than a valuable use of her time, put her through it. Depending on her expertise, the process might uncover either the need to update the training materials and certification process or the holes in her own knowledge that may not have been otherwise evident. The lesson here is this: Let your internal experts build on existing certification programs in order to keep them up to date, relevant, and effective.

The ideal internal certification model for most organizations would look something like this:

- **Basic social media certification**—Mandatory for all employees as a follow-up to your guidelines
- **Advanced social media certification**—Mandatory for all employees with access to official social media accounts
- **Specialist social media certification**—Certifications specific to key social media roles within the organization

Ideally, the organization's social media director, along with HR and the legal team, can create the basic and advanced training programs. For the Specialist certification, it stands to reason that individual departments (public relations, customer service, marketing, and so on) would play a much more active part, not only in developing training materials in collaboration with the social media director and HR, but also in setting the certification standards for roles they are primarily responsible for. Using this model, any organization—and each department within the organization—can create its own customized set of certifications to help ensure that all employees are trained and tested to a minimum standard of competency in this new and sometimes confusing medium.

Social media programs function best when the organizations they serve embrace the importance of putting qualified, eager, well-supported employees at the wheel. This may seem like a trivial matter, but the best social media strategy in the world can be undone in moments because of a poor hiring decision, inadequate employee training, or the assumption that an employee knows the ins and outs of his social media role when he in fact might not. Staffing your program with the best people and equipping them for success is a prerequisite if you want your program to move forward fast and effectively. To that end, always hire with an eye for talent, train with purpose, and certify with confidence.

7

Establishing Social Media Guidelines for the Organization

Compared to social media campaigns and well-executed consumer engagement, the development of internal social media guidelines and policies doesn't seem all that sexy to most social media professionals. It is perhaps for this reason that among all the topics of discussion surrounding effective social media program management, this is one that receives the least amount of attention. Ironically, the establishment of clear, thorough, and well-crafted social media guidelines for employees is one of the most important foundations upon which effective social media programs are built.

Guidelines, Policies, and Purpose

What an organization's social media guidelines should aim to accomplish can be summed up in a few bullets:

- Define a framework of both sanctioned and responsible social media usage for employees of the organization, both internally and externally.

- Clarify expectation of employee behavior, both personal and professional, on the social web.

- Be a resource for best practices, employee safety, conflict resolution, and even training as it pertains to both official and personal social media usage.

Unfortunately, most social media policies in existence today fail to provide thorough guidance for employees, favoring instead a tendency to limit themselves to the legalities of using company-owned equipment such as computers and mobile devices for personal use. They define Wi-Fi, networks, and other forms of Internet access as company property and therefore subject to the same rules as computers when it comes to unsanctioned "personal" use by employees. Some of these policies ban the use of social networks on company property, through its equipment, on its networks, and during business hours. Some organizations even go the extra step of prohibiting their employees from using social networks such as Facebook and Twitter altogether—not just at work but outside of work as well. Finally, such social media policy documents warn employees of professional sanctions, even termination, if these policies are not observed.

The value of such a document is precisely zero. Although it gives an organization the right to terminate an employee if she accesses Facebook from her desk, it does not protect the organization from exposure to criticism online or to PR disasters, for example. It does not allow the organization's various departments to leverage the power of the social web to enhance and amplify their campaigns and programs. It does not prepare employees to deal with conflict online, from personal arguments to harassment, which could have repercussions internally. Finally, it gives no guidance to responsible adults in regard to social media usage that could—and probably will—affect the organization. All such a document does is establish a vague prohibition of a communications medium that a) cannot be realistically prohibited and b) shouldn't be prohibited in light of the fact that the organization plans to use it for business.

For an organization's social media policy document to serve a purpose, it must contain the other elements mentioned previously. Yes, it must define a framework of both sanctioned and responsible social media usage internal to the organization, but it must also address responsible social media usage *outside* the company walls, discuss the organization's expectation of employee behavior on the social web (not an official set of rules, but expectations nonetheless), and be a source of information, insight, advice, and even training materials for employees with questions.

At its core, a properly drafted social media policy document should be composed of ten distinct sections:

1. An employee social media bill of rights

2. Internal usage guidelines

3. External usage guidelines

4. Employment disclosure guidelines

5. Anti-defamation guidelines

6. Social media confidentiality and nondisclosure (NDA) guidelines

7. Official versus personal communications guidelines

8. The employee digital citizenship contract

9. Training resources

10. Social media policies and guidelines for agency partners, contractors, and external representatives

1. The Employee Social Media Bill of Rights

This section of the document states the dozen or so rights that your organization recognizes (not grants—recognizes) are true employee rights when it comes to social media usage. They usually include the following:

- The right to use the social web as a means of personal communications and self-expression outside of work.

- The right to personal digital access: Just as with other forms of communications, employees' right to access digital social networks for personal use on their own devices and networks should be recognized.

- The right to equal access to the social web: Access to the social web for personal use should not be restricted to one group of employees. (Note the inclusion of the term "personal use.")

- The right to digital privacy: In regards to data, this includes information and conversations not available in the public stream. This would protect employees from invasive "spying" by employers using privacy-bypass software.)

- The right to digital dignity: No employee who uses social media should ever have to worry about being harassed or bullied (online or offline) by co-workers, supervisors, fellow employees, or management.

- The right to know: If employees are allowed to use social media at work and/or are using company equipment and networks, the company must notify them if their communications and content are being captured, browsed, shared, or intercepted. This can be done proactively by notifying employees that any data sent or received through company networks or devices is company property, for example.

- The right to own and manage personal accounts on various social media networks without interference from the employer.

You get the idea. A social media bill of rights starts things off on the right foot: It treats employees with respect and acknowledges them as responsible human beings rather than dangerous little children. Building your document upon a foundation of trust, respect, and acknowledgment of personal privacy sends the kind of message to employees they should return in kind: We trust you and value you as human beings. Be worthy of that trust.

Creating your social media employee bill of rights can be a group exercise (and probably should be). Who should be involved? Human Resources, legal counsel, and IT, of course. Bringing in employees with an advanced understanding of social networks to participate in the drafting of this document would also be advantageous. (Drafting an employee bill of rights without the active participation of some employees probably won't work.)

However, many "management" members of this drafting committee should be matched by the number of nonmanagement employees. This way, if an element or the language of the proposed draft is being contested by one side or the other, neither can exercise veto power over the motion. The importance of this seemingly insignificant detail is this: The validity of a social media bill of rights for employees depends squarely on whether or not employees recognize its legitimacy. If the document falls short of its purpose, the workforce may reject it altogether. The objective here is not to breed cynicism. It is to express to employees that the organization recognizes their rights as private individuals to use social media as they please for personal use. Limitations, rules, and exceptions relating to the organization's sanctioned usage of social media come later.

2. Internal Social Media Usage Guidelines

This section should include a detailed list of rules, preferably in bullet form, that touches on the following subjects:

- Personal use of social media during work hours.

- Personal use of social media using company-owned equipment.

- Company bandwidth usage guidelines for personal use.

- Disclosure of company policies and rights dealing with data privacy in regard to communications sent and received via company equipment and networks.

- Official/sanctioned use of social media to conduct company business during work hours.

- Security protocols in regard to file downloads, file uploads, and access to websites through unverified shortened URLs.

- Protocols regarding the download of social media–related software, including clients and "third-party" tools on company computers and mobile devices. The IT department needs to be involved with all downloads.

3. External Social Media Usage Guidelines

External social media usage guidelines outline the organization's views on what each employee's responsibilities may be in regard to the role they play as a representative of the business whenever they are not at work, not using a company device, or using the company's networks to access the Internet outside of work.

The purpose of this section of the guidelines is not to impose an organization's will on its employee's personal use of social media. Its purpose is first to remind employees that the lines can easily be blurred between their official role for the company and the personal opinions they may express online outside of business hours and, second, to help them best negotiate this sometimes tricky area without getting themselves or their employers in trouble. Here is why: Customers, journalists, and the public in general may not understand that between 9:00 a.m. and 5:00 p.m. EST (New York time), comments made by an individual with an official social media role may be on message with the brand, but that between 8:00 p.m. and 3:00 a.m., his opinions are somehow divorced from his employer's.

Ultimately, a company should not interfere with an employee's use of social media for her own personal use and on her own time, but it is important to remind employees that the distinction between their work hours and their personal use of social media may not be as clear to the general public as it is to them. For better or for worse, employees with official social media roles within their organizations need to be aware that in the eyes of the public, they represent their employer around the clock, 24/7/365. There is never a time when their comments or social media activity does not impact the reputation of their employer.

Subsections should include detailed guidelines on the following topics:

- Personal use of social media on noncompany devices and networks. Be sure to remind employees that social media usage on company-owned devices or company-owned networks outside of business hours and even off company property is still considered "internal" use by the organization.

- Guidelines regarding official/sanctioned use of social media to conduct business outside of work hours, on personal devices, and/or on outside networks.

In regard to official use/sanctioned use of social media to conduct business, here are a few things to think about:

- All official (company-owned and -operated) accounts on social networks are the property of the organization. The guidelines governing their approved use is in effect 24/7, regardless of where the authorized employee may be or what devices and networks he may be using. This means that whenever the employee posts content or engages in a discussion using an official account, he must consider himself "at work." In other words, the same rules of conduct that apply to business hours apply here as well. Confidentiality policies and guidelines apply in the same manner.

- To help clarify the difference between official company opinions and personal opinions, nonofficial accounts (accounts owned and managed by the employee for personal use) should be tagged with a clear disclaimer stating that all content and opinions expressed by this account (including websites and blogs) are personal in nature and in no way reflect the views and opinions of the employer. This disclaimer should—as a minimum—appear clearly in the account profile and preferably on the home page as well when applicable (blogs and websites). In instances where the amount of characters allotted to an account profile is inadequate for this purpose, either use an abbreviated version of this disclaimer or use a hyperlink to direct readers/visitors to the disclaimer where it is posted elsewhere. Here's an example of a full disclaimer:

"All views and opinions expressed on this (blog/website/etc.) are my own and do not represent the views of (Insert Company Name)."

And here's an example of an abbreviated disclaimer:

"My views are my own."

4. Employment Disclosure Guidelines

If employees are going to engage in discussions that touch on the industry that their employer is involved with, they must disclose their relationship with their employer either in their profile or every time they engage in such a discussion. This is different from the "opinions are my own" disclaimer covered previously. Here, the employee is required to disclose her material connection to her employer or clients in order to eliminate any risk of confusion in the public's mind as to a potential bias on her part. This is particularly important in social media, where marketing messages can easily be mistaken for genuine conversations or independent opinions when company affiliation is not clearly disclosed.

This portion of the policy document can also be used to help employees differentiate between discussion topics for which disclosure is required versus topics for which disclosure is not required by giving them concrete examples.

As an example, here is a list of topics where employment disclosure for an individual working in the automotive industry is either required or not required:

- Responsible pet ownership: Not required

- Sports other than motorsports: Not required*

- Diet plans: Not required

- Politics: Not required

- Last week's fishing trip: Not required

- Personal computing: Not required

- Any discussion regarding cars: Required

- Motorsports: Required

- Automotive topics: Required

- Automobile reviews: Required

- Any opinion relating to preference in the automotive world: Required

This type of disclosure is required (and depending on what country you operate in, sometimes legislated) in order to eliminate any possibility of clandestinely tampering

---

* Any instance in which a sponsorship or partnership by the employer or a competitor may touch on the topic would make disclosure required. An example might be where a cycling team sponsored by a competitor would shift discussions about cycling into the required disclosure category.

with the public trust. It is important to educate all employees as to their responsibility to obey the law and act ethically in this area, as fines, criminal prosecution, and damage to a company's reputation can result from both deliberate and accidental infractions.

5. Anti-Defamation Guidelines

Anti-defamation guidelines are an important component of a social media policy document. They help protect employees and the organization from unnecessary lawsuits from offended parties.

Because some legal details are beyond the scope of this book, I recommend that you work with your organization's legal team to incorporate anti-libel, slander, and defamation guidelines into your policy document. Employees must understand how not to get themselves and their employers in trouble, and this area can sometimes be tricky for social media denizens. This section should incorporate a clear definition of libel, slander, and defamation, as well as recommendations geared to help employees avoid getting in trouble.

To get you started, here are some basic definitions of libel, slander, and defamation:

- **Libel**—A false and malicious statement printed for the purpose of defaming a living person. A written or pictorial statement that unjustly seeks to damage someone's reputation.

- **Slander**—Words falsely spoken that damage the reputation of another. Same as libel, but spoken. In the world of social media, typical platforms for slander would be video posts/vlogs, webinars, and podcasts. Anything spoken rather than written.

- **Defamation**—The communication of a statement that makes a claim, expressly stated or implied to be factual, that may give an individual, business, product, group, or organization a negative image. It is usually a requirement that this claim be false and that the statement be communicated to someone other than the person being defamed.

Note the difference between an *opinion* and a *false statement*.

A corporate blogger responding candidly in a comment thread with a statement such as, "I think that our competitor is in completely over their head when it comes to this new market," constitutes an opinion. Although not particularly friendly, it does not constitute a false statement.

The same corporate blogger responding the same comment thread with a statement such as, "Our competitor owes at least half of their business to government bribes and false advertising," when this is in fact not the case, constitutes a false statement and probably qualifies as some form of defamation.

To significantly minimize the potential risk of legal exposure that comes with social media activity (sanctioned or not), employees need to understand what constitutes defamation, libel, and slander. The more well versed your organization is on this simple but poorly understood topic, the better protected it will be.

6. Social Media Confidentiality and Nondisclosure (NDA) Guidelines

This section may be one of the shortest in your policy document, but make sure not to omit it. What you want to clearly convey to your employees is this: Whatever your organization's policies and guidelines are in regard to confidential information and any information protected by nondisclosure agreements also apply to the world of social media.

It may be a good idea to cut and paste in your existing policy on confidential information so it is clearly stated in this document as well. Don't make your employees have to go digging for it.

The rule of thumb for confidentiality is this: Confidentiality is media-agnostic. If information is not to be shared verbally, in print, by phone, via email, or by fax, it should also not be shared via social media channels. Although this may seem like common sense, do not assume your employees will figure it out on their own. Make it clear for them.

7. Official vs. Personal Communications Guidelines

This section comes with a bit of good news and bad news.

The bad news: It may seem a bit repetitive given that much of its content has already been covered in internal and external usage guidelines. The good news: Much of the content for this section has already been written, so it should not require a lot of work to put together.

The obvious question then is this: If much of the content of this section has already been covered in other sections, why bother? One word: Clarity. Employees, in browsing through a social media policy document, need to be able to find answers to their questions with the least amount of friction. Modulating the context in which content is presented can serve that purpose. Here, you want to once again create a clear distinction between official, sanctioned company use of social media and personal use of social media outside of work. You also want to create a detailed framework of rules and behaviors proper to each type of communication. Because personal use falls mostly outside the "jurisdiction" of the organization, that subsection of the guidelines should be shorter and less detailed than the subsection that focuses on official communications. For obvious reasons, let's take a quick look at the latter.

Here, you have an opportunity to let employees know exactly what is expected of them when they represent the organization on social networks. Make the most of it. Be as detailed as you need to be. If it makes sense to also create further subsections that outline policies and procedures for specific roles (customer service, community management, and so on), do it. In fact, I recommend it. Take your time with this section. Update it often. Make sure it remains relevant. Every guideline in this section must be realistic, so don't expect to write it once and then forget about it. If experience serves, you will be updating it often.

8. The Employee Digital Citizenship Contract

"The *what*?" I hear you cry. The *employee digital citizenship contract*. Think of it as an agreement by employees to be polite and kind to other people (and each other) online. Why is this needed? To drive this point home: Improper or combative behavior, harassment, and bullying online is a bad idea and will not be tolerated by the organization.

At face value, this section may seem a little silly: Having employees sign a declaration of intent that lists items such as "I promise to be polite and kind, I promise not to be condescending to anyone online, I promise to represent my employer responsibly..." seems a bit unnecessary, right? The truth is that this is as important a component of your policy document as any other.

On the one hand, it lists in very simple terms what ideal online behavior entails and asks employees to commit to it. The clarity of these expectations, along with the commitment, helps move expectations off the page and into the real world.

On the other hand, it provides an opportunity to address two specific types of negative activities not mentioned in detail anywhere else in the policy document: online harassment and bullying. This point is important.

To give you a frame of reference, let's focus on *bullying* for a moment. You may be surprised to know that this type of problem does not end with high school graduation. It is alive and well in the world of grown-ups as well. Here are some staggering statistics published in 2010 by The Workplace Bullying Institute ("The 2010 WBI Workplace Bullying Survey," www.workplacebullying.org/research/WBI-NatlSurvey2010.html) concerning workplace bullying:

- Thirty-five percent of the U.S. workforce (an estimated 53.5 million Americans) report being bullied at work.

- Half of all Americans report having directly experienced bullying.

- Sixty-two percent of bullies are reported to be men. Fifty-eight percent of bullying targets are women.

- The majority of bullying (68%) is same-gender harassment.

- Bullying is four times more prevalent than illegal harassment.

What about bullying online, outside of work (also called *cyber-bullying* and *cyber-stalking*)? The National Crime Prevention Council's definition of cyber-bullying is as follows:

> "When the Internet, cell phones, or other devices are used to send or post text or images intended to hurt or embarrass another person."

By the way, here's the difference between *bullying* and *harassment*, according to BullyOnline.org:

> "Bullying differs from harassment and discrimination in that the focus is rarely based on gender, race, or disability. The focus is often on competence, or rather the alleged lack of competence of the bullied person."

Now, imagine the situation an HR (or PR) department of an organization may find itself in if an employee were found to be using social media to harass or bully a potential customer, a direct report, or a co-worker.

A good way to reduce the risk of bullying and harassment through social media channels is to address it head on—that is to say *proactively*—by bringing them to light in your policy document. Here is how:

1. Define them.

2. Qualify these behaviors as unwanted.

3. Elsewhere in your employee handbook, be sure to address the possible consequence of all forms of harassment and bullying, both offline and online.

In this section, however, simply including a statement such as "I agree never to bully and/or harass anyone through social media channels" should do the trick.

9. Training Resources

This is pretty self-explanatory: Consider this section a repository of information and training materials for all employees in regard to social media usage. This can and should include lists of approved software and statistics, login procedures, best-practices documents, company social media org charts, SME contact information, and so on. Whatever resource does not fit in other sections of the document can find a home here.

10. Social Media Guidelines for Agency Partners, Contractors, and External Representatives

Because some elements of your social media program may be managed or touched by external agencies and partners, it is essential for your policy document to include a section that addresses these particular situations. This document should be written for two audiences: an internal audience (your employees) and an external audience (your external partners and contractors). It is essential that your external partners not only be given visibility to this section but that they be briefed as well. Though this section can be as thorough as your organization wants it to be, it should at the very minimum clearly cover rules of disclosure and confidentiality (including legal language where applicable), conduct guidelines, and collaborative and reporting processes.

I strongly recommend spending some time reviewing other organizations' social media policies and guidelines to help craft your own document. A quick Internet search should put dozens of them at your fingertips, starting with IBM's, which is still considered by many professionals to be among the clearest and most helpful social media policies in existence today.

Finally, remember that the best social media policy is the social media policy that works for *your* organization. As long as you remember to focus on clarifying expectations for your staff rather than drafting a set of rigid corporate rules, you will most likely end up with a worthwhile social media policy document that will serve your company well for years to come.

8

Laying the Operational Groundwork for Effective Social Media Management

No matter what its size and complexity, a social media program needs some kind of reporting and collaboration process in order to function. Without this structure, the various business functions involved in the program will not be able to work in concert with one another, and their social media activity will be as unfocused as the flow of information between them.

Program structures can usually be divided into two parts: vertical and horizontal. The vertical structure is the *reporting* structure, or *leadership* structure, and it maps hierarchy and authority within the program. The horizontal structure maps all operational connections between cross-functional teams and establishes patterns of workflow and collaboration.

Establishing a Social Media Program's Organizational Structure: Leadership and Reporting

In this section of the chapter, we focus on the first of these two elements: the vertical leadership and reporting structure.

The best place to start is by identifying every social media role in your program—from the program director on down to the most junior staffer who will touch social media for the organization. First, make a list that includes digital customer service representatives, community managers, programmers, bloggers, IT support, and so on. Anyone who touches the program in any way, shape, or form should be included in this list.

Second, move beyond the scope of your social media program and map your entire organization's structure. For most companies, this type of mapping is commonly referred to as an *org chart*. If one doesn't already exist for your company, create one, starting with the CEO at the top and working your way down into each department. The object of this exercise is simply to map hierarchy and authority up and down the organization in order to clearly see who answers to whom, understand how budgets are assigned, and track vertical paths of information, both from the top and from the bottom.

Third, use your social media function list to identify who in your broader org chart is involved in the program. Put a check by their names, highlight them, circle them, or underline them—it doesn't matter. The object of this step is to connect each social media function with specific individuals and job titles on your org chart.

Fourth, using your annotated org chart, create a *new* org chart showing *only* the social media–related roles. This should create the basis for your vertical structure (see Figure 8.1).

In creating your vertical social media org chart, bear in mind the difference between direct reports and program authority: Although your org chart may show that one individual answers to two bosses, the reality of a management structure is that no man can serve two masters.

For example, a newly hired digital customer service representative whose function is 100% focused on social media may be told by his recruiting manager that he will answer to both the social media program's manager *and* the customer service manager. Although from an everyday operational standpoint this may seem reasonable, it is not: Sooner or later, the CSR will find himself being pulled in two completely different directions by bosses with temporarily incompatible objectives.

Figure 8.1   Social media program planning: identifying roles.

An example would be an instance in which the social media program manager asks the digital CSR to compile a thorough report of recent customer service activity on Twitter for his quarterly presentation while the customer service manager has asked him to take on a second CSR's load for a few days. From a time-management standpoint, doing both is impossible. When push comes to shove, he will have to choose which task to perform and which boss to disappoint. This type of situation can be avoided by *properly* mapping vertical paths of authority within the program org chart, as shown in Figure 8.2.

Note that Figure 8.2 clearly shows that the two digital CSRs involved with the program fall under the direct authority of the customer service manager and *not* the VP Social Business (the program's manager). A social media program org chart that does not clearly capture this unique direct report pathway (or the absence of a social media program org chart altogether) would create confusion at some point in the program's life cycle. The distinction between direct reports and program authority may seem trivial at first, but a program can find itself derailed—even damaged—by a lack of clarity in this particular area: Turf wars, operational confusion, and even intangibles such as resentment over past turf wars are poison for programs that require fluid collaboration across a number of departments. If an employee cannot serve two masters, how then should a social media program manager view his authority over individuals attached to the program who are not his direct reports? Our example of the digital CSR attached to the organization's social media program provides us with a few clues.

Figure 8.2   Social media program planning: creating an org chart.

Note in Figure 8.3 the direct connection between the VP Social Business and the customer service manager. This is one of two principal pathways of influence the social media program manager can use to exert his authority on our digital CSR and one we might call *indirect authority*. In this type of interaction, the VP Social Business and the customer service manager might discuss common objectives, synergies, and areas of mutually beneficial collaboration, and his needs will be communicated down through the organization's recognized departmental chain of command to the digital CSR.

The other path—that of *direct authority* (see Figure 8.4)—is faster than going through the CSR's manager but can create conflict between the CSR and his boss if communications between all three parties are not open and fluid. In this type of interaction, the VP Social Business might reach out to the CSR directly and ask him to perform a specific task, for example. The obvious advantage of this type of interaction is speed. In the event that the social media program manager and the digital CSR have to work on a crisis or particular project together, bringing the customer service manager into every exchange just might not be feasible.

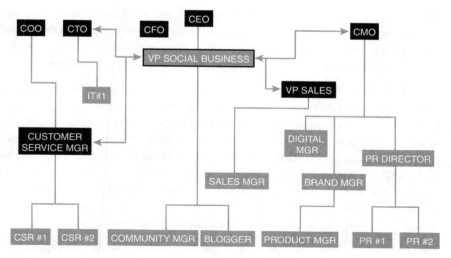

Figure 8.3   Social media program planning: management collaboration.

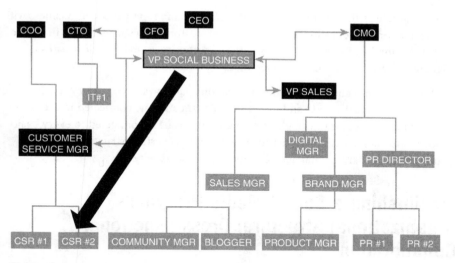

Figure 8.4   Social media program planning: illustrating direct authority.

In our example, the VP Social Business would be well advised to discuss this type of eventuality with the customer service manager ahead of time and obtain his approval. Outside of our example, this type of planning applies to all individuals performing social media functions and their managers.

The risk of not discussing this type of scenario with a manager whose direct report you could be "borrowing" from time to time in the scope of the social media program is twofold: First, the individual in the social media–related function may disregard a social media program manager's authority without being given the green light by his manager. If speed is of the essence, this can prove problematic. Avoid delays by making sure that protocols are in place for this type of situation.

Second, the individual's manager may resent having someone boss his direct report around without his permission. This, more than any other action taken by a social media program manager, can cause damaging friction between various departments and the social media program itself. Tread carefully: Be both conscious and respectful of managers' tendency to feel territorial about their staff and departmental activities. Approach managers with some degree of deference about the need for management overlap in certain situations. Don't demand anything from them. Simply state the facts and then let them suggest courses of action and protocols but do work with them on drafting these. Their department, their rules.

Direct authority also works in reverse: Depending on the situation, the digital CSR may opt to seek the approval or advice of either manager while opting to give both some degree of visibility to these communications.

An example of this would be the digital CSR emailing the VP Social Business with information or a question and including the customer service manager in the "cc:" distribution list. Establishing clear paths of authority establishes clear paths of reporting and vertical communications.

Once leadership and vertical communications pathways have been established and operationalized, the CEO and his executive team are now connected to the entire social media program through its manager, just as he is connected to every basic social media–related role under his influence. This vertical structure forms the basis of the program's management and reporting activity.

Establishing a Social Media Program's Organizational Structure: Cross-Functional Collaboration

Because social media programs touch virtually every facet of a business, they are at their very core exercises in cross-functional collaboration. And as with the vertical leadership and reporting mechanisms just discussed, this horizontal—or *lateral*—aspect of the program's flow of information, expertise, and support cannot exist without some kind of structure. First things first: Identify and map lateral networks (see Figure 8.5).

The idea is to keep things simple. To that end, try to organize lateral networks by tiers, as we have done in Figure 8.5. In our example, the uppermost tier is composed of senior executives and the organization's upper management, the middle tier is made up of departmental managers involved in our social media program, and the bottom tier is composed of the social media program's worker bees: the individuals who do most of the day-to-day social media–related work.

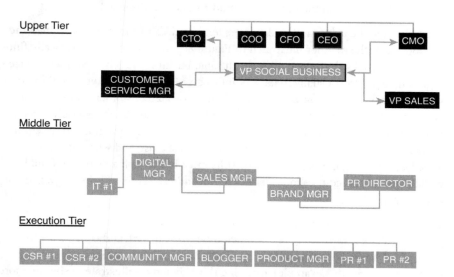

Figure 8.5   Social media program planning: lateral collaborative networks.

In this model, you can clearly see that the VP Social Business's lateral collaborative network includes the Chief Technology Officer (CTO), the Chief Marketing Officer (CMO), the VP Customer Service, and the VP Sales. Most strategic decisions regarding the social media program's direction, the assignment of resources, and the allocation of budgets will be made at this level.

The middle tier, composed of departmental managers such as the PR director, brand managers, sales managers, and the digital manager, coordinate activities, supervise staff, and ensure that the objectives and targets driving social media activities are met and that all departments are on the same page of music. Brand managers work with the PR manager, sales managers, and other department heads to coordinate activities surrounding a new product launch inside of the scope of a social media program in the same way they do outside of it. In fact, you may notice that mapping lateral collaboration networks at the departmental management level for a social media program tends to yield surprisingly familiar results: More often than not, they are identical to non-digital collaboration networks within your organization.

Unlike the upper and middle tiers, the execution tier tends to be unique to social media programs in both structure and degree of collaboration. First, structure: Community managers, bloggers, and digital customer service roles are fairly unique to social media programs. You would be hard-pressed to find a community management role in a traditional sales, marketing, or product management department. For that reason alone, the structure and makeup of this execution tier is going to seem less familiar than the upper and middle tiers just discussed.

Second, while the upper and middle tiers tend to already coordinate activities and collaborate in the manner illustrated in Figure 8.5, the execution tier typically finds itself operationally disconnected. In traditional business models, customer service representatives don't usually make a point to give PR representatives visibility to some of the feedback they are receiving from frustrated customers, for example, and certainly not in real time. Likewise, product managers don't generally receive feedback from digital content producers. For a social media program to function properly, however, this degree of collaboration must exist, and where it does not already exist today, it must be created. At its most basic, such a degree of fluid lateral collaboration requires four elements: procedures, training, technology, and adequate supervision.

The procedures and training refer to the dynamics by which elements of the program will share information, rely on each other for support, and collaborate to respond to the social media program's needs. Looking at the program as a whole (all three tiers, for this example), mapping these dynamics illustrates a slightly more complex diagram, as seen in Figure 8.6.

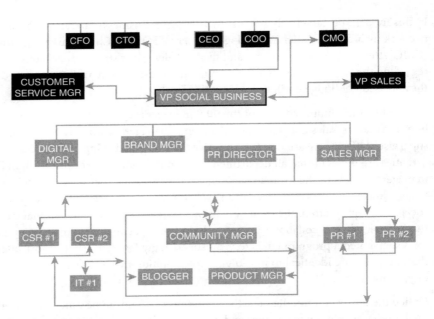

Figure 8.6 Social media program planning: lateral network dynamics.

The difference between mapping lateral networks (Figure 8.5) and lateral network dynamics (Figure 8.6) is that the latter illustrates the interactions within lateral networks. Elements of each network are not merely connected. They are now interacting with one another. In the upper and middle tiers, you see that all management roles are sharing information with one another. The same thing is happening in the execution tier: Digital customer service representatives are sharing information with each other as well as with the rest of the execution elements. Our lateral network dynamics show the interconnection of all these elements through some sort of collaboration mechanism.

In terms of procedures, each of the arrows in the diagram represents a specific type of communication for specific types of situations, each relying on a specific technology. This is where procedures begin, followed by training, followed by the selection of hardware and software that will enable each collaborative procedure, followed by its execution, which will need to be supervised by upper tiers through the mechanisms we observed in this chapter's first section.

Once lateral network dynamics have been roughly mapped out in this manner, you can begin in earnest the process of mapping specific response and collaboration mechanisms for various types of scenarios likely to be encountered by elements of your social media program's execution tier. Scenarios will vary from program to program but usually include every kind of situation requiring the involvement of more than one person in the program. These types of situations can range from crisis response and online reputation management activities to awareness campaigns and forum-style discussions.

Basic Technical Requirements

It isn't enough to simply create procedures and mechanisms by which collaboration and reporting will take place within your social media program if the technology to make these processes possible is not in place. Computers, mobile devices, access to the Web, and social media platforms are not enough. The basic technical requirements of a social media program at this juncture must now focus on tools that will help coordinate activities, share information, and collaborate vertically as well as laterally (see Figure 8.7).

Figure 8.7 illustrates the basic technology structure that should sit at the center of your social media program's communications and collaboration enablement. It consists of three distinct elements: a communications system that allows elements of your social media program to share information with each other, a customer relationship management platform (CRM), and a social media activity management dashboard.

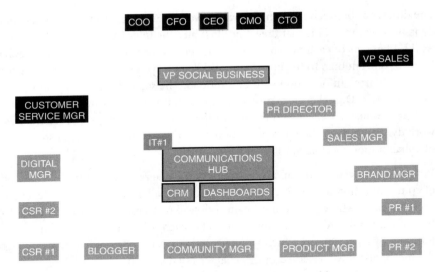

Figure 8.7 Social media program planning: collaboration enablement.

Because technology changes so quickly (and because zeroing in on specific products would make this book's content obsolete before it gathers its first layer of dust), consider any type of internal communication tool relevant to the communications hub component of this enablement structure. SharePoint servers certainly qualify, but you may be surprised that the telephone does as well. So do instant messages, whiteboards, and Post-It notes. Some companies do away with the need for technology altogether by simply placing all of the elements of their social media execution tier together in the same room so they can see, hear, and talk to each other. (This is easier to accomplish in centralized models than decentralized/pirate ship models.) *That* is their communications hub, and for some organizations, "simple" works pretty well. Always remember that the best tools are the ones that work for *you*. That said, also take the time to learn what collaboration tools might best serve your program and test them to see if they have value for your organization.

If you are looking for something simple and easy on your budget, start your search with Assembla, HyperOffice, Ice3, FMYI, Project2Manage, Code2 Public Folders, DeskAway, and even Stixy. For more robust collaboration tools that may fit better in a large organization accustomed to enterprise-class tools, look into what Radian6, Lithium, HootSuite, and Alterian have to offer. When it comes to dashboards, also look into companies such as Netvibes, Involver, MyWeboo, Spredfast, HootSuite (again), CoTweet, TweetDeck, Seesmic, and MediaFunnel.

The CRM component is a little tricky still, mostly because the promise of social customer relationship management (or "SCRM," as industry insiders like to call it) has yet to be fully realized. Essentially, social CRM lives at the intersection of traditional CRM systems (where companies store the data they have acquired on their customers, such as transaction history, profiles, preferences, interactions, average transaction amount, buy rate, and so on) and social data (such as the information shared on Facebook, Twitter, Foursquare, and slews of other social platforms). The idea behind social CRM is to be able to smoothly combine what your business knows about its customers from its own CRM system with the wealth of information that they share on social networks. As important as social CRM will be to your business in coming years, I only bring it up here to point out that the more smoothly your CRM system plugs into your internal collaboration tools and social media dashboards, the more fluid the management of your day-to-day social media activities will be.

At this juncture, social CRM manifests itself in two ways: CRM vendors whose products offer some degree of integration with social web platforms, and CRM vendors with fully loaded SCRM products. Among the former: SAP CRM, Sugar CRM, Oracle Siebel Social CRM, Microsoft Dynamics, RightNow CRM, and NetSuite. The latter include Jive Software, Visible Technologies, Lithium Technologies, and Concourse.

You will find that certain companies are already hard at work combining all three components of this technological puzzle: Combining team collaboration, social media activity management dashboards, and social CRM. At the top of that list are Radian6, HootSuite, Alterian, Lithium, and CoTweet. In your search for the perfect tool, make sure not to stop there, though. Keep an eye on new technologies, stay abreast of new software, test new offerings, and make sure your tools are always as up to date as they can be.

Now let's take a look at how this type of technology makes it all work. For our example, let's use an instance in which an irate customer has been complaining on social media channels about very poor treatment by company employees at a retail store. The digital customer service representative, finding herself unable to solve the angry customer's problem, begins the process of entering information about the incident in her system and triggers an alert to let the rest of the social media program team that they may want to participate in the process (see Figure 8.8).

The technology automatically shares the information with other systems within the program's communications infrastructure, as shown in Figure 8.9.

The system, prompted to alert the rest of the social media program team, catches the attention of several other program elements. Two choose to respond: one through the program's communications hub and the other through her dashboard. This is shown in Figure 8.10. In this example, the PR uses the communications hub to address the digital CSR internally and advise her as to how to handle the situation from a PR perspective. The community manager chooses instead to respond through his dashboard, jumping into the conversation alongside the CSR and addressing the customer directly.

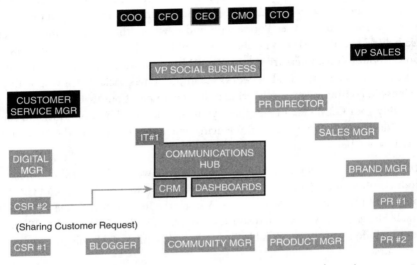

Figure 8.8   Social media program planning: basic collaborative dynamics.

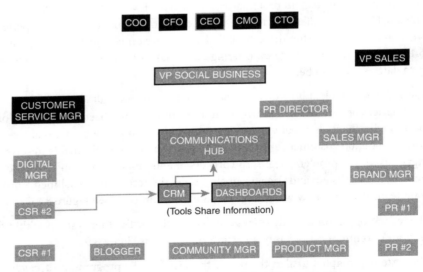

Figure 8.9   Social media program planning: collaborative technology.

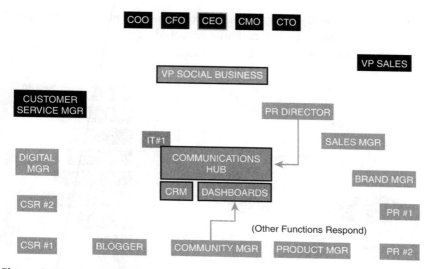

Figure 8.10   Social media program planning: basic response dynamics.

Figure 8.11 illustrates what happens next: The dashboard, CRM, and communications hub both capture and direct communications in regard to the situation and the response to the customer becomes a collaborative exercise. This is what the process looks like internally.

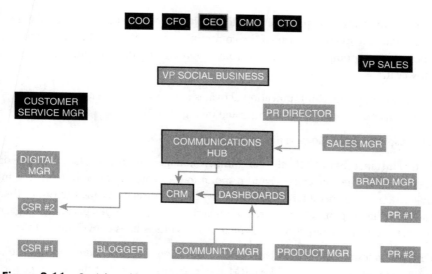

Figure 8.11   Social media program planning: open response dynamics.

Externally—that is to say, from the perspective of the customer—the process looks very different. In this example, a customer has asked a question that the digital customer service cannot answer (see Figure 8.12).

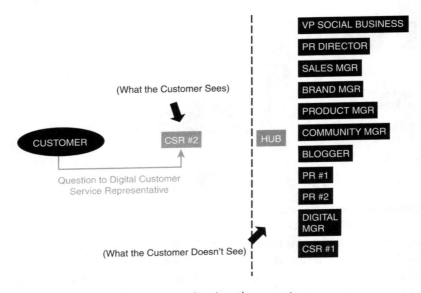

Figure 8.12   Social media response planning: the prompt.

Seeking an answer, she puts the question to the entire social media team; Figure 8.13 shows the manner in which the communications infrastructure distributes the question and prompts involvement from anyone within the program who can help answer it.

In our example, the communication activates a product manager, a community manager, and another CSR, as illustrated by Figure 8.14.

The response that follows is illustrated by Figure 8.15.

In this instance, both CSRs, the community manager, and the product manager opt to join the online conversation and respond to the customer directly. Note that in this instance, the customer is interacting with them directly. While the rest of the social media program elements remain inactive in regard to this particular engagement, the customer can clearly see the four individuals he is conversing with.

Once the question is answered and the conversation dies down, members of the team can politely disengage. The CRM system keeps a record of the exchange for future reference, analysis, and reporting.

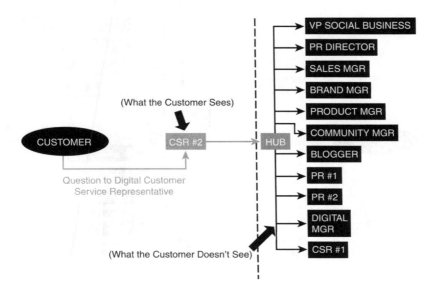

Figure 8.13   Social media response planning: event visibility.

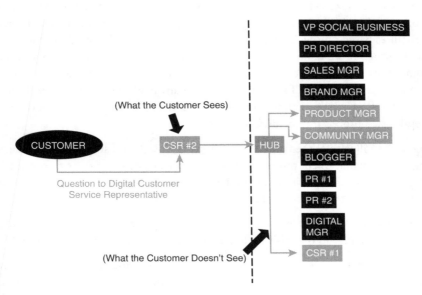

Figure 8.14   Social media response planning: network triggers.

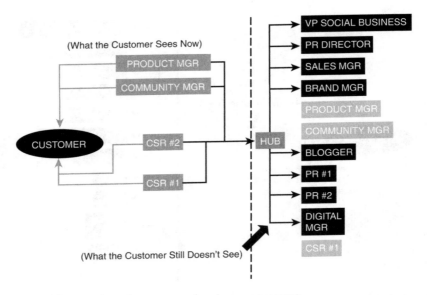

Figure 8.15   Social media response planning: engagement.

Once you get a sense for how every element of your social media program needs to work together, use your technology to start connecting your horizontal and vertical structures based on specific types of scenarios: Ask yourself who within the social media program should be involved in a crisis response process, for example. PR and community management probably need to be on that list, but who else? Begin to run through every type of situation your company may need to create collaborative procedures for, map functions and roles within each scenario, and start developing step-by-step procedures to address each situation.

Figure 8.16 illustrates the type of basic mapping you should start with when devising a crisis management process that begins with a customer service complaint. The diagram connects key roles to each other with the technology element at the center and lists some of the roles' key functions.

From this basic structure, we can now begin to think of each element in terms of the roles they will play in the crisis management process, as illustrated in Figure 8.17:

This type of mapping exercise can help you define roles and create fluid collaborative procedures between lateral and vertical networks within your program. In this example, the VP Social Communication's role is clear: He is to oversee the response, provide leadership and support if needed, and debrief his execution elements once the situation has been resolved. The community manager's role is to assist the lead element (in this case the customer service representative) as needed and follow up with the customer after the incident is over to make sure that the problem was solved. This type of process mapping ensures that response scenarios are adaptable and fluid enough to give every element of the program the flexibility to be effective. Note that the technology element, without which this degree of awareness, reporting, collaboration, and tracking would not be possible, can always be found at the center of the process.

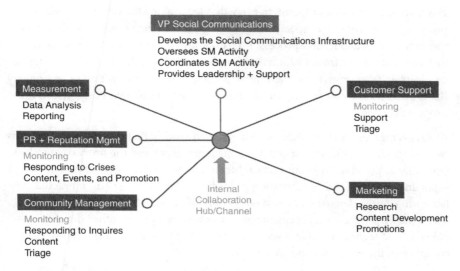

Figure 8.16   Social media program operationalization: function mapping.

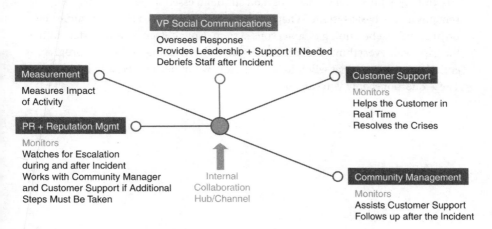

Figure 8.17   Social media program operationalization: share of response.

Though technology cannot take the place of a human being in social media, its role is crucial in facilitating collaboration between elements of the program, giving visibility to key elements of the program as to an activity that requires immediate human attention, quickly connecting elements of the program to a customer or member of the public, and recording the activity for future reference. Though doing all of this using only email and Post-It notes is possible, simple tools exist to make this degree of collaboration, organization, and data analysis easy to manage.

From an operational standpoint, the way that technology fits into the collaboration process puts its role in perspective: Technology should never guide the design of the program's collaboration process. If technology comes before the process, the program may suffer from its limitations and may not be able to adapt to changing conditions. If, however, the collaborative process guides the selection of technology, the process will be able to guide adaptations in the technology in response to the program's needs.

Always remember that software is a lot easier to modify than complex collaborative processes. What matters most is that the structure work and the processes work as smoothly as possible: Map out vertical hierarchies and lateral networks. Establish reporting channels and collaboration procedures. Work out the kinks. Practice collaborating across departments on a daily basis. Make sure that everyone in the social media program gets accustomed to working as a group rather than as individuals. Find technology that does what you want it to and simplifies rather than complicates the processes you have in place.

Finally, test, test, and test again. Learn what doesn't work and figure out how to make it work. Learn what works and then find ways of making it work better. The structure of your social media program, although essential to build early on, remains a very basic system. What you have at this point is a skeleton, some key organs, and the beginning of a nervous system. Now it is up to you to start filling the gaps with everything else. From this point, the "fleshing out" of the program is entirely up to you: What will it look like? How will it behave? How will it develop? These questions, only you can answer.

9

The New Rules of Brand Communications in the Age of Social Media

Social media's impact on brand communications is a game-changer in the same way that the fax machine, the Internet, and email were in the late twentieth century. In a way, you can look at it as the next evolution of human communications.

Social Media's General Impact on Brand Communications

Here is a brief history of human communications:

10,000 BC: Stories around the campfire. Oral tradition. Cave paintings.

4,000 BC: Clay tablets in Mesopotamia.

2,400 BC: First evidence of an official courier/mail system in Egypt.

1440 AD: The first printing press is assembled in Germany.

1839 AD: The telegraph makes its debut in Great Britain.

1880s AD: Telephones and motion pictures make their debut.

1920s AD: Radio broadcasts begin.

1930s AD: The television becomes commercially available.

1935 AD: Invention of the telex.

1957 AD: First radio transmission through a satellite.

1970 AD: Commercial introduction of the fax machine.

1979 AD: Japan creates the first 1G network for mobile phones.

1990s AD: Commercial adoption of the Internet, the first smart phone, and blogging.

2002–2005 AD: Introduction of the Blackberry. Launch of MySpace, Facebook, and YouTube.

2007–2009 AD: Introduction of the iPhone and e-readers. Launch of Twitter, Gowalla, and Foursquare.

2010 AD: Introduction of the iPad and the first 4G smart phone. Facebook passes 500,000,000 user mark. Twitter passes 100,000,000 user mark.

Up until just a few years ago, the vehicles through which organizations communicated with the public (their customers, stakeholders, and the rest of their audience) were essentially top-down and one-directional in nature: print, radio, TV, and the Web were messaging *delivery* channels. Advertising agencies, marketing departments, and PR firms focused for the most part on crafting a message, packaging it for maximum impact, and pushing it outward to the public through whatever channels seemed most appropriate. Rarely did marketers focus on creating a dialogue between consumers and brands, and in their defense, the one-directional nature of mass media channels made any such endeavor almost impossible. People couldn't reach marketers through their TV, radio, or magazines. Yelling up at billboards did not provide a direct line of communication with an advertiser. It just didn't work that way. Over time, the marketing profession and all of its key disciplines (except for market research) became so accustomed to the one-directional nature of mass media channels that they naturally began to see their business as a mostly outbound model.

I remember sitting in a conference room as late as 2006, chatting with a Global VP of Brand Communications for a very, very, *very* large PR firm and being told in no uncertain terms that the public would *never* have a voice. Her assertion was that PR would always be about one thing—creating and controlling *the message*—and that the advent of blogs and Web 2.0 would not change anything. Had she made this claim in 1986, she might have been right. In 2006, however, she was 100% wrong: Because of blogs and the social web, what had until then been a carefully controlled monologue became a fluid and not so easily controlled mass dialogue between not only consumers and brands, but consumers and other consumers. The golden age of *command and control* in brand communications was effectively breathing its last breaths. What was already emerging in its place was a more hybrid model in which the crafting and distribution of marketing messages now had to be carefully balanced against inbound and peripheral messages being created and shared outside the marketing wire, not by professional marketers but by hundreds of thousands of consumers.

Jump only a few short years ahead, and what you have now is a fully scaled version of what our friendly Brand Communications VP didn't want to accept in 2006: With hundreds of millions of people now talking to each other on social networks, posting videos from their phones and documenting every relevant moment of their lives, the game has radically changed for marketers. Expertly developed marketing depicting companies as purveyors of perfection, superior quality, and outstanding customer experiences can no longer afford to allow dissonance to gap the message from the reality of the products and services they deliver. With mass communications now as much in the hands of consumers as marketers, the days of hiding poor quality, lousy customer experiences, and shady business practices behind marketing and PR spin are effectively over.

For brand communications and brand management as a whole, this means consumer experiences must now closely match expectations created by the marketing messages surrounding them, or consumers will rebel. Where a decade ago, most personal tales of unmet expectations might have reached a dozen people at a time, today every single unmet expectation can be instantly shared with millions of people around the globe. The "United Breaks Guitar" campaign launched by a United Airlines customer who saw his guitar damaged by the airline is an excellent example of this process.

Angry customers are not the only voices that can potentially shed a light on dissonance between a brand's marketing and the reality of its activities. Microblogging platforms such as Twitter or Facebook spread rumors, information, and links to content across the globe in seconds. A video shot from a mobile phone can post a company employee doing something awful on YouTube or Facebook in moments, potentially damaging the brand in the minds of millions. The impact of this change on brand communications is massive.

Seven areas in particular affect organizations and their marketing partners directly:

1. **Velocity has accelerated**—Ten years ago, Corporate Communications departments enjoyed at least a day or two after the break of a scandal or potentially negative story to respond. That buffer allowed crisis response teams to meet with their legal departments and key executives, consider all of their options, take their time drafting responses, and finally go to bat with what they hoped would attenuate the problem. After a week, news cycles came and went, pressure waned, and response teams could begin planning the next phase of their responses.

   Today, Corporate Communications departments have about less than an hour to start responding to a crisis once it starts spreading across the social web. When I say less than an hour, I really mean about ten minutes.

   Consider the difference between a 24-to-48-hour response cycle and one expected to be executed less than one hour. Back yourself into the crisis management process, into the time it takes to first be alerted to the problem, then make the right phone calls to the right people, set up a meeting or conference call, draft a response, get it approved, send it out, and begin to manage a crisis in earnest.

   Ten minutes without some kind of response once a crisis begins to emerge, and things can start to snowball immediately. Ten hours, and you might be a trending topic on Twitter. Twenty-four hours, and you could easily be a news item. Actor-director Kevin Smith's ordeal with Southwest Airlines is a perfect example of the speed with which one bad experience can become national news in under 24 hours because of social media. This radical transformation of the velocity with which news spreads and stories scale requires an equally radical degree of adaptation by brand and corporate communications professionals. The channels alone haven't changed the game; the velocity with which information spreads has as well.

2. **Awareness is no longer passive**—Because of the speed with which a negative news item can spread, organizations need to constantly *monitor* social web channels for signs of trouble. If your corporate communications team takes a day or two to alert senior executives that a PR crisis is occurring on the Web, it is already too late. To spot trouble early enough to break a scandal's momentum before it grows out of

control, organizations have to keep a *constant* watch on conversation trends that goes far beyond traditional market research and the acquisition of customer insights. To be able to respond quickly and effectively to potential crises, a new degree of awareness must be engineered into corporate communications: Inbound communications must now become as important as outbound communications. *Listening* has become as important as talking.

3. **Competencies have multiplied**—Crafting messages and managing one-directional communications once dominated the brand and corporate communications field. The advent of the social web has now expanded the list of necessary skills and experience well beyond copywriting and media buying. Communications professionals now also have to develop an operational fluency with channel monitoring, social dynamics, the mechanics of word-of-mouth (WOM), digital crisis management, online reputation management, engagement strategies and tactics, community management, as well as understand the nuances between competing social networks and know the ins and outs of dozens of digital platforms. The field of brand communications has become exponentially more complex than it was just a decade ago, and there is no getting around the need for a radical change in the types of skills and abilities now required of professionals in this area.

    Although it may seem logical to look for social media or social communications "experts" to bring an adequate level of competency to a traditional brand communications practice, this is not a realistic approach in the long run. As the entire field of brand and corporate communications adapts to this change, it falls upon communications professionals to expand their skill sets to *incorporate* social communications into their own individual practices. Social media expertise is not a separate, add-on component of brand communications. It is now an integral part of it. Though further specialization in the communications profession is sure to follow, a practical fluency with social media is now increasingly required of any professional in the field hoping to remain relevant beyond the millennium's first decade.

4. **Psychological profiles have shifted**—Skill set is one thing. The ability to operate in a dynamic, real-time, highly social environment where the slightest mistake can worsen an already shaky situation is another. Working in the social space requires more than knowledge and technical know-how; it takes a very specific type of personality as well—the kind that thrives in complex social environments, one that doesn't run away from risk or pressure, one that doesn't lose its temper easily—or ever—and one that is inherently...well, social. Communications

professionals must now be able to make split-second decisions about not only content but tone. They must be able to switch from *customer service* mode to *evangelist* mode to *voice of reason* mode in moments, without having to consult a manual or a supervisor. They have to *love* engaging with people in the social space. It isn't for everyone. Now that social media has begun to merge with traditional channels, communications professionals with a tendency to be easily rattled by tough questions or a flood of negative comments are not necessarily well suited to hold public-facing positions in brand or corporate communications anymore. Times have changed.

5. **Communications are becoming more decentralized**—Ten years ago, few individuals were allowed to represent the company in mass media channels: perhaps a spokesperson, an executive, and whatever staff obtained permission from the top in the context of an interview or special event. Nowadays, anyone working for an organization can become a company representative, with or without permission. This can be a good thing and a bad thing, depending on the situation. On the one hand, untrained staff can accidentally embarrass their employer even if they don't "officially" speak for their organization. Likewise, one well-trained (or social media–savvy) employee with a little initiative and good timing can save the day when "officially sanctioned" staffers fumble. Any employee capable of forging relationships with potential customers on social channels can, through effective engagement, attract new customers and even generate revenue for his employer. He can fix a customer service problem or put an end to a damaging rumor. He can be friendly and helpful when no one else in the company will. This growing decentralization of communications is a bit of a double-edged sword, with its own set of advantages and disadvantages. Finding ways of dealing with this change should be high on any organization's list of priorities. (Chapter 7, "Establishing Social Media Guidelines for the Organization," focuses on how to get started.)

6. **Communications are becoming less "corporate"**—You may have noticed that social communications are not stuffy and corporate. The more "human" and colloquial the conversations and content, the more effective they are. Conversely, the more carefully crafted and "professional," the less genuine they seem. Corporate and brand communications now need to adapt to a communications environment that requires a more honest, down-to-earth, personal tone and vocabulary. Stuffy old press releases and robotic copy won't cut it anymore.

7. **Trust is everything**—The human brain is wired to notice dissonance. Because it naturally looks for patterns, it also notices *breaks* in patterns.

Such breaks alert us that something is afoot, that perhaps danger might be close. Our "instincts" are essentially this: Our subconscious mind triggering an alarm when it detects a break in a pattern or a dissonance in our surroundings. The same mechanism applies to communications: If messaging and the reality of our experience do not match, our brains trigger not only an internal alarm but prompt us also to trigger the alarm for the rest of our social group—our tribe. This was difficult to do before the advent of social media, but now that we are all connected to hundreds, sometimes thousands of people—themselves connected to thousands of people, and so on—via social networks, this alarm bell can be heard around the world in a matter of minutes. In other words, marketing "spin" is dead. Truth—or "transparency" as we see a bit later in this chapter—is now the new cardinal rule of brand communications in the age of social media.

While other business functions and departments have been only partially impacted by the development of social media, the *communications* function has been fundamentally transformed by this new evolution in communications technology. This is where social media's impact on the organization is most intensely felt and where adaptation must occur the fastest.

What is most important to grasp here is that when it comes to brand communications, social media cannot be treated merely as another set of channels. Facebook and Twitter are not simply new *reach* vehicles. Organizations whose leadership makes this mistake end up not only failing in the social web but exposing themselves to a slew of negative sentiment and missed opportunities to strengthen their brands with the public. Beyond issues of transparency, opacity, confidentiality, and disclosure lie hundreds if not thousands of procedural changes that will inevitably ripple across your organization.

Transparency, Opacity, Confidentiality, and Disclosure

Transparency is not a social media buzzword. It is a legitimate business term that applies to policies of disclosure within an organization, especially in regard to endorsements and material connections with individuals or organizations acting as agents for the brand. A material connection could be as straightforward as a digital agency singing its client's praises on Twitter or as subtle as a blogger writing a positive review of a new piece of software after receiving a free copy in the mail along with a free T-shirt from the software vendor. Policies of transparency in communications help organizations not only establish ethical disclosure practices that help protect consumers from fraud but also positively impact consumer trust. The more transparent an organization, the more likely it is that it will establish a strong foundation of trust with consumers on social channels. In other words, in the age of social media, transparency tends to be good for business. But can being too transparent be a liability?

Ideally, the truest form of transparency would amount to letting the outside world look into your organization as if with X-ray vision. No walls. No magic curtains. Unlimited access to what is going on backstage. This is, of course, impractical for most organizations. So right off the bat, the term finds itself in a pickle: Transparency, in business terms, in communications terms, quickly becomes subjective and conditional. Take confidential information, for example, or trade secrets. Prototypes, creative drafts, employee pay, the P&L, research projects, partnerships being negotiated, acquisitions being contemplated—all of these things require some level of confidentiality that too much transparency would realistically threaten.

Transparency, then, when applied to business processes and the reality of running a business, quickly becomes *relative* transparency. One might call it *conditional* transparency even. You can be *transparent* about some things but not others and even so, at varying degrees. It just doesn't work. What you have is at best *opacity*: a relative absence of transparency. Good or bad, right or wrong, opacity trumps transparency in most day-to-day communications stemming from social media programs, with the exception of one specific thing: disclosure.

Luckily for us, the rules surrounding disclosure in social media are relatively clear, at least in the U.S. The Federal Trade Commission (FTC) took the time to review the risks of nondisclosure in this new space and drafted a document that answers most questions you may have on this subject. It is a little long to include in this chapter, so I recommend that you familiarize yourself with it and incorporate it in your social media policy document. The FTC's document is commonly referred to as "the FTC's guides concerning the use of endorsements and testimonials in advertising," or simply 16 CFR Part 255.

Here are some of its most important rules:

- Bloggers (and by default anyone posting to a microblogging platform such as Facebook or Twitter) are now required to disclose material connections to companies whose products or services they discuss or recommend.

- Regardless of what platform is used, adequate disclosure must be clear, prominently displayed, easily understood, and unambiguous. Disclosure cannot be hidden deep in copy or printed in a font or color that is difficult to read.

This means that anyone who blogs, tweets, manages a Facebook page for an organization, or is materially connected to that organization *must* disclose that relationship in a way that leaves no room for confusion or obfuscation. The reason behind this is simple: In a space where word-of-mouth, consumer recommendations, and nonmarketing communications have the power to influence millions by spreading across trusted peer networks, the risk of false recommendations and reviews is too great to leave to chance. Consumers and organizations alike must be protected against unethical practices. What makes this particularly relevant to this discussion is that organizations can be held responsible for nondisclosure infractions perpetrated by their "agents." In other words, if a blogger who was remunerated in some way in the hopes that he might publish a positive review of a company's product does not disclose this "material connection" in his review, the company could be looking at a hefty fine. In the U.S., for example, organizations could be looking at fines up to $10,000 per instance of nondisclosure.

To avoid even the appearance of wrongdoing as well as hefty fines, it falls not only on an organization's agents (anyone having received some form of payment, even if not implicitly tied to a request by the organization to express a positive view or endorsement) but on the organization itself to make sure that any and all agents disclose any material connection with the organization in their reviews. The disclosure statement can be delivered in a variety of ways, but a common one looks like this:

> Disclosure: Company XYZ is a client.

Or...

> Disclosure: Though a fan and in no way influenced by my relationship with Company XYZ, they are nevertheless a client.

Or even...

> Disclosure: I have received no payment for my opinion other than free product samples.

To make sure that no ambiguity exists, I would recommend that if a material connection ever existed between the blogger and the organization—even if this connection is in the past—that it be disclosed as well.

In the same way, employees, partners, agents, and contractors hired by an organization in any way, when speaking about their company, one of their competitors, their industry, or any topic that might constitute even the slightest conflict of interest, should err on the side of caution: Better to disclose a material connection unnecessarily than not. When in doubt, disclose.

Because the Word of Mouth Marketing Association (WOMMA) focused much of its attention on digital recommendations and influencer marketing before most of the rest of the business world, it began to develop ethical disclosure best practices early. Its website provides one of the clearest and most concise explanations I have found on the topic:

> *Consumers have a right to know the sponsor behind advertising messages that could influence their purchasing decisions, but key information is not always adequately disclosed in a social media context. Thus, for testimonials and endorsements delivered to consumers through social media— whether by consumers, experts, celebrities, or organizations—the FTC requires advertisers and bloggers to disclose all "material connections."*
>
> *Such "material connections" may be defined as any connection between a blogger and an advertiser that could affect the credibility consumers give to that blogger's statements. Important examples of "material connections" include (a) consideration (benefits or incentives such as monetary compensation, loaner products, free services, in-kind gifts, special access privileges) provided by an advertiser to a blogger, or (b) a relationship between an advertiser and a blogger (such as an employment relationship).*

As more and more marketing conversations and content shift to social media channels, the line between marketing and genuine consumer opinions can easily become blurred. In 2006, retail giant Wal-Mart and its public relations partner Edelman PR both suffered a bit of a media black eye when it was discovered that "Wal-marting Across America," a blog that appeared to be written by a couple named Laura and Jim, a couple of Wal-Mart fans driving across America in an RV, turned out to be an Edelman creation. What the blog, Edelman PR, and Wal-Mart failed to disclose was that both Laura and Jim were not just random fans with a blog but brand advocates being *paid* to publish the blog. The duplicitous nature of the blog and Edelman's actions resulted in a firestorm of outrage against Wal-Mart and Edelman PR alike and helped crystallize the need for adequate disclosure in brand communications that fall outside of traditional media channels. Edelman's CEO published a heartfelt apology admitting the firm's "error in failing to be transparent about the identity of the two bloggers," but the damage was done.

In 2006, the need for disclosure in social media and brand communications was merely an ethical discussion. Today, with regulatory bodies such as the FTC acting as watchdogs over the marketing communications space, proper disclosure is also increasingly becoming a matter of law.

Confidentiality and Data Protection in the Age of Social Media

On the flip side of the disclosure discussion is the issue of confidentiality and even secrecy. What if a company's success depends on its ability to keep a special formula, its latest strategy, its prototypes, or other information a complete secret? How does the introduction of social media into the communications landscape interfere with matters of data security?

In Chapter 7, we discussed how to put together a social media policy document that outlines employee protocols in regard to their usage of the social web at work and outside of work. Confidentiality and secrecy protocols must be included in this document. Whatever rules already apply to email, fax, and other forms of communication and communication technologies must now be applied to social media as well. Do not expect employees, partners, and agents to figure it out on their own. Tell them. Once they have read and signed off on the policy document, incorporate this into their basic training. Whatever information is confidential or not for public consumption must not be discussed regardless of the medium or technology. Twitter, Facebook, SMS/txt, Foursquare, and so on, are off limits to this type of data.

This is not limited to pasting super-top-secret blueprints to a tweet or publishing the secret chemical formula on a personal blog. This also includes more subtle types of information that may not seem implicitly off limits. Every organization views data and information differently when it comes to confidentiality and security, but let me draw from my military past to point you to some silly mistakes employees, partners, and agents might make without realizing it:

- **Example 1:** If your competitors are watching your every move (and they are), how would you feel about your employees tipping them off to the fact that they have made five recent trips to a city where a company you might want to acquire happens to be headquartered? How might this happen? In 2007, they might have posted their visit on Dopplr.com. In 2008, Facebook. In 2009, Twitter. In 2010, Foursquare or Gowalla. Such inadvertent little bits of information could let the cat out of the bag on a very big secret. Disclosing confidential troop movements is not only a security threat for military organizations. Similar threats apply to the corporate world as well. Make sure that employees know not to disclose confidential trips in any way through social media.

- **Example 2:** Employees start geo-tagging specific locations within your buildings via Foursquare, Gowalla, or another location-based service. They now start competing against each other to earn badges or rewards. Harmless fun, right? This wouldn't be a problem if they stuck to conference rooms and the water coolers, but it might become more of an issue if your design engineering lab and testing facilities start showing up on Google Maps as well. If certain areas of your facilities need to be kept secret, make sure that employees know not to play geo-tagging games around them (or at all).

For the sake of clarity, I recommend to all of my clients that they adopt a confidentiality scale for all internal data and communications, to indicate the level of confidentiality of every bit of information. It is as follows:

- **Green: Suitable for public consumption**—This can be tweeted, posted, discussed, shared, and so on.

- **Yellow: Company-confidential**—This information is not for public consumption. Employees may only discuss this with fellow employees. It is an internal matter only.

- **Red: Group-confidential**—This information is not for mass internal consumption. It is intended only for a small and clearly identified group of individuals within the organization—recipients of an email, for example. Red-tagged information must clearly list who is authorized to have access to it with every printed or digital communication.

The benefit of such a system is twofold: First, it is painfully simple. There are only three levels of confidentiality, and they are essentially this: open, confidential, and secret. They outline the conditions of confidentiality and permission to share and discuss. Second, it ensures that the confidentiality level of every communication across the organization is clear to all employees. This coding can be easily integrated into emails, conversations, voice messages, diagrams, slide decks, and so on. Does this completely eliminate the risk that confidential information will end up being shared through social media channels? No more than the risk that the same information will find its way out via email, fax, lost laptops, memory devices, the trash dumpster outside, or a loud-talking employee in a restaurant, but it does serve to considerably reduce that possibility.

Social media's impact on brand and corporate communications is sure to continue to evolve in the coming years, with new technologies, software, and cultural shifts further disrupting traditional methods and channels. The good news is that changes of this scale don't have to be scary: This evolution in mass communications presents boundless opportunities for communications professionals focused on understanding how to leverage them. The more we familiarize ourselves with these changes, the quicker we adapt to them, and the sooner we will be able to put them to good use within our organizations' own communications practices.

III

Social Media Program Management

10 Listening Before Talking 127

11 Social Media and Digital Brand Management 135

12 Real-Time Digital Support: Fixing Customer Service
Once and for All 157

13 Social Media Program Management—Putting It All Together . . .173

Listening Before Talking

One of the most common questions asked at the inception of a social media strategy is, "What are we supposed to talk about on blogs and Facebook and Twitter?" Because marketing communications professionals are used to producing and pushing out content, they tend to approach the social web with the same frame of mind. It isn't that the question is wrong. It is actually valid. It just isn't the question organizations need to focus on when beginning the management phase of their social media program. Let me explain.

Everything about human biology leans toward aiding in our survival, from the millions of nerve endings inside our nose to smell when danger is close to our ability to feel pain when we are injured. The human head is equipped with two eyes, two ears, two nostrils, but only one mouth. This is because gathering information about our surroundings, learning, and taking in the world around us are much more valuable than our ability to speak. From a survival standpoint, the more we know about our environment, the better we understand it, the more we can both react to it and adapt to it. Knowledge is power. Insight is golden. This is why listening and observing are much more important than talking. In this, the business world is no different: The more a business knows about market conditions, about consumer tastes, about their competitors' latest failures and successes, the better strategic position it can find itself in. Unfortunately, businesses have not benefited from millions of years of evolution, and their listening mechanisms are not particularly well developed. Market research can be remarkably difficult to manage, is often slow and laborious, not to mention cost-prohibitive for many companies. For all these reasons, in the weeks and months leading up to the official launch of your social media program's operations, make sure that you focus on building for it a solid monitoring and listening practice: Do not immediately concern yourself with campaigns, the creation of content, and "push" activities. Instead, begin your operations by learning how to use social media to listen, observe, and learn everything you can about the types of topics of conversation taking place on the social web that may shape the future of your organization.

Business Intelligence and Search

Imagine yourself a stranger in a strange land. You don't yet speak the language or know the customs. You don't know where to buy clothes or food. You don't know the laws very well yet. You have no idea where the cool coffee shops, restaurants, and bars are. During your first few months in this strange land, would you immediately procure a soap box, find a busy street corner, and start singing your own praises to the crowd, or would you quietly observe and learn what you can before contributing your views to this new environment? Social media is no different.

When organizations start with "What should we say?" they generally put the cart ahead of the horse. What organizations should be starting with is, "What should we listen for?"

Consider the question. "What should we listen for?" is not a social media question. It is a business intelligence question. As a consultant, my answer to that question is generally this: "You tell me. What *should* you be listening for? What kind of information would be most valuable to you?"

This is where social media programs should begin: with focused listening rather than unfocused publishing.

In case elements of your organization don't know right away what they want to listen for, let me get you started with some simple ideas. The first thing you should know is that most of the content published on the social web is searchable by keyword and/or topic and indexed by search engines such as Google. This means that whatever is being discussed online is searchable. Your company, your products, your competitors, your industry—all of these topics can be searched at any given time. Every online mention of your company can be captured, cataloged, organized, quantified, and analyzed.

Begin by performing an audit of your company by using traditional search engines: Google, Yahoo!, Bing, and so on. What turns up? Your main company site, some news stories, and, probably, YouTube videos, blog posts, Twitter content, and the like. (Search engines increasingly capture content from the social web.) If your brand has had any impact on culture whatsoever, you may find a treasure trove of fan sites or hate sites. You may discover user-generated content that aims to either flatter or insult, promote or damage. This is a good start. Don't just stop with mentions of your company. Also look for keyword combinations, like your company's name and "good" or "bad." Add "service" and "quality." Dig into "best" and "worst," still attached to your company name. Bring industry, product category, and other keywords into your searches as well. You can start with general searches about your company and see where they take you, or you can be specific with a search by seeking to answer questions such as, "What are people saying about our latest product?" "What are people saying about the experience of doing business with us?" or "What are people saying about our decision to purchase one of our competitors?"

Now, dive deeper into popular social media platforms. Most of them should have on their front pages some kind of search box. Use it. Begin with a search of your organization's name and see what turns up. The result could be very little, or it could be overwhelming, depending on the size and visibility of your organization. This alone is a great place to begin: Are you starting with very little exposure or an overwhelming amount of data? If your starting point is very little exposure, your program's emphasis will probably be aimed at increasing your presence and relevance across digital channels. If the amount of mentions of your organization is overwhelming, your initial focus will probably be to manage this sea of data and insight and make sense of it.

Already, just by listening, an organization can see the genesis of a six-month strategy begin to form. It may discover that the public's focus in regards to its brand touches on poor user experience and inadequate customer service rather than the new product releases it has been working on for the last eight months. By identifying a problem that the organization had missed until now, it has an opportunity to react and improve both its UX and its customer support mechanisms. By doing so, it may not only solve two problems it wasn't aware needed attention, but it also might help turn the public's focus away from these distracting topics and back to what it wants people to talk about: its exciting new product releases. The same mechanism can also help an organization gauge where a campaign is failing or succeeding. Are people talking about how ridiculous your latest print ad is or how much they like it? Are they talking about how much they love your latest fragrance or prefer your competitor's? Are they talking about how badly they want to buy your latest product but can't until the price drops 20%? Can you quantify this data? (Yes, you can.) Could it impact your advertising decisions, the assignment of departmental budgets to fund specific projects, and even your retail pricing schemes? Information is power: The more you know and the faster you know it, the faster you can make an intelligent decision as to your next move. Building a business intelligence component into your social media program gives organizations that crucial tactical edge. It can help you improve your products and services, adjust pricing, identify design upgrades for the next version of a product, and identify areas of opportunity in a market.

The next step is to dive deeper into your searches with monitoring tools. You can use sophisticated enterprise-class tools like Webtrends, Radian6, and Lithium, or simpler, more budget-friendly tools like Tweetdeck, Seesmic, and Hootsuite, to help spot trends, manage social media data, and more. The breadth of tools that can help you manage and monitor your organization's activity on the social web is vast and ever growing, so my advice is this: Familiarize yourself with as many tools as you can. Most of their marketing teams will gladly set up live demos for you so you can experience their capabilities for yourself. Take the time to do so and find what tools work best for your organization.

Bear in mind that whatever tools you decide to use in this capacity should focus on your ability to monitor key channels, search them for specific types of topics, conversations, and information, and help you both qualify and quantify them. While your ability to respond to requests for help, comments, blog posts, and articles will be important to your social media program's operations as a whole, the business intelligence aspect of the program needs to focus primarily on searching for, listening to, capturing, and analyzing information. To this end, whatever tools you choose to use should focus on this specific task first and foremost.

The Power of Real-Time Situational Awareness

Listen long enough, and what an organization should talk about will become abundantly clear through the public's discussion topics and questions. This is why

Customer Support/Service—not Marketing or PR—tends to be the first department to enjoy some measure of well-organized social media integration in organizations that take the time to listen before they speak in the social space.

Consider the thousands of marketing messages bombarding consumers daily across every channel imaginable: magazines, billboards, TV, radio, the Web. What is the value of yet another marketing message popping up in someone's Twitter stream or Facebook page? Zero. Now consider the value of having a question answered or problem solved by a company representative through the same channel used by a consumer to ask the question or request assistance? The value of such a response, of such a service, is incalculable.

In terms of providing value to customers (and potential customers) then, responding to questions and problems is a far better bet than pushing a blog post, a marketing campaign, or a press release, isn't it? This type of value, which generates positive sentiment, positive word-of-mouth, loyalty, and both net new business and repeat business finds its genesis in listening: An organization cannot respond to the needs of its market without first being in tune to its needs. This begins at the individual level, with each mention of the organization, product, or product category. It begins with deliberate and organized monitoring. It begins with situational awareness. At any given time, hundreds, maybe thousands of people may be talking about your organization or even *to* your organization. If you do not have a system in place to capture, analyze, and respond to these mentions, you are too detached from your market to be effective in it. Situational awareness is—both in nature and in the business world—the first rule of survival. You cannot respond to threats and opportunities if you are not aware of them in real time.

We just focused on ways to use listening and monitoring to identify opportunities and help business grow, one customer problem or question at a time. The flip side of the situational awareness coin is threat management: the threat of obsolescence, the threat of missing the next market shift or technological advance, the threat of watching your own customers flock to a competitor because they were more in tune with your market's needs than you were, and even the threat of finding yourself exposed to a PR crisis that your traditional marketing communications mechanisms are not equipped to manage. Crisis management is a recurring topic throughout this book and for good reason: The social web and the velocity with which information spreads around the world now amplifies everything, including failure. The slightest *faux pas* or rumor can snowball into a trending topic or news item in a matter of hours.

News isn't just on 24/7 anymore. It is on 60/60/24/7. Five years ago, CNN, the BBC, and every other news network could not reach me around the clock unless I tuned into them around the clock. Now that their content feeds into Twitter and Facebook—both of which live on my phone—my access to news is hardly ever interrupted by my programming choices or my attention span. Negative news about an organization can swell into a global story in mere hours. Monitoring social channels for signs of PR trouble is another mode of deliberate situational awareness that organizations need to focus on early in the game. PR departments now need to shift from a predominantly outbound, messaging-based core practice to one that emphasizes 24/7 monitoring, rapid response, online reputation management, and digital crisis management. The faster and more effective the response on the social web, the sooner a PR crisis's damage to a brand can be attenuated. Consider that it takes, on average, the better part of an hour for a major news organization like CNN or the BBC to verify the accuracy of a story. In the past, this gave companies somewhat of a crisis response buffer. Social networks on the Web, because they work as an electronic grapevine, can spread a story around the globe in less than ten minutes. News organizations no longer own the scoop. Bloggers—citizen journalists—do, and everyday customers do.

Not long ago, if a restaurant patron found a cockroach baked into his chocolate cake, you might hear about it on the news the next day. Today, that same patron can take a picture of the offending insect with his cell phone, post it to a half dozen social networks in seconds, and see the story spread around the globe in minutes. An irate customer service clerk at an electronics store losing his cool and berating a helpless old lady can be videotaped by a customer with a mobile phone waiting in line and then posted to YouTube on the spot. That simple of an event, which a decade ago would have received little to no attention at all, could nowadays become the image by which a company is defined for years.

In the United States, the TSA (Transport Security Administration) found itself in such a situation in late 2010 when an airline passenger being subjected to a security pat-down turned on his cell phone's video camera and uttered the now world-famous words, "If you touch my junk, I'll have you arrested," to a TSA agent. The video became a lightning rod for the TSA's increasingly intrusive security protocols, galvanizing hundreds of thousands of irate air travelers across the U.S. to organize protests. The video was shown on every news network in North America, and the TSA eventually agreed to review its screening policies. In this instance, the TSA, which was aware of passengers' frustrations with their procedures, was in a wait-and-see mode of response until feedback from the public put pressure on its leadership to make a change. This feedback, though eventually aided by "traditional" news networks, began with social media. One man with a camera and access to the Internet can ruin an organization's day in less than ten minutes. Because most PR crises involving the general public now begin with a complaint, comment, photo, or video published on a social network, it makes sense to establish PR listening posts there early in your social media program's development and to learn to spot potential threats and crises as early as possible.

New Avenues of Market Research: From "I Don't Know" to "Let's Find Out"

The beauty of the social web is that decision makers and business leaders no longer have to guess what is going on in their markets. Business intelligence, market research, and other means of peering outside the corporate bubble are no longer the realm of research firms' "experts" and academics. Anyone with an Internet connection and access to the proper tools can in moments begin to answer just about any question relating to consumer behaviors and market trends with respectable accuracy. Bear in mind that because not everyone uses the social web, your research pool may come with its share of statistical limitations. What is important to note is that today's organizations have access to a much greater breadth of market research options than in decades past.

The benefit of this evolution in access to intelligence and information is threefold:

- **Access**—Anyone in the organization can now manage a research practice, even with virtually no budget. Access to studies, data, information, research tools, and consumer insights is no longer limited to the C-suite, external agencies, consulting firms, and specialized teams. Where the type of purposeful search and monitoring discussed earlier in the chapter falls short of answering a particular question, websites like SurveyMonkey, TwitPoll, and Zoomerang and software tools like Google Docs can help organizations create their own surveys with which to seed social networks.

- **Velocity**—Market research firms are great, but their process can sometimes take so long that by the time the information it has gathered reaches their client, market conditions have either begun to shift or the window of opportunity for a response is already closing. The social web's ocean of data and insights, accessible in real time through a panoply of user-friendly tools and technologies, can make intelligence gathering quasi-instantaneous. What used to take weeks can now take mere days, sometimes even hours. The value of this new paradigm in velocity is that the faster an organization can gather information and intelligence, the faster it can analyze it and act upon it. It is that simple.

- **Accuracy**—Most consumer and market data has a short shelf life. Consider the value of consumer opinions from three months ago versus consumer opinions from just this morning. Trends change. Consumers are fickle. What may have been true three months ago may no longer be true today. One of the advantages of being able to access market intelligence in real time is that the data tends to be fresh. Always fresh.

Another aspect of data obtained via the social web is that when departments conduct their own research instead of outsourcing it, they eliminate some of the "lost in translation" risk that comes with hiring an outsider to answer insider questions. When departments with specific core competencies and a deep insight into their own business and market conduct their own research, they are less likely to have to deal with incorrectly asked questions, poorly collected data, or misinterpreted information.

"I don't know" no longer has to be the end of a conversation. It can now be the beginning of a project, even an opportunity when followed by "Let's find out." In fact, when it comes to business development in general, social media or not, "Let's find out" is always a great place to start. Not only is it at the core of the pioneering spirit that made brands such as Apple, Starbucks, and Nike market superstars, but it also ensures that before any decision is made, the organization's t's are crossed and its i's dotted. Why fly blind? Why fear the unknown and be paralyzed by it when all it takes is a little curiosity and a window into the social web? If you are a pizza company, do what Domino's did and ask your customers how they would improve your pizzas. Then make the change and give your customers an opportunity to share their pictures of your new and improved pizza with the world, to prove that you not only listened but also delivered (pun intended) on your promise to listen. If you are an airline, a restaurant, or a hotel chain, listen to your customers' complaints and praises, qualify then quantify them, and begin making the necessary changes.

If your company isn't sure about its direction, an idea, or an opportunity, turn to your market using the tools they use to communicate with one another: If you cannot infer from their conversations what about your business you should work on improving, poll your customers. Poll your competitors' customers, even. Don't guess. Just ask. Companies like Starbucks, Best Buy, Cisco, General Electric, IBM, and Pepsi have been for years, and now, with the help of social media, so can you.

The lesson here is this: Before you do anything else with social media, build a listening and monitoring practice. Not just a "hearing" practice, mind you: Watch, listen, and learn. Do so proactively. Develop ways to improve your ability to use the social web as a real-time intelligence and monitoring practice and work at becoming better at it with every passing month. Do this, and 80% of the social media puzzle will solve itself: Through this mechanism, you will uncover areas of improvement across your entire business, discover new market opportunities as they arise, increase the speed with which you notice threats and tackle crises, gauge the success of product launches, marketing campaigns, and corporate communications in real time, and build the kind of market research and situational-awareness engine that will give your organization an undeniable tactical advantage.

11

Social Media and Digital Brand Management

One of the biggest misconceptions to plague social media as a discipline—particularly in regard to its integration in the business world—is that it is primarily a marketing function. It isn't. Social media, like other forms of media, can be used by just about every business function—from human resources to project management. At the crux of social media's value to an organization, though, is the role it plays in brand management and particularly digital brand management.

Introduction to the New Paradigm in Digital Brand Management

Before blogs, forums, and digital social networks came along, brand management was a fairly simple affair: A company would build a brand, craft its messaging, distribute this to its audience via vertical mass media channels such as television, radio, print, mail, billboards, and point-of-sale displays, and that was basically that. Occasionally, when something went wrong, a few attorneys and a crisis-savvy public relations team could manage negative press or public outrage until the next news cycle allowed the public to forget what had happened. In extreme cases, an executive or two might have to step down, and things went back to normal. Things have changed.

Nowadays, with social media living on mobile devices and hundreds of millions of people accessing social networking platforms every day to share their opinions, discuss brand preferences, and air out their frustrations with companies, brand management, especially *digital* brand management, has become a much more complex and crucial endeavor. A brand's image can be severely impacted by a tsunami of conversations resulting from a single event. Think back to BP's oil spill, Toyota's accelerator recall, Southwest Airlines' "too fat to fly" incident with actor-director Kevin Smith, and United Airline's alleged breaking of guitars, which inspired a song that became an overnight YouTube sensation.

By the same token, a brand can be rebuilt or see its relevance refreshed through the effective use of social media, as was the case with Old Spice in 2010, and to some extent the Ford Motor Company in the wake of the 2008 financial crisis and subsequent government "bailouts" of competitors Chrysler and GM.

Brand management is now an around-the-clock activity that encompasses a score of disciplines that were, until now, often disconnected from an operational standpoint: corporate communications, PR, marketing, digital, community management, online reputation management, crisis management, product management, customer service (the subject of its own chapter), and advertising. Together, these disciplines form the core of digital brand management.

In order to both protect and effectively promote brands in the era of the real-time social web, brand management teams must now focus not only on the traditional aspects of brand management (such as messaging, content development, trade dress, and marketing), but also on real-time monitoring of conversations on the Web, managing responses, and ensuring that every department or business function that touches digital communications is on the same sheet of music. Organizations that choose to look at social media merely as a *marketing* activity without looking at the broader and much more vital scope of their complete brand management practice are headed for trouble. Leaving out customer service (discussed in detail in

Chapter 12, "Real-Time Digital Support: Fixing Customer Service Once and for All"), let's explore the components of your digital brand management practice and how social media helps bind them together.

Community Management

"The community" refers to anyone who actively participates in the life of the organization or the brand. Communities can consist of customers, users, fans, pundits, and anyone with an opinion to share. iPhone users, for example, form a community. BMW owners form a community as well. Hunters, bloggers, and scrapbookers also form three distinct types of communities. For an organization, tapping into communities that it finds relevant to its world (and more importantly, communities who find *them* relevant to *their* world) can be extremely valuable on a lot of fronts.

The more active an organization is with its community, the more likely it is to know what it is doing right, what it is doing wrong, and to react swiftly to market needs. Companies with active communities also tend to inspire more loyalty in their customers, although an active interest in their community may be a result of this loyalty rather than its cause. When an organization decides to either create or tap into its community of customers or like-minded individuals, it quickly finds that managing these interactions is a full-time job. Enter the community manager.

Before social media came along, "community management" was virtually unheard of as a business function. Today, it is almost inconceivable to have a social media program without some sort of community management role embedded into it. The community management role, which finds its origins in the early days of Internet bulletin boards and forums, has now evolved into one of the most recognizable social media "jobs" and consists of four principal functions: representing an organization in online forums, being the voice of "the community" inside the organization, mediating disputes in online forums, and helping manage the development, publishing, and curating of the organization's digital content. Let's take a closer look at these four functions:

- **Representing an organization in online forums**—By "forums," I mean any type of vehicle through which individuals can share ideas as a group and discuss them. This could be an old-fashioned bulletin board, a blog, Twitter, or a Facebook wall. This part of the role consists of acting as the designated brand representative on these types of channels— or as some will call it, a "brand evangelist" or "brand advocate." When members of the community have a problem or a question, the community manager is typically the first person they turn to.

  Back in early 2009, Scott Monty (Ford's social media director) took on this role when confusion about the company receiving financial aid from the U.S. government following the late 2008 stock market crash threatened to damage the brand's image and alienate a portion of its market. By spending time on social media channels and discussing the issue at length, he was able to set the record straight: Ford had in fact turned down federal assistance and was going to emerge from the recession on its own. The way Scott Monty took on the role of community liaison during this particular episode is a perfect example of what this first facet of the community management role is all about.

- **Being the voice of the community inside the organization**—One way that community managers set themselves apart from typical company representatives is in their propensity to also serve as *customer advocates* within the organization. In other words, when they are not acting as agents of the organization with the community, they act as agents of the community *inside* the organization. They are, in this sense, in an ambassadorship type of role, both furthering the interests of the organization in the land of customers *and* sharing the customers' moods, needs, and concerns with the organization they serve.

The intelligence gathered by community managers can prove invaluable to organizations interested in obtaining critical feedback from the most active segments of their communities. No one else in the organization is *this* thoroughly tapped into their market. As eager as the community usually is to be a source of feedback, this function contributes to the value of the community management role.

- **Mediating disputes as the need arises**—This isn't something that a community manager will do every day, but it happens frequently enough to be a critical function. Community members tend to be passionate, and discussions can quickly turn ugly. A community manager must be able to police the organization's community without ever getting dragged into the negativity. This basically amounts to being a good host, but it also requires vigilance, tact, and a certain degree of maturity.

- **Keeping content fresh and interesting**—Content management is another key role of the community manager. It isn't enough to interact, mediate, and report. Community management is also responsible for keeping the community both informed and interested almost around the clock. Either developing and then publishing content or *identifying* and then publishing content is an essential part of the role. Every new video, blog post, review, article, bit of news, or fresh campaign needs to make its way to the community and generate feedback. The community manager is ideally suited to perform these functions.

Through his everyday interactions with the public, a community manager in essence becomes the face of the brand in social media channels. The community may not be able to interact directly with the organization's CEO or CMO or with the brand's celebrity spokesperson, but they can and do interact daily with the community manager. This degree of availability and familiarity felt by the community, combined with the breadth of reach and depth of attention enjoyed by community managers in regard to their community, makes them the ideal representatives in times of both crisis and good news.

A community manager can kill a rumor before it has a chance to grow, set the record straight if facts were distorted by a news story, answer questions, deepen bonds between community members and the organization, announce new products, special events, and discounts, provide the community with sneak peeks at new releases, and alert the company as to any potential issues (good and bad) it might want to take a closer look at.

Oftentimes when a crisis hits, the community manager is the first line of defense for an organization with a presence on the Web. The *absence* of a community manager within an organization's social media program can create the type of monitoring and response void that Nestlé suffered in early 2010 when Greenpeace "took over" the food giant's Facebook wall. Prompted by an awareness campaign outlining the environmental impact of Nestlé's use of palm oil in Kit-Kat candy bars, Greenpeace members left negative comments on Nestlé's Facebook wall by the hundreds. They essentially turned it into a marketing Trojan horse: Anyone visiting Nestlé's Facebook account during the few days during which the attack campaign raged on would have seen page after page of hateful comments that Nestlé was unprepared to address.

Had Nestlé had a community manager on staff—someone who could have spotted the crisis, known how to deal with it, managed the response, and shifted the community's anger into a productive discussion—the crisis could have been resolved in just a few hours and possibly even turned into a case study in proper digital crisis management.

The role of the community manager may seem abstract to traditional marketing communications executives, but the need for community management in the era of social media is now crucial. Community managers, by virtue of their presence on social media channels, can help build (and often save) brands in the digital space by simply being there every day, listening, setting the tone, and making sure that community channels remain hate-free, relevant, and a healthy vehicle for all manner of communications both *with* and *about* the brand.

Marketing

The way in which you use social media to promote your products and activities can either make you a hero or a villain. Organizations that abuse the trust of their communities of fans and followers by "pushing" marketing content all day will see themselves rewarded with apathy if not outright negativity. Be very careful not to treat social channels as merely another set of marketing channels. Unapologetic self-promotion can actually mean trouble for a brand in this space. Remember that it pays to be *social* in social media. When it comes to marketing, more often than not, less is more. Marketing activity here should be subtle, infrequent, and respectful of the social context of the space.

One of the most common mistakes made by companies in social media is to put too much emphasis on marketing right from the start. A 2010 study by Altimeter ("Career Path of the Corporate Social Media Strategist," November 10, 2010) noted that 41% of social media program managers (referred to as "corporate social media strategists") came from marketing backgrounds. In sharp contrast to this number, social media program managers with primary backgrounds in customer service and product management were rare, comprising 1% each of the surveyed group. It is no surprise that social media programs are so often skewed toward marketing activity, often to the detriment of the companies they serve.

So how much marketing is too much? Think of it as a ratio: If more than 10% of your activity on social media channels consists of linking to a product page, publishing marketing content, or promoting one of your services, you are overdoing it (and probably overthinking it as well). If you are in a marketing role and social media confuses you, take it easy. Relax. It's only social media. You don't have to sell your products every ten minutes on Twitter and Facebook. Don't worry about creating volumes of content just to have something to publish either. Instead, listen to what your customers are saying. Just as importantly, listen to what your competitors' customers are saying.

Every once in a while, sure, go ahead and remind your community that you have something great to sell, but for the most part, let *them* talk. Let them tell you what they want to talk about. Let your community managers and digital customer service staff deal with most of the conversation topics. Work with them to create your content, decide where it needs to go, schedule when your outbound marketing messages will get published and how. Coordinate with the rest of the social media program's staff and don't worry about doing it all.

Here are six tips to help you avoid common marketing mistakes in the world of social media and digital brand management:

1. **Don't fill your organization's feed with marketing content**—Analyze your social media activity: If more than 10% of your outbound activity is marketing, back off. You are overdoing it, and the impact on your brand is probably negative. Seed your social media feed with marketing messages sparingly.

2. **Listen more than you speak**—A crucial function of marketing is the gathering of market intelligence—otherwise known as *listening*. Short of telepathy, social media provides the most efficient mass-listening channel known to man. People talk about what they like and don't like all day long. They talk about you, your competitors, your competitors' competitors, and so on. So start listening. Don't be shy about asking questions either. No one is going to think you are strange for asking questions or polling the online community. Loosen your tie, take your finger off that marketing trigger, and just listen. That kind of wisdom won't hurt your brand. In a business environment that favors speaking to listening, you will stand out as one of the few brands that actually listen to customers instead of talking at them, which can't hurt.

3. **Marketing to your own community of customers is nice, but also consider marketing to your competitors' customers**—Your competitors' customers have communities too, and because they aren't buying from you yet, they are all potential net new customers. Companies that only listen and engage with existing customers are missing the point: Yes, it's nice to take care of your patrons and fans, especially when they have nice things to say about you, but learn to branch out. Unless you are focusing all of your efforts on increasing frequency and yield, remember to pay attention to other communities—communities you haven't reached out to yet.

   This isn't to say that Pepsi should try and win over Coca-Cola customers using social media, for example. Some people simply prefer the taste of one cola over the other, and no amount of cajoling is going to change that. (Some brand rivalries cannot be overcome by social media alone.) But if you are an airline, a sandwich company, a coffee shop, a dry cleaning service, or an auto repair shop, perhaps you can attract new customers by simply participating in communities where your competitors' customers (consumers with an interest in your category) happen to spend time. How? Be nicer and friendlier than your competitor's social media team. Be there more. Be more helpful. Take better care of your competitors' customers than they do, and people will start to notice. The reputation you build online, using social media channels, can help shape the relevance of your brand *offline*.

4. **If the community closes the sale (and it often does), invest in your community**—Spend time there. Do things for them. Create the kind of content *they* want. Don't treat them like cattle or wallets with legs. Respect them, show that you care about them, get to know them better, and see what happens. Content and marketing messages will never be in short supply. Don't sweat that stuff. Focus on building connections with your community. Do this right, and when you do push out your marketing, your community will actually help spread your content. If you don't build these relationships, all they will do is ignore your feed.

5. **Automation is tricky in social media**—Be very careful what you automate and how. Rule of thumb: The more hands-on you are, the better. Here are a few common pitfalls you should try to avoid:

    - Do not schedule all of your marketing messages and press releases to go out back to back at 8:01 a.m. every morning, especially if you have more than two or three at a time. It is one thing to schedule your updates in advance. It is another to show how little you care (or how little you know) by scheduling them all to release at the exact same time. Ideally, you want to wait until the most opportune moments throughout the day to publish your content (a little research will determine when your audience is either most active or receptive), but if you *must* automatically schedule the posting of updates ahead of time, at least try to space them out so as to not turn your Twitter or Facebook feed into machine-gun fire.

    - Avoid auto-DMs on Twitter. (An auto-DM is an automatically generated reply sent by your Twitter account to a new follower.) Nothing says "I care" like a generic, prerecorded text message. Remember that this space is about building relationships. Don't cut corners. Ideally, what you want to do is either reply in person or have someone on your staff do it for you. If the volume of followers makes acknowledging them personally too difficult to handle, consider *not* replying to every single new follower. In most cases, no acknowledgment at all is better than an automated message.

      If you *must* use auto-DMs, keep them short and simple and avoid the temptation to embed a link to your company website, blog, or e-store. "Thank you for following me" is fine. "Thank you for following me, click on this link to claim your free prize" is not. Sell *later*. Saying hello and thank you is not a good occasion to ram marketing spam down your new followers' throats.

    - If you must duplicate updates across multiple channels (for example, using software that allows you to post a question on Facebook and Twitter simultaneously), make sure that you monitor and manage all channels that you post these updates to. Commit to the channels you use. If members of your community respond to you on every channel you published the question to, acknowledge those responses on all of these channels.

6. **Care enough to invest yourself in your social media program**— Companies that publish their token one to five daily nuggets of content on Twitter and Facebook but rarely respond to comments puzzle me. Surely they notice the lack of activity and interest from even their most ardent customers.

    Everyone notices when a company does the absolute bare minimum in social media. The bank with one Facebook update per day, pointing to its randomly selected financial product is wasting its time. (Albeit not much time, but still.) The restaurant publishing what its soup of the day is on Twitter and Facebook every morning but not responding to other questions about the menu, its location, parking, or its hours of operation is also wasting its time. This isn't marketing or even social marketing. It's just being lazy.

When it comes to brand management, what you do with your marketing says a lot about the kind of company you are: Are you respectful of your audience, or are you a spammer? Is your content valuable or self-serving? Are you smart enough to use all of the channels at your disposal efficiently, or are you completely ineffective in your use of social media? Do you understand marketing's place in a social medium, or do you still think that "social" is a marketing term applied to noisy digital marketing channels?

If you manage a marketing function, take the time to understand the social media space, find your ideal place in your company's social media program, and be respectful of the fact that you constitute an important but very small portion of the volume of activity managed by the program on a daily basis.

Advertising

If you want an example of how advertising, social media, and digital brand management plug into each other, look no further than Old Spice's 2010 social media campaign featuring the towel-clad "Old Spice Man," Isaiah Mustafa. The agency behind the campaign, Wieden+Kennedy, decided to leverage Isaiah's popularity through the potential reach of social media channels such as YouTube, Facebook, and Twitter and the potential for a viral effect (content spreading at a very high speed through word-of-mouth and digital sharing tools), and created a series of spots specifically for social media denizens.

Over the course of three days, Isaiah and W+K's creative team pored through thousands of questions and requests submitted by fans and created almost 200 spots in response to their favorite ones, all published through social media and digital channels. What Old Spice did with this project was to create almost 200 customized commercials just for their community in an unprecedented display of "we care *that* much about you" genius. The campaign was enormously successful, increasing the brand's reach almost exponentially in just two weeks, helping make Old Spice "cool" again and boosting sales practically overnight.

The lesson here is this: Advertising is still a powerful medium when it comes to brand communications. Coca-Cola, Levi's, Volkswagen, Las Vegas, Apple, and now Old Spice can all attest to the power of advertising. Building up an image, a narrative, and a visual language can create differentiation, drive desire, and turn promising companies into powerful global brands. Social media has not changed any of that. What social media has done, though, is provide advertisers and brand managers with not only a new set of channels with which to reach their audience, but new methods of reaching them.

Because of advances in technology, ads can now be much more interactive than they have ever been. They can be created and published in minutes, without necessarily requiring a media buying team or a huge budget. They can be customized for a particular audience, or better yet, customized *by* a particular audience. They can be easily shared, which can increase both their reach and their impact.

Advertising strategy must now incorporate not only digital channels but social channels as well. It isn't enough to shoot an ad and post it on YouTube. The intersection of advertising and social media lies in an advertiser's ability to create ads specifically produced for the fan community and specifically designed for consumption on social media channels. These ads can either reinforce a brand's positioning or refresh it—as was the case for Old Spice.

Product Management

Social media programs too rarely touch on product management. This is puzzling because most companies build their brands around specific products. Take Ford's Mustang, for example, or PepsiCo's Tropicana orange juice. Think about the possibilities that exist in social media for the product managers behind each one of these products: Opportunities to discover entire communities of owners, users, and fans, engage with them, find out what they like and dislike about them, how they use them, why they choose them, and so on.

The Mustang's product management team can create digital destinations for Mustang owners and fans, where they can discuss their passion for the car, for the driving experience, share photos, videos, stories, garage tips and tricks, and so on. A product manager for Tropicana can hone in on some of the drinks and foodie recipes in which people use Tropicana juice. He can create environments where fans can design their own packaging, discuss the health benefits of drinking fruit juice, and so on. To a certain extent, these types of activities already exist in both PepsiCo's and Ford's social media practices and could be taken much further if the need for that degree of focus were needed. Any company can do this. Whether you sell cars or orange juice, mobile phones or video games, potato chips or legal advice, product management does have a role to play in social media and digital brand management.

What makes the marriage of social media and product management so powerful is the specificity of the focus: On the whole, it isn't difficult to see how this type of activity might be intrinsically beneficial to the brand, but the light it shines on a company's core business—its *products*, especially those with loyal followings—can make its impact both more meaningful and sticky. Such a depth of focus can give a budding social media program the kind of direction and it needs from the get-go. It can also be easily plugged into the F.R.Y. model of performance tied to a specific products whose sales it aims to support.

Digital

Corporate websites have become the new storefront and the principal vehicle through which consumers interact with brands. From the welcome page to the "contact us" page, web design has to convey all of the brand's positive attributes, ensure easy navigation, provide a pleasant-if-not-remarkable experience, and exceed consumer expectations. Incorporating social media into the mix is not particularly complicated, but it does require both strategic planning and proper tactical execution.

How organizations decide to integrate their traditional web properties and social media properties varies. Every company integrates social media with their websites in different ways, based on their needs, capabilities, and culture. At one end of the spectrum are companies like Skittles (the candy company), which decided in the early days of Twitter to shift its web presence almost exclusively to social media activity. Instead of traditional content and navigation common to most websites, the first things you see on its site might be a YouTube video, Twitter and Facebook statistics, or photos from Flickr galleries. At the other end of the spectrum are companies with more traditional website integration models, where social media is compartmentalized. In these instances, "community" or "follow us" sections are added to the site, indicating what key social media platforms such as YouTube, Facebook, and Twitter are being used by the company.

How many social media platforms companies choose to add to their digital endeavor varies as well. To give you a frame of reference, as I write this chapter,

Coca-Cola and Starbucks list five social media platforms on their respective websites. PepsiCo and Ford list seven. The White House lists eight. The most common culprits: Twitter, Facebook, YouTube, Flickr, and blogs. *More* doesn't necessarily mean *better*, but if your organization is going to have a presence in social media, make sure that visitors to your various websites can easily find your social media information on these sites.

A digital department should also help create, connect, manage, and update social media properties for the rest of the social media team. Creating proper Twitter page designs, customizing Facebook accounts, YouTube channels, and blogs as needed, securing specific plug-ins for the organization's various blogs, embedding content such as video and podcasts into various web pages, developing mobile applications, securing, managing, and renewing accounts, coordinating the cross-pollination of feeds and content—these are among the digital department's crucial responsibilities in the digital brand management process.

Though more traditional in nature than, say, a community management role, the digital department's expertise is nonetheless a crucial component of any digital brand management effort. With the emphasis shifting to conversations and engagement, it is easy to forget its importance. Digital departments make sure that all of the puzzle pieces fit perfectly, look amazing, and are easy to work with.

Corporate Communications and PR

Because social media channels are *communications* channels (and as such, typically the realm of corporate communications and public relations departments), the challenges facing corporate communications and PR teams in leveraging social media aren't always immediately obvious.

First, because so many other departments must now manage their own communications practices via social media channels, the communications role in an organization has evolved into a far less centralized model than what traditional PR and corporate communications professionals are accustomed to. This adjustment can be difficult to adapt to, both culturally and operationally.

Second, because social media channels allow people to talk back and talk to each other when, how, and where they choose, the good old days of "controlling the message"—and even controlling the channels—are essentially gone. Traditional communications teams accustomed to more control over their medium must now adapt to a whole new landscape and to develop new skills and methodologies to practice their craft.

For corporate communications and PR professionals willing to operate outside of their comfort zones for a little while, the challenges brought about by this evolution in communications also come with a wealth of opportunities, especially when it comes to reuniting PR, corporate communications, and digital brand management. Let's face it: Messaging is still important. Brand narratives, stories, news, reporting on business performance, announcing mergers, projects, and major contracts, setting the record straight—none of these things are going away because of social media. The core mission of corporate communications and PR hasn't changed. Only the channels have. The three principal opportunities for this element of your business are reach, search, and feedback.

- **Reach**—Most people don't have an appreciation for how difficult it was for PR professionals, before social media came along, to ensure that their messages reached their audiences. Journalists and key media gatekeepers often held the key to the distribution of outbound corporate information and brand communications. Specific media outlets such as trade publications and newspapers *were* the channel. Depending on editorial calendars, workload, and sometimes even the mood of a particular gatekeeper, stories either made the cut or didn't. None of this has changed, of course, but now communications teams have additional channels with which to spread their message, regardless of what happens in the traditional media space. These channels are virtually free, directly reach hundreds of millions of people through the Internet, and indirectly reach anyone with access to the Web through search engines.

  As a communications professional today, I can build an online network of followers, fans, and connections and use them to help me spread my message. Industry bloggers, category aficionados, customers, users, amateur reporters, and news aggregators are the new filters. Reach out to them with relevant information, and they will reach out to their own interconnected networks to push your message further down the pipes.

- **Search**—Once your information starts to spread on the Web through tweets, blogs, Facebook updates, all leading back through hyperlinks to your content (preferably a press release or other materials published to your own website), search engines can begin to pick it up. Manage your activity properly, and you may become a trending topic on popular social media platforms, news aggregator websites, and other digital media outlets. Granted, the impact of information spread through social media networks will vary from company to company. Apple announcing a new revolutionary device, for example, will spread farther and faster than a faucet company introducing a new line of high-efficiency showerheads. If you are a B2B organization, both your reach and your impact on search engines will be limited mostly to your industry or specific keywords.

That said, don't fret over inequities of net impact between major global brands and smaller niche brands. A brand with smaller reach has to accept the role that proportionality has to play in the communications game: Focus on *relative* impact—or rather, *relevant* impact. If you are a trucking company whose clients are B2B manufacturers, remember that reaching a hundred million consumers with your message isn't necessarily worth your while. Unless they are potential investors and your objective is to sell shares of your company, the general public probably doesn't need to be your focus. Manufacturer networks in your operating radius, however, are. These are the networks populated with individuals who might become new customers, develop a preference for you over your competitors because of the frequency with which they are reminded that you exist, or decide to do more business with you because your latest press release indicated that your latest service offering will save them hundreds of thousands of dollars per year.

Whether searches are active (entering keywords into a search box on Twitter, Google, Facebook, or any other website) or passive (following or subscribing to industry feeds from your digital outlets or other digital outlets that may publish your news), your ability to leverage the Web's search mechanisms through effective outreach can help recalibrate your PR and corporate communications effort in the digital space. Social media can facilitate this process by accelerating the speed with which information spreads, and amplifying it for search engines.

- **Feedback**—Here is where things get interesting for PR and corporate communications professionals. Until now, most of the work that communications departments focused on was meant to be outbound. "Inbound," though important, was secondary to messaging and outbound reach. Because social media is fueled by dialogue and conversations, expecting to simply push messaging out and measure the impact of each message is no longer enough. PR and corporate communications teams now also have to contend with responses, either vertical or lateral. Vertical responses are addressed to the company. Lateral responses are members of the public talking with each other about the company.

Communications teams must now invest equally in outbound and inbound. This means three things: 1) Setting up digital monitoring practices in order to know what people are saying about their company, their products, their latest bit of news, and so on; 2) Setting up measurement practices to gauge the relative impact of both their activity and the feedback they receive through their monitoring practice; and 3) Setting up high-velocity response mechanisms in order to deal with both positive and negative feedback identified through their measurement practice and quantified through their measurement practice:

1. **Building a monitoring practice**—The simplest way to explain how to build a monitoring practice is to build listening outposts across a variety of digital channels that are relevant to the organization. A good place to start would be industry news websites, forums, blogs, Facebook, Twitter, and YouTube. The second step in the process is to either man the outpost around the clock with someone who will scan and filter conversations manually or create an automated keyword search filter across all of these channels. A variety of digital tools can do this for you—some requiring hefty budgets, some requiring none.

   Twitter keyword monitoring can be made simple by using tools such as Tweetdeck, Seesmic Desktop, Monitter, and dozens more. To map how information spreads on Twitter, also try Tweetburner and BackTweets. For blog and broad channel monitoring (also including Twitter), try Google Alerts, IceRocket, Technorati, Social Mention, Spy, monitorThis, or BlogPulse. For Facebook-specific searches, try Trackur and Webtrends. Remember that new monitoring tools launch all the time, so do your research, find out what works best for your organization, and stay on top of every new release that might help you get an edge in this space.

2. **Setting up measurement practices**—This basically consists of putting together a mechanism through which you can quantify the impact of your messages. Here are the types of questions you should be answering: Are people talking about our latest bit of news? If so, how many and where? How did this number change from yesterday, last week, last month? What specific keywords tend to be most often associated with our brand name? Is opinion (usually called "sentiment" in the social media space) becoming more positive or negative, and if so, by how much? Should we focus on increasing the ratio of positive to negative mentions on Twitter, and if so, how? Measurement leads to analysis.

   Analysis, when done properly, leads to effective action. It isn't enough to craft positive and engaging messages. By capturing, quantifying, then analyzing feedback, you can adjust communications to better serve the interests of the organization, most often by elevating the status of the brand in the court of public opinion.

   If the digital tools already mentioned in this section do not provide robust enough measurement capabilities, try these: Alterian, Radian6, Lithium (formerly Scout Labs), SelfService, BrandsEye, Trendrr,

Spiral16, HowSociable, Attentio, and dna13. Again, do your homework. Some of these tools may be replaced by much stronger options as time moves on, so don't stick to this list. Find out what is available and test as many tools as you can to see what works best for you.

3. **Setting up response mechanisms**—This requires no tools. What it does require, however, is a combination of good judgment, experience, tact, and oftentimes speed. The first step in the process is to decide whether or not a response is even necessary. The type of response you may be required to craft will depend on a plethora of factors: Are you dealing with a *potential* crisis, a *scaling* crisis, or a crisis at all? Are you in the early stages of a big release that warrants a lot of online conversations with fans, customers, and bloggers? Should you schedule a Q&A session on Twitter with the brand's CEO or chief designer to answer many of the questions and concerns your monitoring practice identified across the Web? Should you meet with your company's community management and customer service teams to discuss how to address a particular topic of conversation you are currently tracking?

   The topic could be a product recall, for example, or the impact of new legislation on how your product may be used, or changes in your terms of service. It could be a new product release, the appointment of a new CMO, the launch of a campaign, or it could simply be a rumor that needs to be addressed. Setting the record straight should always be high on the list of priorities of every PR team working in the digital space.

What is important for communications professionals to remember is that with the advent of social media, messaging now shares space with dialogue. First and foremost, ignoring social networks and social media channels is no longer an option. Second, ignoring the social and conversational nature of the space in planning for the management of brand communications on these channels is also no longer an option.

Information is still the lifeblood of your communications practice. Social media has not changed that. If people are not talking about your company, they aren't thinking about it either—and that is never good for business. Without corporate communications and PR to share news about your company and seed media channels with information, advice, and valuable content, consumer mindshare becomes difficult to capture. And without their constant vigilance and ability to help manage public perceptions of a brand in an increasingly dynamic and vocal environment, companies can quickly find themselves playing defense.

Effective digital brand management in today's world depends in no small part on PR and corporate communications teams to not only understand and adapt to social media but embrace all of the opportunities it provides in such a way that new communications paradigms become the building blocks of the next evolution of best practices for their profession.

Online Reputation Management

Online reputation management is a simple function that requires only three things: planning, vigilance, and a response mechanism. The premise is simple: Every day, a brand may be attacked by detractors. Online reputation management consists of listening for either negative or incorrect statements made about the brand or one of its assets or products, and when needed, setting the record straight, using the same channels.

This process often falls to an organization's public relations department, but increasingly, community managers and corporate bloggers are leveraging the social media space to respond to attacks and incorrect statements all on their own. How organizations manage the monitoring and response mechanisms is a matter of preference, so don't be afraid to ask your various departments to come up with a company-wide plan that deals specifically with online reputation management using social media channels. The more open your communications are in this regard, the better your online reputation management practice will be. Collaboration between departments here is key.

Make sure you don't allow turf wars to get in the way of effectively addressing this function: Agreeing that online reputation management should be PR's job or customer service's responsibility is not always the best approach. Instead, explore ways in which *all* of your customer-facing departments, especially those connected to your social media program, can coordinate intelligence and response processes.

As with all social media–monitoring practices, make sure your online reputation management begins with the monitoring of relevant keywords and conversations. Unlike other types of conversation monitoring in social media, this one focuses on your brand. Online reputation management does not need to get sidetracked by conversations relating to your competitors, category, or market. You only want to focus on what people are saying about you.

To gain a better understanding of the specific topics dominating these conversations, consider using word clouds around specific keywords. For Twitter, Tweet Cloud, twendz, Social Mention (gives you top keywords rather than a fancy word cloud), and Twitter Stream Graphs are simple online tools that will help you visualize what words are currently being used in connection with your brand name, account, or keyword of choice. For comparative analysis between two keywords, try Twitter Spectrum.

Monitoring sentiment (with an eye toward changes in sentiment) can be a little tricky. Although sentiment analysis tools keep improving every few months, false positive and false negative results are still too common. An update such as "I had a really bad day until I had my Starbucks double-frap" might show up as a negative mention, for example, because the term "bad" was used alongside the keyword "Starbucks," although it is, in fact, a positive mention. It is best to always manually determine whether individual mentions of your brand are positive or negative.

A response mechanism within the scope of online reputation management has the principal aim of setting the record straight. Whether through a community manager, blogger, or spokesperson, once the online reputation management team has all the facts about an attack, accusation, or rumor, it can deliver its response with tact, temperance, and an eye toward enhancing the brand's image. The idea isn't to win an argument or rub someone's nose in a mistake. Be magnanimous and give people the benefit of the doubt. Simply state the facts and make sure that the individuals who triggered the response by publishing potentially damaging content are made aware of the facts you have taken the time to highlight. Never get defensive, never take attacks personally, and never allow yourself to be drawn into an argument. Present the facts calmly and professionally, monitor the impact of your activities on topics relating to your brand and overall sentiment, and either press on with your response or move on.

Crisis Management

Crisis management in social media is an embattled brand's final line of defense. This is where social media and corporate communications teams find themselves when community management, online reputation management, customer support, and other communications processes have either failed or been pushed aside by the sheer force of an attack or screw-up. You know you are in crisis management mode when your brand is under attack by dozens, if not hundreds of individuals, either through negative comments directed *at* you or negative comments being shared *about* you.

When Nestlé's community management team failed to properly address negative comments being posted by environmental activists on its Facebook wall, it slipped into crisis management mode. When public outcry about trains not running in snowy weather in the UK just before the Christmas holidays (leaving thousands of passengers stranded) snowballed into a major news story, European rail company Eurostar found itself battling a brand-rattling PR crisis as well. Could either company have used social media to better manage these PR crises and resolve them faster? Absolutely.

Crises happen. There is no way around it. At some point, your organization is going to make a mistake: Your quality control department might sign off on a faulty product, your CFO might cook the books, your servers might crash, your CMO might say something offensive on national television, and one of your employees might get caught doing something awful. You simply cannot predict or stop bad things from happening. You can, however, create a plan that will help your organization deal with unexpected crises when they strike.

The basics of crisis management plans typically include flow charts that detail communications and activities: who does what, where do they do it, who authorizes responses, what the tools and channels should be, and so on. The first step in managing a crisis is simply to have a plan—and preferably an up-to-date, well-thought-through, often-rehearsed one at that. You don't want to wait until a crisis hits to suddenly realize that you don't know what to do. By that point, it is way too late to try and figure out who should be doing what.

The second step in the crisis management process is to make sure that a portion of that plan focuses specifically on leveraging digital and social media channels. Part of the process deals with monitoring the crisis online: measuring changes in the volume of mentions, changes in the types of keywords being used in connection with the brand name, and changes in sentiment attached to these mentions. If the overall volume of mentions increases, associated keywords focus on the crisis (terms such as *recall, dangerous, terrible, bad,* and *scary,* for example) and your sentiment mix is more negative than usual, you know that you are still in crisis mode. If, however, the volume of mentions starts to return to normal, keywords associated with your brand shift away from crisis-related topics, and positive sentiment begins to increase, you know that the crisis is subsiding.

Knowing where you are in a crisis cycle—and being able to quantify, map, and graph your position along that timeline—is crucial to managing your resources effectively.

The third step in effectively managing a crisis is the response. Every organization will find its own comfort zone, but here are six tips that seem to work both in social media and outside of the digital space:

1. **Acknowledge the problem if there is one**—Do not ignore it and do not delay. As soon as your company finds itself in crisis mode, reach out to your audience. State the issue. State the facts as you understand them. Here are three examples:

   - "One of our employees seems to have acted improperly, and we are looking into the situation."

   - "Several thousands of our customers are currently without power, and we are working as fast as we can to fix the problem."

   - "Salads packaged between January 1st and January 3rd may have been tainted with E. coli bacteria. We are looking into it."

State the facts. Clarify the situation for your audience. Show them that you are aware of the situation. Silence here is not golden. A statement of fact is reassuring: It lets the public know that you are on top of the crisis, and it also showcases your crisis team's effective use of media channels, including social media.

2. **Don't be afraid to buy yourself some time with an update**—It doesn't matter if you don't have all the answers yet. Initially, all the public needs to know is what the problem is, that you are working on correcting it, and that updates will follow. "We are looking into the problem now and will update you in less than an hour" is a perfectly acceptable response. Let people know a) that you are working on the problem, b) that you will update them, and c) when the next update will come.

3. **Create channels for dialogue**—While your company's landing pages are effective at keeping the public informed as to the latest updates regarding your crisis, do your best to funnel discussions into specific areas, preferably away from these major landing pages. A Facebook discussions tab, where specific topics can be featured and addressed in context, is an ideal vehicle for this. Create a discussion topic for the recall inside of your Facebook ecosystem and let the public know about it. Funnel traffic and activity to that specific page and have your community manager(s) mediate the discussion there.

   For Twitter, consider creating a #hashtag (a conversation topic code preceded by the # sign) and even a specific account to address the crisis. In the case of Toyota's recalls, a @ToyotaRecall account could have helped direct discussions to one place. Likewise, a #ToyotaRecall hashtag could have helped both the public and the crisis management team better track and identify conversations and information focused on the crisis.

4. **Tell your audience what you are doing to fix the problem and update them often**—For travelers stranded by Eurostar in 2009 (and their families), one of the biggest pain points was uncertainty, caused by a lack of status updates. Most people had no way of knowing how long they might remain stranded, when their trains might be operational again, what they needed to do in the next few hours, and whether or not they should stay near the train stations or book a hotel room for the night. Had Eurostar planned for this type of crisis, it might have been able to use social media channels such as Facebook and Twitter to update the public as to what the situation was and deliver updates quickly and often to as large an audience as they could.

As more mobile devices find themselves connected to social media platforms, and more and more people carry them everywhere, using social media channels to keep the public informed is a no-brainer. Fit social media channels into your crisis communications plan, and managing crises will become much easier for your communications teams. Keeping the public informed is a way to quell some of the anger and frustration that sometimes turns minor problems into full-scale revolts against a brand.

5. **Ask your audience what they would like to see you do**—Social media is a participatory medium. Use it. Shift the conversation away from why people are angry to how they think you can fix the problem that they are angry about. In essence, if you are going to have a conversation with a mob of angry people, see if you can redirect their energy away from the problem itself (negative) to potential solutions (positive). In terms of engagement, this is far more productive than letting hundreds, even thousands of people tell your crisis management team how horrible the company they work for happens to be at this particular moment. You will derive two distinct benefits from this clever tactical maneuver:

   - The public might actually tell you how to solve your problem.

   - The public will look upon your interest in their opinion and ability to put their advice into action in a very positive light. Note that it is hard for someone to stay angry at a company when the company thinks enough of them to ask them for advice.

6. **Follow up**—Once the crisis begins to die down, keep the dialogue going. Once the crisis is over, put together two reports outlining the entire event: one for internal use and one for external use. Share the external report on your blog, Facebook discussion tab, and whatever other channels were most relevant during the crisis. Detail the causes of the problem, the specifics of the problem, what happened during the crisis itself, what steps were taken to fix the problem, and what the state of affairs is today as a result of the crisis. Give the public closure. Internally, make sure to share what you have learned during the crisis and update your crisis management procedures accordingly.

In the end, how you deal with a crisis is much more important than what caused the crisis to begin with. If a crisis cannot be averted, make the crisis either as short or as painless as possible. React quickly. Adapt swiftly. Use the power of social media to communicate better with your audience, dissipate their anger and frustration, and resolve the issue as fast and efficiently as possible. The faster and more efficiently you manage to do this, the less lasting damage your brand will suffer. Speed and tact are of the essence.

One final note about crisis management in the social media space: The more active an organization is in the social space before a crisis (through community management and customer service, for example), the more effective its crisis management activities will be right from the start. What an organization wants to avoid at all cost is waiting until a crisis hits to suddenly decide to focus on building a presence in social media. The more established your presence, the more respected and trusted your community managers and representatives—the larger your reach, the better.

Putting It All Together

Creating a digital brand management practice in the age of social media is no small juggling act: It consists first and foremost of combining product management, public relations, corporate communications, community management, marketing, advertising, digital, crisis management, online reputation management, and even customer service to create a communications infrastructure that can effectively deal with the growing breadth of media channels used by both the organization and the public to communicate with each other. This requires planning, flexible but deliberate organization, a lot of collaboration, and intense focus on making sure that all the moving parts are working together every step of the way—from planning and creating content, to monitoring conversations and managing interactions with the public.

Managing such a complex structure and mechanism may seem a tall order for most companies that have not yet transitioned to this operational mode. It requires hard work and diligence to get there, but the alternative—a disjointed effort that leaves brands open to market confusion, coordinated attacks, and negative impressions—is no kind of alternative at all. Brand management is too important to the well-being of an organization to leave to chance.

The reality of transitioning to this type of digital brand management model, using social media as both the catalyst and the glue that binds all the pieces together, is that most of the pain points come with the creation and adoption of such a structure, not its *management*. Once created, a digital brand management practice with strong social media monitoring, publishing, and response components isn't that difficult to coordinate. It is only the change itself that is difficult. But a few growing pains along the way will be well worth it once your organization finds itself in a position to effectively manage its brand online in good times and bad.

Remember the endgame: The stronger the brand, the more loved, respected, and aspired to, the stronger its market position tends to be. Brands such as Apple, Nike, and Starbucks are category leaders for a reason. The stronger your brand, the more relevant your company, and the more likely it is that your business will find avenues of growth. Look to social media as a vehicle with which to both protect and build your brand in the digital space—and build your social media program accordingly.

12

Real-Time Digital Support—Fixing Customer Service Once and for All

I don't want to frighten you just yet, but social media may very well completely change the way you think about customer service. From the role it plays in your customers' lives to its importance to your business as a whole, the introduction of social media in the world of business will fundamentally transform customer service and shake its foundations to the core.

Before I tell you what I mean, we need to address a few fundamental facts about customer service, starting with this: Great customer service is good for business. Bad customer service is bad for business. No matter how great your products, how cool your packaging, how pretty your designs, how attractive your price, if you treat your customers like dirt, they will leave.

Now repeat after me: Customer service is a *product*. It doesn't matter if you sell software, faucets, shower curtains, wine, microchips, or professional services. Customer service isn't just a department in your organization or a back-office business function from 9 a.m. to 9 p.m. GMT. Customer service is a product, and it is as important to the well being of your company as the stuff that comes with a price tag. The way you treat customers is as much a part of your brand ecosystem as everything else that fuels your customers' expectations and validates their preference. An automated message that starts with "your call is important to us," for example, because it means the exact opposite, is a bad product. Forcing people to wait on the phone for over 40 minutes (most of which is spent on hold) to finally, after a dozen failed attempts, talk to someone who can *maybe* solve their problem does not create loyal customers.

Bad customer service can invalidate in minutes what you spent years and millions of dollars trying to build. Consider the cost of acquiring a single customer, the effort it takes through research, marketing, PR, product development, advertising, discounting, and scores of other tools to attract customers. Think of the cost of converting mere impressions to actual transactions, then into repeat business. After having worked so hard to acquire, convert, and develop customers, don't let something as trivial as bad customer service undo what you have built.

Now look at your business this way: On the one hand, here you are, spending all your time, energy, and money trying to convince people to do business with you. It's exhausting work, and there's no end to it. It taxes every part of you, and you wish you could spend more time on the company itself than on trying to recruit business. Meanwhile, in another part of the building, poorly trained customer service reps may be actively chasing a portion of that hard-earned business away because they are having a bad day, they weren't properly trained, or they simply don't care all that much.

It can take various departments, such as marketing and sales, months to turn a prospect into a transacting customer, but it takes mere minutes to turn all that hard work to dust. That's why great customer service is *not* an afterthought. It isn't a "necessary evil." It isn't an inbound *complaints department* you outsource to the lowest bidder half a world away. Not anymore.

Because bad customer service creates an accumulation of hundreds, thousands, sometimes tens of thousands of bad customer experiences over time, it can, if left unchecked, bake failure into your brand's DNA. To make matters worse, people *love* to share bad experiences: Make someone happy, and they might forget to tell their friends, but make them angry, and they will tell everyone they know. Before the rise of social media, the recounting of bad experiences might have only reached four or five people at a time, but now, they can reach tens of thousands in mere seconds. In the age of Facebook and Twitter, where hundreds of millions of people are

connected to each other around the clock, where influence has shifted from traditional sources of information to *word-of-mouth* networks and *peer-to-peer* recommendations, the impact of bad customer service can be instantly amplified: The
stakes now are much higher than they were ten years ago, when one bad experience
might have cost you one or two customers. Today, one bad experience might cost
you a hundred, maybe a thousand customers. Because of this, social media has
irrevocably shifted the role of customer service from an easily outsourced, back-
office function to one of an organization's most important tactical assets.

We know that the average Facebook user has between 100 and 200 friends on the
service. Most people I know have several hundred. A few of them have networks in
the thousands. These numbers pale in comparison with the number of people who
"follow" what so-called cultural "influencers" have to say on Twitter. Consider the
PR nightmare actor/director Kevin Smith created for Southwest Airlines in early
2010 when he tweeted that he was being removed from an aircraft for being "too
fat." Armed only with a cell phone and a Twitter account, Smith attracted the attention not only of fans but of every major news outlet, from CNN to *The New York
Times*, prompting a very public "heartfelt apology" from the embattled airline the
very next day.

This is *influence*, and as such, it should not be taken lightly.

Imagine that you are an airline, a restaurant, or a hotel. An individual with significant influence reports that you have provided her with spectacular service and recommends you to her entire network, over and over again. You "wowed" her. She fell
in love with the way you do business, and now she has set you up as the industry
standard by singing your praises on social media channels. Your name pops up
when people ask her, "Who gets it right?" She recommends you every chance she
gets. How do you think this will impact your business? How much new business
might it generate over time?

Now let's look at the same hypothetical situation again, but from the opposite end
of creating good customer experiences: You are the same airline, restaurant, or
hotel, but this time, the same influencer has a remarkably poor experience dealing
with you. She reports everything in detail to her tens of thousands of fans, friends,
readers, and followers, and swears that she will never do business with you again.
How do you think this type of situation might impact your business? How much
new business might you now fail to generate moving forward? How much existing
business might you lose as a result even?

Almost every customer complaint that grows into a public relations crisis starts out
as an avoidable customer service failure.

Great customer service is engineered. It is the result of careful consideration, purposeful design, and continuous improvement. Companies with great customer

service regard this aspect of their business as if it were a marquis product. Every possible type of interaction with customers is scrutinized and improved upon at every turn. Companies such as Zappos have even designed their recruiting and employee development practices to enhance this aspect of their business. Everything they do revolves around being known for their spectacular friendliness and devotion to delighting customers.

Now what does this have to do with social media?

Everything.

The Superhero Principle

"I just need someone to help me." That's what the elderly woman said again and again as she edged in and out of the mass of angry travelers waiting for news about their next flight. The setting was a crowded gate in Dulles International Airport, and as usual, bad weather somewhere was causing a domino effect of flight delays. Thousands of travelers were trying to figure out if they had any chance at all of reaching their destinations that afternoon. Many were tweeting about their predicament from their smart phones, and I was one of them. Needless to say, the three airline employees working the gate were a little overwhelmed, and by the time the woman started to let anxiety get the best of her, they no longer seemed to care. What caught my attention was that while two of the three gate agents were working with their computers to assist travelers, a third was standing behind two of his colleagues, doing nothing. Actually, that isn't exactly right. He *was* doing something. He was staring at her.

After some time, a gentleman standing next to me got up and walked up to her. He asked her if he could help. She explained her predicament: She was a widow, visiting her family in Chicago and didn't own a cell phone. She rarely flew. Anxiety about flying, about negotiating airports alone, about having very little control over the events of this day were now amplified by the notion that her daughter, unaware of the flight delays, might be stuck waiting for her at her destination airport for hours. It was this that worried her the most. She repeated, "I just need someone to help me" three more times, each one of them turning to the gate agents for a sign of acknowledgment.

One of them, a middle-aged woman with some authority over the other two, politely told her to get in line and wait her turn. After the second time, her tone had lost any semblance of empathy.

The gentleman calmed the poor old woman down and offered her his seat. "You won't lose your place in line," he said, loud enough for the gate agents and everyone in line to hear, and offered to call her daughter on his cell phone to let her know her mother's flight might be delayed. As soon as he said this, the woman started to calm down.

Why am I telling you this story? Two reasons: First, never underestimate the power of being a hero for a customer in need of assistance. No matter how trivial, how fleeting the crisis may be, the opportunity to save the day even in a small way for a frustrated or angry customer is pure gold for an organization. The third gate agent—the one doing nothing behind the counter—could have intervened. He and the customer were separated by less than 12 feet. How hard would it have been to show a little kindness to a customer in distress (and an elderly one at that)? Had he walked over to her and treated her with professionalism and kindness (much like our Good Samaritan), he could have resolved the problem in just a few short minutes. The simple act of being helpful and kind in front of so many customers might have influenced dozens, perhaps even hundreds of them to become more loyal to the airline. Some might have even been impressed enough to share what they saw on Facebook or Twitter. Instead, by doing nothing, the airline lost my business and made a bad impression on dozens of people who were also concerned for the elderly woman.

Second, people love to be helped *without having to ask for help*. This is the Superhero Principle—when out of nowhere, a guy in a cape swoops in to save the day, seemingly out of the blue.

What the Good Samaritan did for the stressed-out woman is now something your company can do remotely via social media. As people turn to Facebook, Twitter, YouTube, and other social networking sites to vent their frustrations, complain about bad experiences, and share videos or updates about things happening around them in real time, catching instances in which swift action can turn a bad situation around is becoming increasingly easier. An on-the-ball customer support team focusing on social media channels can, with a little focus and a bit of savvy, save the day, much as the Good Samaritan did in our airport story.

Assume for a moment that someone else at the gate tweeted what was going on or mentioned it on Facebook. This is not a stretch. Not anymore. Many of us at the gate were, in fact, doing just that.

Now suppose that the airline's customer service team was monitoring the Web for mentions of the airline's name and that what's shown in Figure 12.1 popped up on their monitoring dashboard.

Figure 12.1   Airline customer service bait (from Twitter).

They might immediately spring to action and contact the person who tweeted about the incident using the same channel (in our example, Twitter), preferably in the public stream to make the process visible to anyone paying attention. It could be as simple as responding with a friendly, "Hey, this is Jack with [insert airline name] Customer Support. Just saw your tweet. How can we help?"

A dialogue would ensue. The airline's customer service representative might obtain information about the airport, the flight number, and the gate. He might make a few phone calls, even locate a supervisor at the gate's terminal and alert him to the immediacy of the problem. From there, the supervisor might make his way to the gate and check in with the gate agents. The distressed passenger could then be located and the problem fixed. With the right kind of training and foresight, this degree of customer service response could be swift, painless, and absolutely real, all of it stemming from implementing a proactive social media monitoring practice.

By monitoring social media channels, organizations can now spot trouble anywhere in the world and respond to it in seconds, just like comic book superheroes: Superman has super-hearing, Spiderman has spider-senses, and now customer service departments have social media. This is the Superhero Principle. Does this scenario seem like a stretch? Not anymore. Organizations are already beginning to move in this direction for obvious reasons: Great customer service is good for business, and holding on to customers by wowing them with simple positive experiences that surprise and delight them is now easier (and more affordable) than ever. Why focus on creating complicated and expensive loyalty incentives when you can just become someone's hero?

The Basic Social Media Customer Service Model

The incorporation of social media into the customer service process is a proactive endeavor. It isn't something that will happen by accident. It needs to be engineered to produce desired outcomes. The proper types of response mechanisms have to be worked out, the right tone has to be set, and different types of online mentions call for unique types of responses. Let's start from the beginning and construct a framework that can be applied to any digital customer service representative (CSR) practice.

What we have just talked about with our airport example is a basic 1-2 monitoring-and-response mechanism:

1. The customer service team monitors social media channels for mentions of the company.

2. The customer service team responds to online mentions as applicable. These fall into three main categories:

- Positive mention
- Neutral mention
- Negative mention

For each of these types of mentions, the customer service team must decide whether a response is required, as follows:

- Positive mention

  A. This requires an acknowledgement (basically, a thank-you.)

  B. This does not require an acknowledgement.

- Neutral mention

  A. This requires a reply. (If so, what kind?)

  B. This does not require a reply.

- Negative mention

  A. This requires a response. (If so, what kind?)

  B. This does not require a response.

The question of whether or not to respond to negative online mentions comes up often. There is no simple *yes* or *no* answer to it. Each instance is different. A little humor can sometimes help defuse a stressful situation, but it can just as easily inflame it. You just never know. In cases when an organization feels the need to respond, starting with a tone of genuine concern is always a good bet. Ask questions about what brought about the negative mention. Find out how you can help fix the problem or rectify a bad situation. It is difficult to fault an organization for trying to be helpful. If the complaint is genuine, you may turn negative into positive. If the complaint is not genuine, you will have identified the individual making the negative mention as a heckler. Any exchange in which a customer service representative can steer the discussion toward "What can we do to do [insert subject of complaint] better?" is a good one, so start there.

Identifying positive, neutral, and negative online mentions is the first step in framing a basic response model for a customer service department using the social web as a communication channel. Now let's take the process a bit further and separate mentions further by asking a simple question: What is the person mentioning us online trying to accomplish? Typically, online mentions fall into one of six basic categories:

- **Validation**—This is simply someone stating an opinion and looking to have it validated by others in his or her network. Example: "I love coffee!" "Oh yeah, me too!" *"No, I love coffee more!"* ...and so on. Bear in mind that validation can be either positive or negative.

- **Status update**—People are going to be at your place of business. They're already there. They just left from there. They want everyone to know. Example: "I'm going Starbucks" or "Sitting here in Starbucks, waiting for my friends."

- **Research**—This is someone who might be shopping and expects his network to help with the decision. Example: "I'm in the mood for a latte, but I'm torn between Starbucks and Liquid Highway. Decisions, decisions."

- **Observation**—This is someone who communicates either a positive or a negative experience. Example: "Best latte I've ever had" or "These coffee beans smell like a bag of hockey socks."

- **Request for assistance**—This is someone who could use a customer service superhero right about now. She's calling for help on her favorite social network. Example: "I've been driving around for twenty minutes and still haven't found a Starbucks anywhere. I'm starting to lose hope."

- **Window breaking**—This is simply someone out to vandalize your brand online. He doesn't want anything. He just likes to break stuff. "Starbucks kills babies!" "Starbucks beans are roasted on the coals of hell itself!" Usually, window-breakers spew complete venomous nonsense just because they can.

In a traditional organization, where customer service is its own silo, a response model for these six categories of mentions would be pretty basic: A request for assistance would trump all. Research mentions, observation mentions, status updates and validation mentions would be mostly ignored because they fall more to community management topics. The window-breaking mentions would be monitored but not necessarily addressed unless they were mistaken for an angry request for assistance.

Don't get me wrong: This model puts you decades ahead of customer service departments operating either behind a service counter or a 1-800 number, but it falls short of its fullest potential. The breadth of the opportunity can be summed up by this question: What if customer service representatives monitoring social media channels were given permission to be *more* than just convenient remote helpers? In other words, aside from addressing direct requests for assistance, what else could they do?

In terms of addressing *validation* and *observation* mentions, for example, a customer service rep with a presence on Twitter could respond to positive mentions of the brand by just saying something nice, such as "Thanks for the love." That's it. That's all it takes. A little good will goes a long way in creating a positive connection between an organization and the public. This doesn't always have to fall to the community manager. Anyone in the company with an official account should be given permission to do this.

Now let's say the validation or observation mention is negative. Is there an opportunity for the customer service rep to perhaps turn that perception around? There probably is. She could find out what prompted the negative mention. Was it a negative experience? If it was, what happened? Maybe she can come up with a fix. Maybe the interaction alone might trigger a change in perception. It never hurts to try.

Now let's look at status updates. Someone is talking about going to one of your locations. Maybe he's there already or just left, but the implication is that he will be back at some point in the future. What could you do to *reward* the mention? If you want to play it safe, you could ask the customer what location he is visiting (using the same channel he chose to share the status update) and what he thought of his experience. You could even give him a discount code for his next visit. That's always nice. Feeling a little bold? Call the location, talk to the manager, tell her that a special customer is in her store right now (or on the way) and suggest she treat him extra special.

I have seen this done. In 2008, Liquid Highway—a South Carolina–based chain of coffee shops—was already pioneering this method. It played out like this: A customer was sitting at her table, typing away on her laptop. Ten minutes earlier, she had tweeted that she was working from her favorite "remote office"—one of Liquid Highway's locations. The manager, who pulled double-duty as the company's social media customer service department and made a habit of keeping an eye on online mentions of his company, spotted the status update. He immediately made her another decaf cappuccino and took it to her table. "On the house," he said, beaming. "Thanks for tweeting about us." The customer's reaction: Total shock and amazement. All she could say at that moment was "Wow," but within minutes, she had tweeted about what had just happened and posted a comment on her Facebook wall. I was sitting at the next table and watched the whole thing unfold. As a joke, I tweeted "Where's *my* free decaf cappuccino?" It showed up moments later, the manager and I became fast friends, and I became a customer for life.

Needless to say, Liquid Highway's business greatly benefited from this type of engagement with customers—at its core, monitoring social media channels for mentions and responding to them with tact, intelligence, and a big dose of friendliness.

This may seem like a silly question, but when was the last time you deliberately used your customer service department to wow a customer? In the age of social media, wowing just one customer can spread to dozens, even hundreds of potential customers who might, upon hearing about how well your company treats its customers, start doing business with you. This type of tactic costs far less than advertising or special sales promotions and tends to yield far more impressive results.

Responding to research mentions is also a fairly simple proposition: Here, you might want to push your keyword searches a little further than your brand name. Look at category keywords as well. If you are a hotel in Portland, Oregon, for example, set up keyword searches for mentions of "Hotel," "Portland," and "PDX." If someone is asking her network for advice on a place to stay in Portland, you can recommend your hotel directly.

Yes, that's right: I just suggested that your customer service department passively engage in lead generation. Heresy! Well, okay, except for the fact that it is smart. These are the folks you already trust with online monitoring and engagement. Why not give them permission to help steer customers toward your business as well?

Finally, we come to the window-breakers. These are people whose principal intent is to harm your organization, not to complain about a legitimate problem. Most of the time, it is best to let them be, as many feed on attention. Give them any attention at all, and they may never leave you alone again. For the most part, waiting for them to find a new target works just fine. For the few who will not go away on their own, proceed with caution, but address their concerns as if they were legitimate. Without ever allowing yourself to be dragged into an argument, calmly ask them to explain what their complaint is about and how they would like you to address it. Insist on focusing on the facts of their complaint. If you have ever heard of the expression "killing with kindness," this is the type of situation that calls for it. One last note: Window-breakers are not the enemy of your customer service department. Instead, they are the ultimate test of your staff's professionalism. Remember that next time one of them pops up on your radar.

As you can see, customer service on social media channels is not merely "customer service" in the traditional sense of the term. It is much more. When designing your digital customer service program, remember not to make it too specific or rigid. Build into it a deliberate breadth of initiative that will allow your online representatives to help customers in any way necessary. Remember that Customer Service's job is simply to be helpful.

The New Digital Concierge Service and Customer Service 3.0

Every once in a while, I run into an unmanned counter—usually in a lobby—with a little bell sitting front and center. Next to the bell usually sits a sign that reads

"Ring for service." When I look at Twitter and Facebook, all I see sometimes is that little bell.

Consider creating an account on Twitter, manned by your customer service department, to either drive certain types of services or enhance the quality of the customers' experience. Think of it as creating a sort of online concierge service for your customers. This would be a service they might turn to for advice about products, to access information about business hours, or to get help with a decision or a transaction. In short, you can provide anything that would prompt people to do business with you instead of doing business with your competitors.

Say you are an electronics retailer looking to attract new customers. You are already advertising across a variety of media, and you know what kind of impact this type of activity will yield. Now you need something more: a boost of some kind. How might a digital concierge strategy help you accomplish this goal?

Try this: Focus your online keyword searches on every product you carry. (If your inventory is broad, you may either have to assign more resources to this activity or prioritize certain products in order to keep it manageable.) You can use a combination of tools to do this—from Google Alerts and a Twitter application such as Tweetdeck, to more specialized monitoring tools. Your budget and the complexity of your searches will dictate what types of tools you really need. Many are free and simple to use but lack the sophistication needed by large organizations. Others, geared toward the enterprise space, are complex but expensive. Some stand somewhere in the middle. Do your research and find the ones that best suit your needs.

Now that you are monitoring these keywords, you notice several hundred daily online mentions of a particular type of product you happen to carry. Your objective, remember, is to attract new customers. Influencing prospective buyers of a product to buy this product from you rather than from a competitor is a good way of going about it. How might you use these hundreds of product mentions to accomplish this objective? Simple: by making it easier for your community of prospective buyers to purchase the items from you than from a competitor.

First, discard every mention that does not imply a decision is being contemplated:

"I love my new [insert product]" is not as important to this function as "I am looking at buying a [insert product category]. What kind should I get?" The first does not imply that a purchase is being contemplated, whereas the latter does. (Note: This type of selection requires a human being. It cannot be automated.)

Second, respond to mentions that ask for advice. Think about what a concierge does: A hotel guest in an unfamiliar town may inquire about the best local restaurant, or how to purchase tickets to a show, or how to best tour the city. Then, the concierge often acts as the facilitator: Once the advice has been given, he may offer to help the guest make reservations, purchase tickets, or inquire about availability.

The principle here is the same: Answer questions and be helpful but with a bias toward gently influencing the individual toward a mutually beneficial choice and then help facilitate a transaction, preferably with you.

Using your customer service's social media monitoring program for lead generation can conveniently put you in a position to first influence dozens, perhaps hundreds of customers every day to transact with you and then facilitate the process with simple purchase drivers such as securing the best price, arranging for a demo at your closest retail outlet, calling ahead to speed up the checkout process, or even giving the customer directions on how to get there.

From the perspective of the customer, the process is completely opt-in. Shoppers can take advantage of the help or not. If they do, their new digital concierge can help them until the purchase is made, and in some cases, even after the product is installed and in use. If not, the digital concierge disengages and focuses on shoppers who want to be helped. It wouldn't be a stretch to call this "Customer Service 3.0."

A note about maintaining a healthy balance between customer service and sales: The last thing you want to do on social media channels is spend all day trying to sell your wares. The idea here isn't to use your customer service department to sell anything, but rather to make the customers' lives easier *before* their purchase rather than focusing on doing so only after it. If doing so results in a transaction, that's great. If not, they will at least have been introduced to your business and your relationship with them may grow over time.

Digital Conflict Resolution

Sometimes, people just want to fight. Customer Service's job, online, where hundreds of millions of people are looking for a company to either impress or disappoint them, is not the place to have a grudge match with an irate customer. What we are going to talk about in this section is not kung fu. As a matter of fact, the first bit of advice I will give you when it comes to resolving conflict online is this: Don't try to win. Don't even fight.

Let me explain. Remember the golden rule of customer service: The customer is always right. Social media doesn't invalidate this rule. Quite the contrary: Blowing up at a customer over the phone won't generate a whole lot of witnesses, but what about on Twitter and Facebook, at the speed with which incidents are shared digitally? A snarky comment from a customer service representative could become the subject of hundreds of sarcastic of blog posts, all of which will be archived by Google forever. From that moment, every time someone does a search for your company name and the words "customer service," they get to read all about how one of your customer service employees lost his or her cool with a customer. You don't want that.

I am not bringing up this scenario to scare you away from social media. Quite the contrary. My intent here is to remind you that social media is serious business, that it moves customer service from the back office to the town square, and that if you want to do well in the new digital space, you will not only have to put your best people forward but train them for crisis resolution as well.

So here are our rules of online conflict resolution:

- **Rule #1: The customer is always right. (Even if he isn't.)**

- **Rule #2: You will treat every customer like royalty, regardless of how she behaves.** Dignity isn't a gift you bestow upon others. It is a gift you bestow upon yourself. Remember that when you start feeling ill-disposed toward a particularly unsavory customer.

- **Rule #3: Unreasonable customers are not the enemy.** They are merely tests of your professionalism and training. Embrace them as such. Ask yourself this: Are you really going to give some petty little tyrant the satisfaction of having made you lose your cool in front of everyone? (The answer, in case you were wondering, is *no*.)

- **Rule #4: The most effective weapon against an angry customer is a calm, generous demeanor.** You're online. The customer can't see your face. You're hundreds of miles away. Relax. Take your time responding. If you need to go pour yourself a glass of milk, nothing is stopping you. Controlling the pace of the exchange (slowing it down) can be an effective way of defusing the situation.

- **Rule #5: The most effective weapon against a rude customer is politeness.** Breathe. Smile. Relax. Be polite.

- **Rule #6: Recruit your customer into helping you craft a solution.** Once the customer stops ranting and it is your turn to speak, say this: "I understand your frustration. How can I help?" This sentence can be repeated as many times as needed until the customer calms down. In the event that "How can I help?" is not enough, a more direct question, such as "What can I do right now to fix the problem?" can help the angry customer shift from a complaint mode to a solution mode.

- **Rule #7: Never, ever, ever, under any circumstances get sucked into an argument with a customer, especially online.** Don't do it. The objective is to *resolve* a conflict, not prolong one.

- **Rule #8: Don't be afraid to apologize, even if you have nothing to apologize for.** "I'm sorry that your experience with us hasn't been great today" can help defuse a bad situation. It also impresses everyone watching the "incident" unfold on their favorite social network.

- **Rule #9: If the customer's request for a resolution is unreasonable, apologize and say that you can't do that but offer an alternative.** Before you respond, though, offer to take things offline. Tell the customer a manager can contact him and address his request. Move the conversation off public channels now that the customer has agreed to some kind of resolution. Remember that unreasonable demands aren't the end of the world. It's good to know what the angry customer wants. You can always negotiate the settlement down, or better yet, let someone else do it.

Conflict resolution is simply this: taking the pressure out of a balloon. Everything you say and do either *adds* air to the customer's angry balloon or takes air *out* of it. Right and wrong have nothing to do with the matter at hand. What matters is this: Almost all of your exchanges on social media channels can be observed by hundreds, perhaps thousands of people. This means that the way you manage a difficult individual in a public space is at least as important as the subject of the disagreement itself. To add to the precariousness of this new level of exposure in customer service, crowds tend to take sides. Win the crowd by being kind, calm, and professional, and you will win the day, not just for yourself but for your company as well.

 Caution

> If it becomes clear that the angry customer is a window-breaker, excuse yourself from the conversation. "I'm sorry. I don't know how to help you" usually does the trick.

If the customer has been abusive toward one of your staff and is completely out of line, let the customer know. Do it calmly. Let him know he's gone too far and take the conversation offline. A simple way of doing this is to use the individual's name (or screen name) and calmly tell him that you will be happy to continue the discussion at a later time. Example: "John, I can see that you are very upset. Why don't we take a break and talk about this again later when everyone is calm?"

If things start to either drag on or degenerate, don't hesitate to take the conversation offline. Social media channels aren't necessarily the best environment for in-depth discussions. Offer to give the offended (or offending) customer a call or to let him call you. Don't be afraid to ask the individual to follow your account so you can send him a direct message or a phone number where he can call you directly.

No matter what happens, always focus on simply being helpful. Social media or not, that is really what all of this boils down to. With or without customer dramas, with or without the heat of the moment, emotions, and the occasional abrasive behavior, your job is simply this...to be as helpful as possible even under what can sometimes be very difficult circumstances. *That* is what separates professionals from amateurs.

From Risk to Opportunity: Turning Anger on Its Head and Other Considerations

The question I hear most often before a social media program gets the go-ahead is, "What if someone says something bad about us?"

I love this question because the answer to it is so simple: They already are.

Without a social media program—and more importantly, without direct customer service involvement on social media channels—a company is both deaf and impotent. It is deaf because without a deliberate monitoring practice in place, all of the types of customer support opportunities we have discussed in this chapter will likely never be discovered. It is also impotent because without both a monitoring practice and a response mechanism in place, the company will find itself incapable of dealing with complaints, requests, questions, and opportunities to conduct business on social media channels. Regardless of social media, deliberately making your organization both deaf and impotent is never a winning strategy.

What presents the greatest risk? Letting angry customers drag your name in the mud across social media channels month after month or making sure that every complaint reaches your ears so that you can try to make things right?

It isn't a trick question. Angry customers are out there, waiting to be made happy again. The risk in monitoring social media channels for complaints or negative mentions is zero.

Consider the cost of your customer service operations now. Pull out your balance sheet and get familiar with every little cost associated with customer service in your organization. Now consider the speed and efficiency with which customer service issues can be resolved via social media channels. What would be the financial impact of shifting even 5% of customer service requests from an inbound call center to, say, Twitter or Facebook?

How about 10%? How about 25%?

You may never be able to completely detach yourself from your inbound call center, and there is nothing wrong with that, but you may discover that integrating social media into your customer service practice could result in *significant* cost reductions.

Another aspect of the impact that social media can have on a customer service practice touches on the topic of profit: A customer service department doesn't have to merely be a cost center. One of the reasons why so many customer service functions now find themselves outsourced is because their value to the organization sometimes eludes cost accountants. If customer service doesn't drive sales, it is an afterthought when it comes to prioritizing departmental budgets. In many cases, customer service is seen as nothing more than a necessary cost of doing business. Following that logic, the lower that cost is, the better the balance sheet looks. That is how we ended up here: Entrusting modestly paid strangers to take care of our customers when they have a problem. From an accounting standpoint, this is a good model. From a brand management standpoint, it is a complete disaster. Social media offers a compromise.

Without turning customer service into a sales department, its function can be broadened to also play a part in lead generation, customer development, user support, business development, and, yes, even community management. Technical support, for instance, can be proactive. Customer service representatives can help produce video tutorials, address common technical questions on the company blog, host customer support chats on Twitter, and participate in a multitude of other social media activities that help increase both the exposure and value of the brand they serve. Being helpful to customers doesn't preclude customer service from being helpful to the company as well. In fact, with a little help from a well-managed social media program, customer service may very well become one of your organization's most valuable tactical assets.

13

Social Media Program Management— Putting It All Together

Should a company manage its social media activities internally, or should the task be outsourced to an external partner? That is the million-dollar question.

Although the easy answer might be "it depends," the real answer is "outsource as little of your social media program's activities as possible."

Social Media Management: In-House, Outsourced, or Somewhere in Between?

Social media works best when fully integrated into all of an organization's business functions: The closer your social media program is to your business, the more effective it will be in the long run. Outsourcing effectively works against this principle. That said, the reality of program management (social media and otherwise) is that sometimes an organization cannot handle it all on its own. Limited resources such as manpower, technical expertise, creative masterminding, and access to specialized labor can get in the way of even the best intentions. When hurdles such as these emerge, companies may have no other choice than to reach out to an external partner or agency to handle some of the load. There is, however, a difference between hiring an external agency to manage specific elements of a social media program that do not require the personal touch of an employee and handing a significant portion of your program over to them, so proceed with caution. No agency, no matter how brilliant it is, can own the relationship you should have with your customers. Only *you* can.

Success in the social media space is predicated upon an individual or organization's ability to forge and nurture online relationships and to some degree convert them into equally valuable offline relationships. Out of respect for your interlocutors, many of whom may be your customers, consider both the practicality and ramifications of outsourcing your relationships before doing so. How do you build relationships through a proxy agent? Can you? Should you? Figure 13.1 outlines the basic planning process to determine whether or not an element of your social media program can be outsourced.

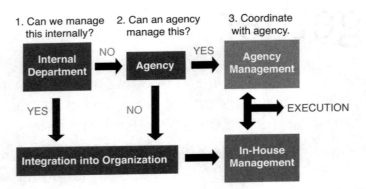

Figure 13.1   Planning for outsourced management.

Whether you are conscious of it or not, the message you send to your customers whenever you outsource a relationship-based social media function like customer service or community management is this: *We need someone to do this because someone has to, but we don't care enough to do it ourselves.* How much trust, affection, and loyalty will this kind of attitude generate? Conversely, companies that choose to manage their engagement roles in-house—companies such as Ford, Starbucks, and Zappos—send a very different kind of message to their customers and the public at large: *We care. We want to have a daily dialogue with you. We aren't in this space just for show.*

The social media space is, lest we forget, *social*, which means that most of the rules common to other social settings apply here as well: treating your interlocutors with respect, being polite, and most of all, not delegating social interactions to a hired agent. Think of parameters of acceptable social behavior outside of the digital universe as a parallel to your organization's behavior in the social media space: Having an assistant to screen your calls, take messages, and organize your emails is perfectly acceptable. Sending a lookalike to a client meeting because you can't be bothered to, however, is not. Asking an intern to follow you into meetings, do research for you, and learn how to sort through lists of email addresses for an upcoming campaign is also well within the bounds of acceptable delegation. Asking her to chat with customers while pretending she is you is not.

Specialists and skilled professionals play a part in simplifying your day, from the barista brewing you the perfect latte first thing in the morning to the dry cleaner pressing your suit for a late afternoon pickup. These types of specialized technical tasks can be outsourced because they have little bearing on your social interactions. You cannot, however, outsource your relationships. When it comes to delegating tasks relating to your social media program, any aspect of the program's activity that touches relationships in any way cannot and *must* not, under any circumstances, be delegated to an outside agency or partner.

There simply is no way around the fact that building *real* relationships with customers and potential customers is at the crux of any social media program's ultimate success. It is the glue that binds all other activities together and makes them stick. If you overlook this aspect of your program or if you choose to ignore it, no amount of effort, attention, or content you throw at your program will make it successful.

So the question begs asking: What elements of your program can you safely delegate to an outside agency? The answer is this: You can usually delegate any function that does not focus directly on building and managing relationships with your audience. The three safest of these are monitoring, measurement, and campaign management.

Monitoring and Measurement

Monitoring keywords isn't a bad place to start with light activity outsourcing. Expect some overlap with customer service and other in-house monitoring practices, but with clear focus and fluid communications between in-house teams and the outsourced monitoring team, this type of delegated activity can be manageable.

Two types of monitoring in particular come to mind. The first is general keyword monitoring coupled with measurement, whose purpose is to track and quantify fluctuations in online mentions. Working with an outside agency that specializes in collecting and measuring predetermined data sets can save an organization time and money, and in some cases yield more precise results than if a moderately experienced employee tries to add this type of activity to an already full schedule. Uses for this type of service range from gathering consumer insights throughout a product's lifecycle to quantifying the impact of a product launch or marketing campaign.

The second touches on online reputation management, public relations, and crisis management and serves as an early warning system for organizations whose monitoring practice may not be "on" around the clock. Companies now have to watch for trouble on the Web 24 hours per day, 7 days per week. When they cannot afford to fund around-the-clock social media monitoring in-house, they can hire an outside agency to scan for trouble at a fraction of the cost. Companies that find themselves frequently targeted in smear campaigns by environmental groups, for example, would find this type of outsourced service helpful.

The extent to which the agency will get involved with the management of a crisis once it develops is the topic of another discussion altogether, but at the very least, the monitoring agency can, if it sees a potential problem on the horizon, ring the alarm, so to speak, and bring it to the attention of the client's crisis management team. This type of service can provide a business with peace of mind when its employees clock out for the day or the weekend and does not interfere with the relationship-building aspects of a social media program.

Campaign Management

Marketing and advertising campaigns are often the realm of external partners and agencies. Because public-facing campaigns are likely to include content and components specifically tailored to social media channels, especially if the client organization has a social media program it can leverage, agencies must play a role in the development and management of these social media components. For the sake of continuity, it makes sense for the agency creating content and managing the campaign to also handle some of its social media components. The following are some tips on how to make sure that an agency's management of specific aspects of a campaign involving social media yields the desired results:

- **Content**—A simple way of keeping the agency and client boundaries clear when it comes to campaign management "duties" is to divide the social media ecosystem thus: The social media *channels* are managed by the client, while the *content* associated with the campaign is both produced and inserted into these channels by the agency. In other words, both the agency and the client have access to the program's social media accounts, and the agency uses them to publish content and collect data as needed.

  A word of caution: The emphasis on delivering content works well in the context of a campaign, but it is secondary to the one-on-one engagement with the public that is the focus of your overall social media program. Be careful not to let marketing firms' tendency to favor content over social engagement take over your overall program strategy. Outside of specific campaigns (which may focus primarily on delivering content in the form of videos, blog posts, and other information), listen more than you speak, pull more than you push, and focus on monitoring and responding more than you do creating "content." Remember that when "content" is at the center of your campaign, the channels may be social, but your activity no longer is.

- **Characters**—A question that sometimes comes up touches on the characters created for a campaign. Characters, in the context of this discussion, are not real people. They are made up, like Betty Crocker's Green Giant, The Keebler Company's elves, and Dos Equis' "most interesting man in the world." Occasionally, the public will begin to relate to the campaign and the product or brand it serves through the character driving the campaign's narrative. What do you do then? Create Facebook and Twitter accounts for the character? Sure, why not. But if you do, someone is going to have to manage those accounts, and that someone is going to find himself not just "creating content," but answering questions, having conversations, and "bonding" with the public, in character.

  Consider the ramifications of this type of endeavor: First, the person managing the character's account will become the voice of the brand. Who is best suited to handle this responsibility? An agency creative or a member of your own brand management team? Are you certain that you want to entrust your brand communications on social media channels to an outside partner? It can work, but you need to be absolutely sure that the agency can handle both the task and the commitment.

Second, bringing a fictitious character to life in a way that appeals to the public demands tact, intelligence, and wit. If the conversations are not humorous or entertaining, if the individual behind the character's accounts takes himself too seriously or turns out to be a stick in the mud, the idea probably won't work. Third, plan for continuity once the campaign is over. Will you simply retire the character's accounts when the campaign wraps up? Will the accounts suddenly become unresponsive to consumer comments and questions, or will you incorporate them into your program once the campaign that led to their creation runs its course? Tough questions, all.

Don't just run with a "cool idea" without thinking about what happens next: The reality of bringing a character to life in the social media space is that you cannot let its accounts go dormant one day without effectively creating a void in the lives of the character's fans. People who become accustomed to interacting with a character will invariably become attached to it. They will notice the sudden death of activity, and the impact on your brand will ultimately be negative. Once you start on this road, plan on traveling it for a very long time.

- **Data**—In regard to data, the agency should collect and analyze its own as it pertains to its campaign, including data from its social media activity. A word of caution: Although it may seem repetitive, perhaps even unnecessary, the client should also collect campaign data on its own, to make sure that the agency is on the right track. This for two practical reasons. The first is that weekly and monthly reports won't do when it comes to making on-the-fly adjustments, and the agency may not have the time or resources to report to a client daily or hourly. Velocity is crucial in the social media space, and even a 60-minute delay from the time an opportunity or a problem occurs to the time the client is in a position to react can make an enormous difference. For this reason alone, monitoring and measuring the effectiveness of a campaign *in-house* is a simple failsafe mechanism.

The second is that the agency may not be measuring the effectiveness of its campaign the same way you do. The software and methodology the agency uses may be different, the keywords and channels it selects may only tell part of the story, and dozens of small details may add up to gaps in both data and analysis. A second opinion (in this case, your own) can't hurt. Although it is important to trust your agencies and campaign partners, it is never a bad idea to make double-sure that campaign data is accurate.

- **Creative**—Let's face it, agencies and marketing firms often come up with pretty good ideas. Their creativity is one of their most valuable assets. Even outside the context of a campaign, don't hesitate to reach out to external partners for advice on how to be more creative and effective with certain elements of your social media program. They might be able to help you develop awareness campaigns, create beautiful microsites, help you customize your social media properties, help craft messaging and tone, and otherwise be a bubbling brook of clever ideas. Leverage their access to talent. Tell them what you want to accomplish and see how they can contribute creatively to the process by which you plan to get there.

One last bit of advice: Bring your campaign partner or agency into the fold by giving them visibility to your sales data. Ultimately, if all a campaign influences are impressions, visits to a website, or activity on social networking sites, chances are that it failed to help you meet your business objectives. In far too many agency-client relationships, the agency has no idea if its campaign has any impact whatsoever on the business itself.

Do not allow a disconnect to exist between your outside partners' activities during the course of a campaign and the business metrics that the same campaign are expected to influence. If the campaign is producing impressive nonfinancial outcomes, that's a great start. If, however, it falls short of producing key financial outcomes—such as an increase in sales or growth in net new customers—you should show the agency the hang-up. Help it connect the dots between activity and outcome. Give it visibility to what is working and what isn't so it can react accordingly. By treating an agency as if it were an extension of your program rather than a separate, detachable, almost mercenary entity, you will be far more likely to engineer success into your collaboration.

Eleven Key Best Practices for Social Media Program Management

Now that we have discussed the outsourcing of certain social media functions, let us turn our attention to best practices for overall program management, both outsourced and in-house. The following is a list of 11 that should form the basis of your organizations' social media program management best practices checklist:

1. Make sure that all roles are clearly assigned and that everyone involved with your social media program understands exactly what their responsibilities are.

2. Make sure that all objectives and targets are clearly outlined. Program objectives should be made clear to the entire organization. Team objectives and targets should be communicated and assigned accordingly, on down to individual objectives and targets.

3. Use an organizational chart so that participants in the program and other company employees and agents have visibility to who does what in regard to the program. This chart should list and map all key social media program participants, provide a description of their role and their contact information, and be kept up to date.

4. Because technology is at the center of your social media program, it is the social media program manager's responsibility to work closely with the IT department and other technology partners to ensure that all of the program's technical requirements are met. All technologies—from software and interfaces to bandwidth and licenses—must also be updated, maintained, and properly deployed. This too is the social media program manager's responsibility.

5. Make sure that all procedures and guidelines pertaining to social media activities and protocols are routinely reviewed and being followed by the staff. Monthly reviews will work for most organizations, but be prepared to make changes to your guideline documents on the fly if need be.

6. Ensure that all social media–related training for employees and outside partners is either completed or scheduled to be completed.

7. Project schedules should be posted and available to all employees and outside partners. The schedule should include upcoming meetings, media releases, product releases, special events, editorial calendars, and all activities pertinent to the social media program.

8. How to best manage communications between all elements of a social media program, including external partners and agencies, is a matter of personal choice, but three simple daily activities usually take care of most of program's communications planning:

    - **Start every day with a short team briefing**—First, review the overall objectives and update everyone on where they stand in relation to their individual targets. Second, if any events of note are coming up (such as a product launch, a magazine review, or a tradeshow), this is a good time to bring it up. Start with the most immediate events and work your way into what may be pertinent that week, then that month. Third, bring up some key issues from the previous day. This is a good time to ask members of the team to briefly talk about anything of note: how they dealt with a difficult customer, how the new software is difficult to manage, and so on. This is also a good time to answer questions, get some clarity or closure about something that happened the day before, and then move on.

Lastly, state any particular kind of item you want your team to focus on that day. Wish them a great day and let them get back to work. Daily briefings should last no more than 10–15 minutes. Share notes from the meeting by either posting them to a shared file or sending them via email.

- **If your teams are spread out across a number of offices and locations, find a system that works for everyone—** Videoconferencing with each individual team is an option. If your program management structure is layered, consider delegating some of the briefings specific to individual teams to their supervisors. Also be sure to invite anyone who wants to attend.

- **Stay in constant contact with your social media program team—** Internal collaboration is key if the program's day-to-day management is going to go smoothly. If the public relations team is not in regular contact with the community manager, for example, their activities will eventually fall out of sync. One of the program manager's responsibilities is to make sure this never happens.

  Every business function and department (including external agencies) needs to have visibility to what everyone touching the social media program is doing at any given time so that the program can run smoothly—from the coordination of overlapping monitoring and response mechanisms to the orderly distribution of content across specific channels at specific intervals.

- **Share information with the rest of the organization—**Meet with other departments. Find out what they are doing and planning and share what you are doing and planning. The elements of a company's social media program should not be the only ones with visibility to what the rest of the team is doing.

  It is important for the entire organization to be briefed on its activities, its challenges, its successes, and its capabilities; in turn, you need to be aware of what other elements of the organization are working on. The more information about the social media program flows across the entire organization, the more its value can be understood, and the more likely it is that its capabilities will be increasingly leveraged by key departments.

What's more, knowing what else the company is focusing on will help you adapt the social media program's focus to better serve the organization as a whole and help engineer more wins. This will further the adoption of social media into the organization's culture and potentially help secure more funding for projects, head count, and other resources as time progresses.

9. Be a leader, not just a manager. It isn't enough to merely manage a social media program's schedule and oversee its activity and communications. In order to successfully develop, deploy, and then grow a social media program into a successful endeavor, you must also understand how to blend both *business mechanics* and *social dynamics* to build its value within the organization and for customers and fans outside of the organization. You have to be intimately familiar your organization's strengths, weaknesses, and capabilities so that you can leverage outside agencies in the right context when needed, as well as know when not to. You have to be able to manage, mentor, and supervise sometimes dozens of otherwise unconnected teams across not only your own organization but outside agencies as well. You have to be supremely organized yet ready to completely rewrite complex plans and improvise at a moment's notice.

More than anything, you must have a clear vision for the program and be capable of articulating it clearly to everyone involved with it. You have to be both a leader and a manager, which is not always the easiest thing in the world. It takes hard work, complete dedication, and a lot of patience.

10. Measure what matters and do it well. Do not settle for basic social media metrics such as reach (the number of followers, fans, connections, and so on), volume of online mentions, "likes," click-throughs, and volume of comments on your blog. These things are important, and you should measure them, but they are a small part of what you should be looking at. Remember the business objectives your program is tasked with supporting. Think about the targets that were set for those objectives. Measure progress there as well.

If one of your business objectives is to acquire new transacting customers by using social media, measure conversions from net new followers and fans to net new transacting customers.

If one of your objectives is to improve public perception of your organization, benchmark sentiment at the start of your program, and track changes in sentiment in online mentions over time. Track changes in keywords to see if topics of conversation regarding your organization are shifting away from negative topics. *That* is how you prove the value of your program and how you know that your activities are yielding the desired results. Connect the dots and do so empirically. Do not assume. Do not guess. Measure. Track progress. See where you are having an impact and where you are not and make the necessary adjustments. Measurement holds the key to adaptation and improvement not only for your program, but for the entire organization. The better your measurement practice, the more effective your program will be.

11. Reporting to the company leadership is a key component of the program management role. If the CEO and other senior executives either don't know what the program is doing or aren't completely clear on the value it brings *daily* to the organization, its importance to them will always be questioned. A social media program manager must not only give complete visibility to the program's activities to the executive team, but create reporting mechanisms that serve a variety of purposes— from funneling market intelligence to the right decision makers to reporting on successes and challenges at proper intervals. Reporting, although rarely brought up in best practices discussions, is not only crucial to the program's well-being, it is one of the central duties of a program manager. Chapter 17, "Social Media Program Analysis and Reporting," is entirely dedicated to this topic.

Staying Focused on Business Objectives: How Marketing Campaigns Should Fit into Your Social Media Program

Perhaps the most crucial aspect of bringing all of the pieces of your social media program together deals with effectively incorporating social media–related *campaigns* into your overall social media *program* in such a way that they will support both your short-term *and* long-term business objectives. To understand how this process works, let's take a closer look at the relationship between campaigns and the program—or rather, the mechanism by which campaigns help drive the growth of a social media program in support of specific business objectives.

To understand how campaigns typically work, consider the impact of media spend on attention and sales illustrated in Figure 13.2.

Typical Campaign Cycle

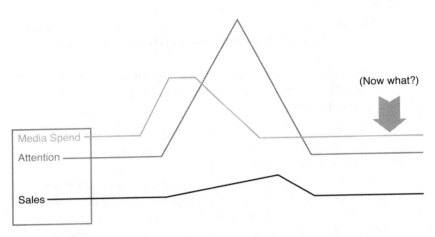

Figure 13.2   Typical campaign cycle.

Campaigns are all meant to work pretty much the same way: When sales need a boost because they are flat or not growing fast enough, the company spends money on a campaign to drive attention and influence consumer behavior. Campaigns exist essentially to convert dollars into attention and attention into transactions. Figure 13.2 shows the relationship between these three metrics, starting with the funding that generates the campaign itself, followed by an increase, then a peak in attention, and a relative increase in net sales as a result. So far, so good. This is simple stuff. Now notice what happens to the attention and sales metrics once the funding stops and the campaign ends. That's right: Attention falls back to pre-campaign levels, as do the sales numbers. In other words, when the funding ends, the campaign ends, and the desired business outcomes end as well.

Now let's see what a series of back-to-back campaigns look like over time (see Figure 13.3).

On their own, campaigns work, but their impact is usually short-lived.

Figure 13.3   Campaign cycles over time.

What Figure 13.3 shows us is a series of campaigns (the arrows), and their impact on attention and sales over time (the peaks above each arrow). Note that each campaign creates its own little increase, but that once a campaign is over, sales tend to slump back to where they were before. (For the sake of simplicity, let's assume that the business is growing year over year but that this growth is imperceptible in our example.) What you see when you look at successive campaigns plotted along a timeline is that they are essentially microcycles: They are relatively short lived and come at somewhat regular intervals to inject net new activity into the business.

For most businesses, campaign microcycles tend to support short-term goals, ranging from a few days to up to a year. If a campaign is particularly successful, its concept may be extended into the next microcycle—for example, Burger King's "king" series of campaigns, or Subway's "Jared" campaigns, which both lasted several years in the United States (in fact, Jared is still going strong as I write this very paragraph). But no matter how many times a theme or concept is repeated and extended for continuity, campaigns remain short lived. They are always microcycles, whose immediate goals are to support short-term objectives such as generating a boost in sales on a particular day, week, month, or quarter. This is not a bad thing.

What Figure 13.3 shows us is the basic flaw that is the result of campaign mindset: Though campaigns tend to create spikes in activity, the impact of campaigns over time is limited at best. High levels of activity seen at the peak of each campaign are simply not sustainable without a regular injection of funding. This is a problem. What organizations want to see is sustained growth over time, as shown in Figure 13.4.

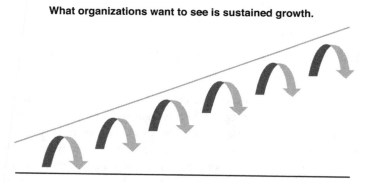

What organizations want to see is sustained growth.

Figure 13.4   Campaigns and long-term growth.

The trick, then, is to see if carefully combining campaign activity with a social media program with clear business objectives might help solve this sustained growth problem. The answer, of course, is yes. The best way to think about how this works is to think about what happens between campaigns when regular contact between the organization and the audience whose attention it captured during each campaign continues, even once the campaign is over. For a company that has no social media program, that degree of interaction simply isn't possible. For a company with an active social media program that encompasses community management, customer support, marketing, PR, product management, and other roles across a variety of departments, that degree of interaction is built into the business model.

Attention and reach don't have to recede when a campaign comes to an end. With each new follower, fan, connection, or subscriber activated by a campaign, an organization now has the ability to keep that new connection activated without having to harass them with promotional messages they may not want. Figure 13.5 shows how building social equity during and between campaigns can help this happen.

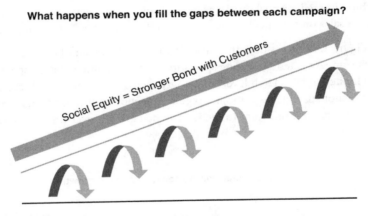

Figure 13.5 Social equity and long-term growth.

Now that you understand the concept, let's see how it actually works. If you are familiar with endurance training, you will recognize the staircase pattern in Figure 13.6. If not, let me introduce you to plateaus. A *plateau* is essentially an area of stagnation in performance that is represented on a graph by a relatively flat, horizontal line. Plateaus occur in all manner of performance when a natural balance is achieved during an adaptive process. In the case of business activity, a plateau can occur once the public adapts to the novelty of a campaign or once sales level out after the initial frenzy of a popular release, for example. When an organization plateaus, it finds itself in a sort of recovery and planning mode until the next campaign launch sends it once more into a frenzy of activity.

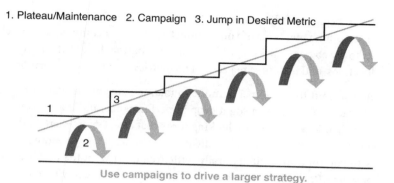

1. Plateau/Maintenance   2. Campaign   3. Jump in Desired Metric

Use campaigns to drive a larger strategy.

Figure 13.6   Campaigns, social equity, and ever-adaptive plateaus.

Rather than looking at campaigns as short-term boosts in performance, treat campaigns as triggers that propel the organization's performance to its next plateau. Just like long-distance runners gradually manage small bumps in mileage, allow their bodies to adapt to the demands of their new level of performance, then jump to the next level again, use campaigns to drive business activity up to where it naturally settles and hold it there until this new plateau becomes the new baseline. If you look at Figure 13.6, you will notice that this occurs as a three-step process:

1. Start with your current baseline: your current plateau. This can represent sales, conversations on Twitter, number of people you interact with on Facebook every day, and so on. The KPIs are yours to choose based on your business objectives.

2. Use a campaign to drive a rapid increase in activity or performance for that metric (or set of metrics) as you would with any other business.

3. Establish a new plateau. This step is important because it is what makes the difference between the long-term outcome of a traditional campaign mentality and the successful outcome of your social media program's strategy: Do not allow the boost in performance generated by your campaign to fall back to pre-campaign levels, as illustrated in Figure 13.3. Plug your social media program into the campaign to make it stickier with your audience. Enhance the impact of the campaign by driving discussions, by amplifying its reach, by filling attention gaps, and making it more than a mere campaign.

As you notice that your key metrics (your chosen KPI) begin to peak, your job is now to use your social media program's assets to start taking over and maintain that level of performance or activity even as the campaign begins to fade. This could be measured in volume of conversations, online mentions of your product, customer recommendations, visits to a web page, clicks of a "share" or "like" button, foot traffic to retail locations, and of course net sales. The metrics are yours to determine.

As you shift from campaign mode to maintenance mode (your new plateau), you may see a slight drop in performance, and that is okay. Don't panic. What you are looking for is that sweet spot where both your organization and your audience, now either larger or more active with you (or both), will naturally settle. You don't want the performance of your KPI to slip too far, but let it find a place where it will hold steady and work to keep it there.

What you are driving at with this method is a deliberate adaptive process focused on steady cyclical growth. The campaigns do the fast, heavy lifting, and your social media program then steps in to brace up the new level of performance. It helps the business adapt to this new level of performance at its own pace until it is no longer a challenge to manage, and then the process starts over again. This method incorporates campaigns and other activities into the program's long-term strategy in such a way that short-term tactics always support both short-term targets and long-term objectives. Meanwhile, the program's long-term vision in supporting specific business goals gives campaigns both purpose and continuity. *This* is program management with purpose.

Final Thoughts on Social Media Program Management

Distilled down to its core, social media program management is simply a product of purpose fueled by opportunity: The *purpose* is to help an organization perform better, provide a higher degree of value to its audience, stakeholders, fans, and customers, and drive organic and sustainable business growth. The *opportunity* lies in doing this by leveraging easy-to-use technologies and channels that help humanize organizations, significantly increase the breadth of their reach, and build deep, lasting relationships with their customers and fans—all this at very little cost.

Depending on the organization and the depth of its ambition, this can be either a simple affair or a juggling act of epic proportions. The trick here is to be able to be clever about it. Never underestimate the value of cleverness, especially in this space. An effective social media program manager must be able to improvise quickly and often. No two companies are the same. No two industries are the same either. Every social media program in the world is as unique as the thumbprint left behind by its social media program manager, and no social media program manager will ever build the same social media program twice. Although many of the mechanisms and basic concepts are the same no matter where you go, the execution built around them is always utterly unique. Ford and GM's social media programs are completely different from one another. So are Coke and Pepsi's.

The beauty of social media program management is that when done right, it is at its core an exercise in functional cultural design applied to the business world, and in the right hands, that can be very exciting. Once you master the fundamentals, the management of the program itself can become a laboratory for business best practices that aims to improve every facet of an organization's operations, from seemingly non-social business functions like internal collaboration and marketing campaign integration to more customer-facing disciplines like experience design and community management.

Don't be afraid to experiment, test new ideas, and try things other social media programs haven't yet tackled, but whatever you do, don't ever lose sight of your organization's business objectives, as they will always guide you, give your program purpose, and ensure that your social media program yields measurable, relevant results.

IV

Social Media Program Measurement

14 Creating a Measurement Practice for Social Media Programs 193

15 ROI and Other Social Media Outcomes 207

16 F.R.Y. (Frequency, Reach, and Yield) and Social Media 239

17 Social Media Program Analysis and Reporting 257

14

Creating a
Measurement
Practice for Social
Media Programs

Because most companies look at business communications, marketing, and business development as mostly an outbound model, it is easy for executives to forget that the same channels and mechanisms can be used for inbound purposes as well: If you can use these channels to spread content and increase reach, you can also use them to seek feedback, measure it, analyze it, and make course adjustments as needed.

This is the ultimate triple-value of measurement in the social media space: discovering what elements of a campaign or program work and don't work, doing so in real time, and being able to make on-the-fly adjustments to achieve specific goals. This is why no social media program can be effective without an adequate measurement practice.

Before the *How*, the *Why*: Keeping an Eye on Objectives and Targets

We started on this journey by talking about objectives. More specifically, we started by emphasizing the need to tie a social media program to very specific, measurable business objectives and targets. In Chapter 2, "Aligning Social Media to Business Goals," we outlined the need to narrow down objectives from vague, abstract generalizations ("We need to sell more stuff.") to specific measurable targets ("We need to sell 245 more red bicycles in this year's Q4 than we did in Q4 last year.").

Tying a social media program to measurable business objectives is crucial for the following reasons:

- Business objectives give purpose to a social media program.

- Business objectives give momentum to a social media program.

- Business objectives makes everyone involved with a social media program accountable to the rest of the organization.

- Adequate measurement of a social media program gives managers timely information and insight into what parts of the program are working and not working.

Without an adequate measurement practice in place, success, progress, and even failure, cannot be properly measured in either the short run or the long run—that is to say, along the entire life cycle of the program. On the one hand, understanding what works, what doesn't, and why is crucial to the proper management of a social media program because it allows an organization to make adjustments on the fly. This is particularly important in the social media space because of the velocity with which opinions and attention can shift. On the other hand, being able to justify investments (in particular, elements of a social media program) over time depends on the organization's ability to effectively measure the investment's value to the organization.

A social media program, in order to be effective, needs to be measurable within the context of the business it serves: measurable, in other words, against the very objectives and targets it aims to influence.

A Word of Caution Regarding Measurement in the Social Media Space

It is easy to get sidetracked by typical social media metrics that don't have much of a bearing on business objectives. Focus on establishing a social media program measurement practice that caters to an organization, not a celebrity. Popularity and popularity metrics are not necessarily what you want to spend a lot of time and energy on.

The value of a follower on Twitter or Facebook or any other social networking platform can be measured in many ways, all of which are tied to the ultimate success of the organization. Someone merely clicking a button that reads "Follow" or "Like" and then moving on without further contact is of little value. Now imagine 1,000 of these ghost followers—10,000, even. These are empty numbers. They may look great on paper, but in the end, the value of that portion of your network, until these followers have helped you meet a business objective, is precisely zero. Forgetting to tie the easy numbers to something of substance can send your program down the wrong measurement path.

Likewise, it is easy to become obsessed with fleeting "moment-in-time" metrics. Brand mentions will rise and fall every week, every day, every hour. Positive and negative sentiment within those mentions will also fluctuate all on their own. I have seen people obsess over short-term changes like these, to the point where the wrong kind of focus paralyzes the entire program. The social media space, given its breadth of metrics, provides its own stress fuel for people who easily get sidetracked by too much data.

Measurement, analysis, and reporting therefore require context: A single metric, taken at random, is as relevant or worthless as one chooses to make it. But as part of a greater whole, supported by a plethora of data points telling their piece of a bigger story, that piece of data can be meaningful and find its true value.

The Cornerstones of Your Measurement Practice: Monitoring, Measurement, Analysis, and Reporting

Your measurement practice will be built on four cornerstones: monitoring, measurement, analysis, and reporting. They are four distinctive disciplines, and they are important because, together, they connect the dots between observation, data collection, the development of insights, and the conversion of data into business intelligence. Let's take a closer look.

Monitoring

Monitoring, also frequently called "listening" in social media circles, is often confused with measurement, and that can sometimes be dangerous for a social media program. Monitoring consists of establishing listening outposts and using them. That's it. Monitoring is listening with purpose. It does not, in and of itself, seek to quantify or "measure" anything. Monitoring's role relative to measurement is merely the identification and sorting of data that may need to be measured. It qualifies data but doesn't quantify it.

Measurement

Once data has been qualified as relevant, it must be quantified. This transitions the process from monitoring to measurement. In the simplest of terms, measurement is the systematic assignment of an empirical value—or as it is sometimes explained, "a magnitude of quantity"—to data. You might measure the number of visitors to a website, the number of clicks on a link, or the number of views on a YouTube video. You might also measure changes in data sets over time or the velocity with which a video, blog post, or story spreads across a variety of channels. Measurement focuses on assigning values and hard numbers to any point of interest relating to your social media program.

There are only two rules when it comes to measurement: Be precise and measure what matters. Start with your objectives and work your way back into metrics that support these objectives. Then make sure you quantify the degree to which they illustrate the types of changes in behavior you are looking for.

Analysis

Analysis is the interpretation of data once it has been measured and quantified, with the aim of drawing insights from it. Without analysis, measurement serves no purpose. (What is the value of data if the organization does not take the time to apply it to its decision-making process?) This is where many organizations fall short: Too often, measurement serves merely as a step in the internal reporting process, a means of quantifying data to simply print it on a page. This is shortsighted. Do not merely report. Data, assuming it was collected and measured properly, is only worth something if the organization knows how to extract from it actionable insight. Without focus and deliberate analysis, data is just numbers on a page, points on a chart, content for a pointless game of show-and-tell.

Your social media program's measurement practice finds its value here, in analysis. As the business unit and program management team pore over their data, analysis is guided by how the data relates to the objectives set forth at the inception of the program or campaign. The object of properly focused analysis is to create a comprehensive narrative for your social media program's progress over time, to show where actions have been successful (or not), why and how, and what this means to the program as a whole. Analysis allows the program team to see where it must focus its efforts and resources next. It identifies success and failure, opportunities and risks, potential improvements, and new courses of action.

Another point worthy of mention: Measurement is not static. In other words, your measurement methodology should constantly be evolving, particularly in the social space. Why? Because technology advances at breakneck speed, and every few weeks, a new tool emerges, bringing with it a new evolutionary step in measurement. Whether it allows you to measure deeper, more precisely, or along multiple channels at once, every new tool, every new feature can and should impact your ability to measure your progress.

Reporting

How data and analysis are reported, by whom, and under what circumstances is also crucial to the success of your social media program. Why? Because chances are that if you are reporting your progress to someone, your success will be *judged* by that person. If decisions need to be made at his level, delivering not only the data but relevant, actionable insights *in the right context* will go a long way toward producing the internal outcomes that will best further your aims. We dive deeper into this topic in Chapter 17, "Social Media Program Analysis and Reporting."

Best Practices for Performance Measurement

Best practices for performance measurement could fill the pages of an entire book. Unfortunately, it would have to be rewritten every few months in order to stay current. So for now, we focus on simply building a *framework* for best practices, one that leaves enough room for you to fill in the gaps and create a flexible and adaptable measurement practice that fits your organization's needs.

Here's a list of the fundamental best practices of a measurement framework:

- Maintain a list of everything you *can* measure.
- Maintain a list of everything you *must* measure.
- Stay current on the best measurement tools.
- Ensure the neutrality of the employee(s) tasked with the measurement of your social media program.
- Tie everything you measure to business objectives.
- Test, measure, learn, adapt, repeat.

Maintain a List of Everything You *Can* Measure

Keep this list updated as it grows. Among the types of things you should look at are the following:

Number of Twitter followers

Volume of outbound updates per day

Volume of inbound tweets per day

Number of outbound re: (replies) generated per day

Number of RT (retweets) generated per day

Number of click-throughs (inbound via Twitter)

Number of Facebook fans (even if they aren't called "fans" anymore)

Volume of updates per day

Number of "likes" per day

Number of "likes" per update

Number of comments per day

Number of comments per update

Number of "shares" per day

Number of "shares" per update

Number of click-throughs (inbound via Facebook)

Other activity on Facebook (discussions, downloads, event RSVPs, and so on)

Number of daily visitors to the blog per day

Number of unique visitors to the blog per post/article

Number of comments per day

Number of comments per post

Number of daily inbound visits to website from blog

Number of inbound links visits to website from blog per unique post

Number of views and downloads (video)

Number of downloads (audio/podcast)

Number of downloads (PDF/White paper/Study/other content)

Volume of mentions (brand and assorted keywords) across channels

Net positive mentions* across channels

    General praise for the brand

    Praise for the brand directly addressed to a company account

Net negative mentions* across channels

    General complaints about the brand

    Complaints about the brand directly addressed to a company account

Customer Support or Service requests on Twitter per day/per hour

Average number of re: (reply) updates to complete a customer service request

Average amount of time to close out a customer service request

Net number of positive outcomes to customer service requests (resolution)

Net number of negative outcomes to customer service requests (no resolution)

Net potential reach

Net frequency of interactions/touches per customer in a selected group/subset

Net unique visitors to website

Net number of unique visitors inbound from seeded links across SM channels

    Net per channel

Net online transactions (e-sites)

Net product reviews (total volume, positive, negative)

Net recommendations across all channels

    Net per channel

Brick and mortar store traffic

Response to promotional offers (track codes, hashtags, and so on)

Event attendance (physical and/or virtual)

Net number of transactions

Net sales volume (total, by product, by category, by location, and so on)

Net number of transacting customers

Average buy-rate/frequency of transaction in a selected group or subset

Average yield/dollar amount per transaction in a selected group/subset

Conversions (yes, any and all of them)

Maintain a List of Everything You *Must* Measure

From this list, create a list of everything you *must* measure. Figure 14.1 shows an example.

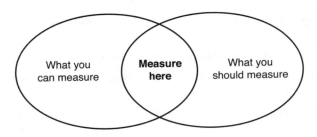

Figure 14.1   Measurement matrix.

What makes sense to measure is likely to depend on each department in your organization because each will focus on its own set of relevant metrics. Tread cautiously here because the social media program manager will also need to measure the effectiveness of the program as a whole, across all business functions. Think of this as a dual model of where *micro* measurement will take place at the departmental level, and *macro* measurement will take place at the overall program management level.

Here are two examples of what micro measurement might look like:

- An online reputation management team may choose to focus only on sentiment, positive mentions, negative mentions, volume of specific keywords (such as "recall" or "unethical"), volume of negative comments left on the organization's Facebook wall and blog, and other sentiment-related metrics.

- A business development team, on the other hand, may focus on a completely different set of metrics: net new fans and followers, click-though volume, volume of "shares" and retweets, and online purchases.

For macro measurement, the program manager would have to consider each team's data relative to its specific objectives as well as overall KPI for the program as a whole. Here is a general list of key performance indicators typical of a macro-measurement focus:

Total volume of mentions (brand, product[s])

Sentiment mix for each

Create a word cloud of keywords associated with your brand

Create a word cloud of keywords associated with your product(s)

Create a word cloud of keywords associated with your competition

Net new followers, fans, subscribers, and so on (individual channels)

Net number of direct mentions (the account, not just the brand)

Net number of clicks to source content by individual channel

SMS/text activity data, if applicable

Email activity data, if applicable

Traditional mail response data, if applicable

Retail store traffic, if applicable and measurable

Net transacting customers, if measurable

Net number of transactions (Total, by brand, by category, by product)

Net revenue (Total, by brand, by category, by product)

Other conversion data

Regardless of your focus (macro or micro measurement), what you are looking for in these data sets is change. What you want to see are shifts in behavior indicating that something you are doing is having an effect.

Consider, for example, the importance of knowing that this month online mentions of a particular product in your catalog have doubled or that sentiments for that particular product and your brand in general have shifted from 57% positive to 72% positive. We have discussed the importance of being able to see the heart of these conversations in real time, pinpoint their source, and respond. In terms of measurement, what we want to do now is track changes in data relating to this outside activity over time: Is the volume of mentions and conversations increasing? Is the sentiment mix increasingly positive? Are we still seeing some of the same negatives we were concerned about three months ago? Is this an indication that a problem still has not been solved, and if so, to what extent?

This is all valuable, actionable business intelligence. Not measuring this, not tracking changes and progress from measurement period to measurement period is a lot like driving blind.

The same is true of every other metric mentioned earlier, from net *followers* and *fans* to net *revenue by product*. Every individual bit of data, in the way it either changes or *doesn't* over time, tells you a little bit of the story you are trying to piece together. Each gives you a snapshot of what is happening between the initial investment and the ultimate *return*. The question every change begins to answer is this: *Is what we are doing having an effect?* If yes, how much of an effect is it having? From there, the puzzle left for you to piece together is, *how is this all connected, and what is affecting these specific customer behaviors?*

Once you understand that A leads to B leads to C, you can start testing different methods, types of content, campaigns, activities, and so on. You can turn your social media program into a lab: If something works, you know it instantly and to what degree. If something doesn't work, you also know right away.

Stay Current on the Best Measurement Tools

Make sure you review measurement tools often to ensure you aren't using last year's (or last month's) technology. This could be a completely integrated dashboard that does everything for you or a panoply of smaller tools with their own unique specialties and strengths. Keep in mind that if you are not careful, the tools you use may end up determining what you measure instead of your measurement imperatives driving the adoption of tools that will best serve your needs.

Companies sometimes fall into a trap here, and it can come in two forms:

- An agency or outside partner may offer to handle the measurement of a program or campaign for you, using their own tools or dashboard. Although the tool may be adequate for their own purposes as an agency, it may not be adequate for the particulars of your social media program.

- Your company may have committed to a suite of measurement products before understanding what the program really needed. Held in place by a sizeable upfront investment, you may find yourself forced to use software that does not suit your needs. Try to avoid committing too early to software and measurement services that may end up not being the most adequate for your program.

A good rule of thumb to follow is this: If you own your social media program, you must also own your measurement practice, which means having control over your program's measurement software. There is no shortcut here. Everything you outsource, you run the risk of losing control of, not the least of which is measurement. Even if you choose to outsource some of the execution dealing with your social media program, be very careful about outsourcing its measurement: What you may end up with are nice monthly reports, but not a lot of actionable intelligence.

When it comes to measurement software, the best thing a company can do is continuously test what is available on the market. See what works for you and what doesn't. Don't be afraid to experiment with tools of every category—from enterprise-level dashboards with hundreds of features, to free tools that measure only one thing (but do it well). The best toolkit for your program is the one that works for you, not the one your agency or consultant is trying to sell you. Become the expert. *Own* your measurement practice through and through, from the methods you employ to the tools you use.

Ensure the Neutrality of the Employee(s) Tasked with the Measurement of Your Social Media Program

It is easy for a social media program's measurement practice to become either derailed by a lack of operational focus or tainted by politics and personal agendas. In the first instance, problems can emerge from an erosion of perspective, and in the second, by a lack of objectivity.

In terms of perspective, it is worth noting that if an individual's focus is intended to target engagement with the public or content creation, asking her to also focus on measurement may distract her, even impede her ability to perform her primary function. A community manager, for example, needs to focus on building social equity, producing content, and moderating discussions, not measuring the value of each interaction. If her focus shifts to measurement, even part-time, she may not be able to remain effective in her engagement role. You don't want that. If you can, it is usually best to let the *social* people on the team be social and the more data-driven people on the team focus on the program's numbers.

Because objectivity in your measurement practice is crucial, assigning measurement to someone whose contribution isn't at the crux of the program's success can help avoid detrimental conflicts of interest. Though analysis is subjective, data collection and measurement should be unbiased and pragmatic. Assigning the measurement piece of your program to someone whose performance doesn't depend on what the data will reveal ensures that the *full* data set—not just the convenient parts—will be delivered to the analysis team. You don't want to open the door to the picking and choosing of what data should be reported based on whether that data will benefit or hurt a manager involved with your social media program.

Tie Everything You Measure to Business Objectives

Twitter followers, for example, speak to reach, which in turn branches off into impressions, mentions, sentiment, click-throughs, retweets, and engagement. This in turn can feed a conversion funnel that eventually results in net new transactions. (We cover this in the next few chapters.) The point is, see the whole field when it comes to measurement. Understand that every bit of data you gather should measure the impact of your activities on consumer behavior. If what you are measuring has no bearing on your business objectives, you are probably measuring the wrong thing.

Test, Measure, Learn, Adapt, Repeat

Your entire social media program is driven by trial and error, adaptation, and repetition. Let your measurement practice be your compass: Focus on what works, don't waste your time on what doesn't, and be patient. Over time, your social media measurement program will yield deeper insights, grow simpler to manage, and may even become your social media program's most powerful asset. It will take patience, diligence, and focus, but the work you invest into it now will pay off in the end.

Building Velocity and Specificity into Your Social Media Measurement Practice

Thirty years ago, one of the biggest pain points for businesses was *intelligence*. Sales numbers were the only true benchmark by which companies gauged their success from month to month. Some retailers also looked at net receipts, and the smart ones measured foot traffic as well. Ad agencies and PR firms mostly reported on estimated reach and impressions, based on the media they had secured for their clients. Comment cards were another source of data, along with the occasional satisfaction survey. All in all, though, in terms of business intelligence, what we were looking at was as full of holes as a block of Swiss cheese—and an old moldy one at that. (How old were those customer satisfaction surveys by the time a full report reached the company?)

Then came the Internet, and suddenly web analytics brought a little more information to the table. Not just *more* information, but *real-time* information: How many people were visiting the company website? What pages did they seem to like? How did they get there? How many clicked the red button? If a company created an e-commerce site, some transaction behavior could be tracked online as well. Our moldy block of Swiss cheese was thrown out and replaced by a fresh slab of Emmentaler.

Jump to today: We now have social networking platforms populated by hundreds of millions of users worldwide, freely sharing demographic information, freely talking about their likes and dislikes all day, all night, all around the world. What this amounts to is a giant database of constantly refreshing opinions and personal information at your fingertips, all in real time.

By setting up monitoring outposts on Facebook, Twitter, blogs, news sites, Foursquare, and whatever other channels seem relevant, an organization can capture an instant sampling of likes and dislikes. It can see whether its latest bit of content, messaging, promotional genius, or discussion topic is a hit or a miss—and why. If the public likes or dislikes a new product, that information can be quantified immediately, and in minutes a marketing team can create a poll to clarify a point or validate a hunch, push it out to its online community, and begin measuring its impact. The velocity with which organizations can collect specific data, gather business intelligence, and measure the impact of a particular activity at any given time by using social media is astounding. Two rarely discussed key benefits to emerge from the marriage of social media and business measurement are velocity and specificity.

Velocity is important to the success of a social media program because the speed with which intelligence reaches a decision maker will impact the speed with which he can respond to a market opportunity. Like a driver seeing the obstacle sooner allows him to safely avoid it instead of having to slam on his brakes, providing a decision maker with business intelligence in quasi real time instead of data collected three weeks ago allows for quick course corrections and better decisions. The fresher the data, the more valuable it is to an organization. This is especially helpful during a public relations crisis, but it is also vital to a social media program on a day-to-day basis.

If something is working, the organization knows it immediately. It can opt to dig deeper into more specific types of measurement and see exactly how, why, and where it is working and (this is key) take advantage of its current momentum.

If something isn't working, the project team can immediately shift into problem-solving mode, look for the source of the problem, and adjust course. Perhaps the situation can be salvaged. What if a company were spending a million dollars per week on a campaign that wasn't hitting its mark? What would be the cost of finding out three weeks into the campaign that something isn't working as expected? What would be the benefit of finding out within hours?

The other advantageous aspect of incorporating the social web in a business measurement and intelligence practice is that the information you drill for can be *specific*. Think about the old way of gathering market intelligence: customer surveys. More often than not, the quality of the answers you obtain from a survey were directly tied to the questions you asked of your audience. The inherent flaw of the customer survey model is that asking the wrong question will keep you from obtaining the information you really need. Absent specificity, customer satisfaction data can completely miss the mark. Because surveys presuppose a certain range of dispositions toward a brand or product, they can fail to give consumers the opportunity to voice their most relevant concerns. Look at most surveys still floating on the Internet these days (see Figure 14.2 for an example).

Rate your level of satisfaction with our product:

Not satisfied   Very satisfied

1   2   3   4   5   6   7   8   9   10

Figure 14.2 Traditional customer satisfaction survey (detail).

What if instead of guessing at what questions to ask, you monitored conversations about your brand and products in order to *isolate* what your customers and users are praising you for and complaining about? You might discover that among a dozen topics of discussion, poor service in a particular store and a design defect in a product are the real issues needing your attention *today*. You could immediately reach out to the people who inadvertently alerted you to the problem and collect more data. The ability to capture, qualify, and target topics eliminates the need to guess at what questions you should be asking.

Because social media allows you to increase both the degree of specificity with which you can target data and the velocity with which you can acquire it, your organization can leverage its social media measurement practice to adapt to market conditions almost instantaneously: If a message isn't hitting the right triggers with your market, you can tweak it and try it again until you get it right. If customers hate or love something that you are doing, you can take appropriate action right away.

This ability to test campaigns, measure quickly and efficiently, adapt, and test again will be one of your social media measurement practice's most valuable contributions to your organization.

What you decide to test is up to you: It could be messaging, a print ad, a promotion, the popularity of a microsite, a demo, or an event. It doesn't really matter. Testing any activity through social media channels by measuring specific feedback associated with it in real time will allow you to determine its value to both your social media program and to the organization as a whole.

Once you get something to work, you will have learned something about the structure of success: You will know what triggers work under certain conditions, how information spreads, and why certain activities or types of content work better than others. From this bank of insights, you will be able to start building an architecture of success by repeating what works and discarding what doesn't and by continuously testing, measuring, learning, and adapting to the market's mood in real time.

15

ROI and Other Social Media Outcomes

Before we get into the definition of ROI, let's talk about one of the principal reasons why the subject so often comes up in discussions before a social program gets the green light from the C-suite: business justification.

In some instances, when you're first considering or proposing a social media program to bosses or clients, they will embrace the idea with open arms, understanding the intangible value of the social web to their business. They will see the value of establishing listening and monitoring outposts with which to enhance their business intelligence, online reputation management, and customer support practices.

They will understand the value of building online communities, bridging gaps between offline and online experiences, and communicating more fluidly with their customers. They will jump at the chance to establish vibrant embassies in new and exciting channels. You won't have to sell them on the why of social media. But not all bosses and clients fall into this category. Most, in fact, don't.

ROI and Business Justification

It isn't that the majority of decision makers are necessarily anti–social web or not web-savvy. I mean, they may very well be, but a CEO or CMO's reluctance to jump into a social media program typically has little to do with a lack of social media sophistication. What is really at work here is a simple process of budget justification. Here's how it works: First, we know that an organization's overall budget is finite. Sure, I've run into a company or two that may have been printing money in their basement (I won't name any names), but for the rest of the corporate world, dealing with limited resources is a daily reality. Most companies simply don't have an extra few hundred thousand dollars to throw at a new program just for the heck of it. Usually, every bit of funding they own is either already assigned to a business unit or is earning interest while not in use.

In other words, unless like Scrooge McDuck, a CEO likes to keep cash sitting around in giant vaults so he can swim in it, 100% of a company's budget is in use in some way shape or form 100% of the time. Let me repeat that because it's important: 100% of a company's budget is in use 100% of the time.

Now let's take that thought one step further: 100% of that total budget generates 100% of the company's revenue. In other words, every single dollar the company can call its own is put toward driving business at all times. (Technically, even cash is an investment...but we won't get into that. Different book.)

How budgets are assigned is a complex process, but here are a few rules of the road that will help shed some light on budget allocation:

Rule #1:   Necessity is the mother of all business decisions.

Whatever the company's resources may be, they will always be allocated first and foremost to the most necessary business functions: the core of the business, the things the company cannot do without.

Rule #2:   Winners get funding. Losers don't.

Here's how that works: Picture two new business units. Each gets a budget of $1,000,000 for the first fiscal year. At the end of the year, Business Unit A has generated $10,000,000 in net new revenue. At the end of the same timeframe, Business Unit B has registered a net loss of $800,000.

Now imagine you are the CEO. You look at these numbers. Budgets for the next fiscal year are due in a few months. What do we do?

One group generated $10,000,000 in new revenue. The other lost almost a million dollars. You have $2,000,000 worth of annual budget to invest. Last year, you split that mount 50/50 between those two groups. Will you invest that budget in the same way again?

Maybe, but probably not.

You just did two things. First, you made an ROI calculation. Whether you are familiar with the equation or not, you did. You instinctively inferred that Business Unit A produced a 900% return on investment. (Once it generated its first $1,000,000 in revenue and paid back its budget, it became cost-neutral. Every dollar of revenue generated after that point was pure profit.) Likewise, you inferred that Business Unit B, with its loss of $800,000, didn't exactly meet expectations. By all accounts, the $1,000,000 the CEO invested in that business unit was a flop.

You see, when confronted with a business decision dealing with budget justification, ROI becomes almost instinctive. Your mind moves to analyze the situation.

The second thing you did—perhaps without realizing it—was to consider *opportunity* cost.

If you have never taken a business management course, now might be a good time for me to briefly explain what *opportunity cost* is. Quite simply, it is the cost of choosing one course of action over another. Most of the time, opportunity cost isn't easy to define upfront. It is by definition a hindsight type of exercise. Only after decisions have been made, costs recorded, and outcomes arrived at can you calculate the true opportunity cost of a decision. But sometimes, you get a pretty good idea of where things are going, as with our example.

You are the CEO and are considering where to spend your $2,000,000 budget for the next fiscal year. Business Unit A is a no-brainer: It is a revenue-generating machine. There is no reason why you wouldn't renew its $1,000,000 budget this year. But what about Business Unit B? Hmmm...what to do, what to do? The numbers look bad. Do you try again? Renew its $1,000,000 budget and hope for the best? You might as well burn that money, and you know it. You start to look at other opportunities. Where else could you put that money to good use?

The question becomes this: Where would that $1,000,000 investment generate the greatest *return*?

The process of determining where a company's budget will yield the greatest return, what we just talked about, is at the heart of budget justification. Choosing between one program and another, one project and another, one campaign and another— that process of considering the opportunity cost of investing in one idea instead of another is what you are dealing with when you come up to a CEO or CMO and propose a social media program.

Although your idea may sound grand, and everyone may love it, the reality of running a business is that profit and loss (P&L) ultimately drives every business decision requiring any sizeable investment. If a company is going to invest in a program, it needs to know that its choice to fund that program will yield better results than where that money had been invested before.

Here comes the kicker: When you approach a CEO or marketing manager about your social media program idea, and she considers your proposal, she now has to look at all the programs and budgets currently under her care and decide which one(s) will be cut to fund yours.

That's right: The reality of finite budgets and limited resources is that in order for you to obtain your funding, in order for your resources to be approved, someone else somewhere in the organization is going to have to give up his. To fill your bucket, someone else's has to be emptied. This is the basis of opportunity cost. The lesson here is this: If ROI is a factor in the assignment of budgets in your organization, your social media program is competing for budget dollars against other programs based on their ability to show a positive return. Ideas typically don't get funded just because they have merit. Ideas get funded when they can be shown to yield results.

For you to get your funding, the decision maker has to believe that your program will yield better results than someone's current program. How will you measure this? How will the decision maker measure this? It's simple. You do it the same way you instinctively evaluated the performances of Business Units A and B in our example—by weighing the potential of one program over another and using return on investment (ROI) as the litmus test.

Financial Outcomes vs. Nonfinancial Outcomes and a Word About Conversions

Before we go on with our *measurement* and ROI discussion, it is important to draw a clear distinction between two types of outcomes: financial outcomes and nonfinancial outcomes. This is important because ROI falls into only one of these two categories: financial outcomes. Return on investment never falls into the nonfinancial outcomes category.

A good way to look at the difference between financial and nonfinancial outcomes is that financial outcomes manifest themselves in two ways: cost reductions and increased revenue. Nonfinancial outcomes are everything else.

Here are some examples of nonfinancial outcomes:

An increase in unique website visitors

A change in positive mentions

A change in negative mentions

Net new Facebook fans

Net new Twitter followers

Net new requests for information

A 25% increase in RSS subscriptions

An increase in visits to a brick-and-mortar retail outlet

Increased time spent on a website

A change in volume of impressions

A 300% increase in YouTube video downloads

The number of times an article was liked or shared

The number of comments on a blog post

The following are examples of financial outcomes:

A 16% reduction in cost by shifting a portion of customer service tickets to Twitter

$1,200,000 in net new sales

A 16% increase in online sales during a Facebook promotional campaign

Decreased *cost per impression* from $2.62 to $0.76 by leveraging SM channels

$320,000 in sales attributed to net new customers acquired through Facebook

The difference between financial and nonfinancial outcomes is simple: The first can be measured in currency, in legal tender, in a dollar value. The second cannot.

This is important for two reasons: First, because the investment, the gain, and the return must be measured in the same currency (the unit of measure of the investment, the gain, and the return must be the same in order for the ROI equation to function), only a financial outcome can qualify as a proper gain or return. In other words, financial outcomes are the culmination of any investment. This is where return is always measured. It cannot be measured anywhere else.

Second, nonfinancial outcomes are intermediate metrics. They fill the gaps between the investment and the subsequent gain and return. They tell the story by capturing changes in customer behavior. They give us snapshots of what happens between the time a program is assigned its budget and the time it yields a measurable return.

Consider then that a sequence of events happens between the initial *investment* and the *gain* (that is to say, the financial outcome) on that investment. There is a structure to this, as shown in Figure 15.1.

Ignoring possible cost reduction outcomes for a moment, let's focus on the *revenue generation* aspect of a social media program. What you see in Figure 15.1 is a typical sequence of events tying the investment in the program or campaign with the ultimate financial outcome. Note the placement of nonfinancial outcome in this sequence. It precedes financial outcomes. It is a transactional precursor, which is to say a precursor of ROI.

Let's look at an example of how the sequence works (see Figure 15.2). First, the company decides to invest $25,000 in the program in Q1 to test the waters. Let's call this a proof of concept: "Here's $25,000. Show me what you can do."

$$$
Investment ➤ Action ➤ Reaction ➤ Nonfinancial ➤ $$$ Financial
                                    Impact   Impact

Figure 15.1 Sequence of events between initial investment and gain.

$$$
Investment ➤ Action ➤ Reaction ➤ Nonfinancial ➤ $$$ Financial
$25,000   Impact   Impact
for Q1

Figure 15.2 Example with $25,000 investment in Q1.

In this scenario, Facebook's user statistics seem to promise the best opportunity: greater reach, a breadth of marketing options, and more opportunities for conversions. The program manager decides to start there (see Figure 15.3).

The launch of the company's Facebook page is the *action* in this case. Had the company decided to invest more funding into the program, the action could have been more than just the one thing. It could have been *actions* (plural), all leading to their unique sets of reactions and outcomes. What happens next is the public's reaction (see Figure 15.4).

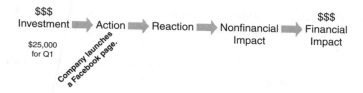

Figure 15.3 Next step: launching a Facebook page.

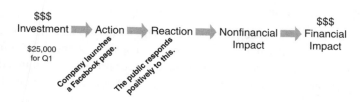

Figure 15.4 Public reaction.

In this scenario, based on the types of conversations turning up (keyword analysis, sentiment, volume of mentions), the public seems to like the idea. People notice. They don't ignore or rebel. This is a good start.

We now move to what the public does next (see Figure 15.5). What is the nonfinancial impact of the action—or activity—funded by the company?

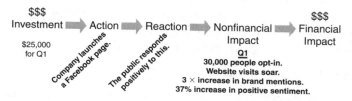

Figure 15.5 Nonfinancial impact.

Here, we see several specific types of nonfinancial impact being measured throughout Q1. (Because the investment had a specific shelf life, the program manager opted to use the funding period as a benchmark.)

The first thing you will notice is that while the page may have touched untold numbers of people on Facebook, the program manager decided not to estimate impressions, but rather to focus on a more telling number: how many individuals opted in. In the early days of Facebook, these would have been *fans*. As I write this book, these are *connections*. Bottom line: During Q1, 30,000 people clicked to opt into the page and can now receive updates, engage with content, share it, and so on.

The program manager also listed three other telling metrics: website visits, an increase in online brand mentions, and an increase in the percentage of positive sentiment in these mentions. As limited as this information is and devoid of context as outsiders, we can still infer that perhaps (emphasis on *perhaps*) the Facebook page has affected consumer behavior in several ways.

First, 30,000 people just opted to interact with the brand more than they already were. The opportunity to reach out to them—to increase their appreciation for the brand and to increase mindshare—is not negligible.

Second (and this is trackable), the Facebook page seems to incite visitors (whether they are among the 30,000 or not) to click links and visit the company's official website. This increased exposure to the brand and its products could impact perception, preference, and ultimately purchasing behavior at some point in the future.

Third, awareness and word-of-mouth are also seeing a boost. Evidently, the Facebook page is generating not only introverted interest (opting in and website visits) but conversations, discussions, and opinions. This is good as well, and we have seen the impact that lateral engagement can have in helping a brand's reach.

Finally, a 37% increase in positive sentiment means that not only are people talking about the brand three times as much as they were before the start of Q1, the perception of the brand has shifted. This is key: A 37% increase in positive sentiment means that the brand is now more favorably perceived. Does this increase the probability that consumers will shift their preference accordingly? That's a safe bet. By how much remains to be seen, however, because the outcomes of the investment and subsequent activity have only yielded nonfinancial results: that is, increased reach, increased exposure, and improved brand image.

Let's now look at what comes next, the financial impact (see Figure 15.6).

Here we see that the program manager has added some transactional data. For the sake of simplicity, let's assume for now that sales were flat for the last few quarters and that no one would have a reason to suddenly start buying more from this company: no new products, no price reductions, no cool advertising campaigns. Let's say that this company makes old-fashioned wooden yoyos. What we have, then, is a scenario in which the company's only change in activity was the creation of a Facebook page, which yielded 30,000 "fans," a significant increase in visits to the website and brand mentions, and a significant shift in sentiment.

Now we find that the company has sold 12,000 yoyos more in this quarter than it is accustomed to. This could be Q over Q (quarter over quarter) or Y over Y (year over year, basically comparing last year's Q1 with this year's Q1). What we do know is that the 12,000 increase in the volume of transactions yielded $120,000 in additional sales revenue in Q1 than was expected.

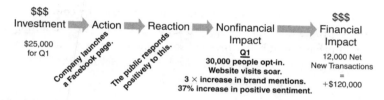

Figure 15.6 Financial results.

The sequence of events (investment fi action fi reaction fi nonfinancial outcome fi financial outcome) and the role of nonfinancial impact relative to financial impact tell a story (or begin to anyway). The more you start connecting the dots, the more dots you realize must be uncovered in order to fill the gaps and satisfy your curiosity. More on that a bit later.

One final note before moving on to what ROI is and isn't: Ask yourself what this sequence really illustrates. Is it cause-and-effect? Maybe. Is it correlation? Probably. That is what we are trying to establish at the very least. Those are two good guesses, but we are after neither. The real prize, when the analysis is all done, when the dots have been connected, speaks to *conversions*.

Every step of this process—from this simplified conceptual illustration to deeper, more complex versions (incorporating dozens if not hundreds of actions)—is simply a conversion flowchart. It's the story of how your investment turns into gains and how return is mapped not in random data points but as a narrative whose chapters are steps in a daisy-chain of conversions, ultimately ending in a change in transaction behavior.

If your program is not driving conversions and if your measurement practice does not focus on identifying and measuring conversions every step of the way, you cannot measure a program's success—financial or otherwise.

What ROI Is and Isn't

ROI is simply an acronym for one of the most fundamental business terms: *return on investment*. No more, no less. ROI has been as the root of business measurement since...at least before the dinosaurs, and it has always meant the same thing: You invest money into something with the expectation of getting money back from your investment (preferably more). There's even an equation that clearly defines ROI. (No really, there is.) It looks pretty much like this:

ROI = (gain from investment − cost of investment) ÷ cost of investment

You can see from this equation that ROI is traditionally expressed as a ratio, percentage, or a relationship between investment and return. Most companies are happy to see a positive return on investment. For example, if a company invests $100,000 in a program, it will be happy to see a $101,543 return. Assuming that the money couldn't have been better invested somewhere else (now we are getting into opportunity costs), that's basically a win. Right? Right. Because the ratio is positive: The return was greater than the investment.

Some organizations, however, have very specific expectations of return. I spent some time in the distribution channel a few years ago and worked closely with Microsoft. As a vendor, Microsoft funded marketing programs through its distributors. In other words, the company invested in marketing programs, hoping to see its investment drive boosts in business. From day one, it was made clear to me that the expectation of return was that for every dollar Microsoft invested in one of our programs, it expected to see ten dollars back. That's right, Microsoft's ROI expectation was in the order of 1:10.

Most often these days, ROI is expressed as a percentage, as in, "The ROI on this campaign was 167%," "Your investments have yielded a 29% return so far," and so on.

This is how ROI is typically expressed. It doesn't matter if the activity touches print advertising, outbound call centers, e-mail marketing, or social media. ROI is media-agnostic: The principle remains the same no matter what the activity or medium.

As an example, let's assume that the cost of a campaign (the investment) was $10,000, and that the return on that investment was $15,389 in net new sales (attributable to the campaign). Therefore, the equation would look like this:

$$ROI = (\$15,389 - \$10,000) \div 10,000$$

For every dollar invested in the campaign, the company made $1.5389 back, for a positive ROI of 153.89%.

Another way to express ROI is simply with a net dollar value. (Percentages and net numbers are great, but net amounts give results context.) This is done by removing the last element of the equation:

$$ROI = (gain\ from\ investment - cost\ of\ investment) \div cost\ of\ investment$$

What you end up with is this modified ROI equation, which speaks to net $ values:

$$ROI = (gain\ from\ investment - cost\ of\ investment)$$

Using the same example as before, let's again assume that the cost of a campaign (the investment) was $10,000 and that the return on that investment was $15,389 in net new sales (attributable to the campaign). The equation would look like this:

$$ROI = (\$15,389 - \$10,000) = \$5,389$$

The net return on investment for the campaign is thus $5,389.

Pretty cut and dry, right? You would think. Unfortunately, there seems to be some confusion in regard to ROI when it comes to social media, possibly because a large chunk of social media aficionados don't come from business management backgrounds and have never managed a P&L or been responsible for maintaining positive ROI in a project. We touched a bit on this earlier in the book: Not everyone who works daily in the social communications space comes from a business background, and nor should they.

Let's take another look at our four main categories of roles working in the social space (see Figure 15.7)

The third category (management) focuses on human interactions. Those with this role worry about quality, not quantity, and measure success in terms of depth of engagement, loyalty, sentiment, social equity, and trust. Their world hinges on emotions and intangibles. They shake hands. They kiss babies. They make people feel good. It's what they do. They are believers and advocates. Their world is intuitive and empathic.

Figure 15.7   Four main categories of roles in the social space.

The fourth category (measurement) deals with numbers—with data, with tables, targets, and measurement. Loyalty for those in this role isn't a feeling, it's a set of metrics. Engagement is expressed in numbers. The nature of ROI is not open to debate. It is what it is, and we just covered what it is.

It is important to realize that these two roles have very different world views: One is *empathetic* whereas the other is *empirical*. One focuses on relationships whereas the other focuses on hard, measurable data. Each is bound to have a completely different perspective of return on investment.

Let's think about what the management group considers the investment to be: people, time, conversations, engagement. In this world, the investment "currency" isn't financial; it is human. The measurement group, on the other hand, sees the investment from a business perspective: People, time, conversations, and engagement are all items on a P&L. Every community manager, every man hour, every unit of bandwidth has a specific cost attached to it. When these folks think of return on investment, they see this:

ROI = (gain from investment – cost of investment) ÷ cost of investment

But bloggers and other adepts of "engagement" first evangelized and adopted the social web, not cost accountants and data analysts.

Let's set a few basic rules when it comes to social media ROI:

- **Rule #1:** ROI is a *business* metric, not a *media* metric. (See Rule #2.)
- **Rule #2:** ROI is 100% media-agnostic.

  The definition of ROI doesn't change from one medium to the next. Whether you are calculating the return on an investment in stocks, in machinery, real estate, or a social media program, ROI is always calculated in the same way:

  ROI = (gain from investment – cost of investment) ÷ cost of investment

- **Rule #3:** The values used in the ROI equation are nonvariable.

  Here's what I mean by that: If your *cost of investment* is calculated in a particular currency, then the *gain from investment* must be calculated in the same currency. Dollars to dollars. Euros to Euros. Pounds to pounds. You cannot calculate ROI if your investment is calculated in dollars and the gain from it in something else.

Tip

ROI is business measurement, not alchemy. Transmutation doesn't live here. If your equation shows a cost value expressed in dollars and a gain value expressed in Twitter followers, you're in the weeds.

Remember that at the core of ROI lives a very specific equation—in other words, *math*. Let me illustrate. Have you ever tried to calculate something that looks like this?

ROI = 30,000 Twitter followers – $10,000) ÷ $10,000 = X

What would be the value of X? Dollars or followers? Exactly. It doesn't work. (Unless you attempt to assign a dollar value to followers, as some people do.)

- **Rule #4:** ROI stands for "return on investment." This is not debatable. ROI does not need to be reinvented, retooled, reframed, or altered in any way. It is a rock-solid, tried-and-true, logical, and dare I say essential, immutable business metric.

  While it may be tempting to reinvent the wheel and want to put a fresh new spin on grandpa's old business measurement acronym, first learn what ROI is. Accept it. Embrace it. Become fluent with it. Apply it to social media as you would any other business endeavor.

 Note

Still not convinced? Ask yourself: What is the unit of measure (the currency, in other words) of inspiration? How about imagination? Innovation? Relationships, even? How will you calculate intangibles? How do they fit into the following equation?

ROI = (gain from investment − cost of investment) ÷ cost of investment

 Tip

Return on investment is always a calculation. If you cannot define an empirical unit of measure for the elements of your equation, you are on the wrong track.

- **Rule #5:** Every resource you assign to a project has a monetary value.

  Typically, these resources fall into one of four categories: personnel, technology, time, and miscellaneous.

  Personnel have salaries or hourly fees and perhaps benefits. They may receive bonuses and other incentives. Your people, in other words, cost money. That money counts toward your investment.

  Technology could be an assortment of elements contributing to your social media program: servers, computers, portable devices, software licenses, monitoring tools, community management dashboards, bandwidth, all the way down to light bulbs and the security locks on your office doors.

  Time can manifest itself as overtime or a percentage of time spent on your program by employees or contractors not necessarily assigned to it full-time (your legal department, for example, or design work by your digital department, or any workload managed by outside agency).

Miscellaneous costs might include travel to and from social media conferences, registration for training programs, webinar attendance, consultant fees, industry reports, Facebook ads, and just about anything you can dream up that doesn't fall into the other three categories.

The point is this: Social media is not free. Everything you put into a social media program has a cost attached to it. The total sum of that cost is the dollar value of your investment in that program. You cannot calculate the ROI of a program if you cannot first wrap your head around your program's cost accounting. Building a social media program isn't as simple as assigning a few interns to hang out on Twitter and report what they see.

- **Rule #6:** ROI can only be calculated *after* the investment has yielded a return. It cannot and must not be *estimated* beforehand. Ever. Under any circumstances.

If an executive asks you to predict the ROI of your program before you have even put it into play, before it has begun to yield results, consider it to be a trick question. You might as well try to predict the weather or the value of a stock in a company three months in advance. Don't do it.

If you have data from previous programs that you want to put forward, go for it and talk about trends and expectations. Fine. If not, focus on what you *want* your outcomes to be. Discuss specific objectives. Narrow them down to targets. Ask "What kind of ROI would you like to see from this program?" Explain how you will get there. Paint a picture that outlines the process, the structure, the drivers, and the reasoning behind the program's momentum. Outline your measurement methodology. Speak to ROI. Be professional, realistic, and responsible. Never be afraid to ask an executive what he has in mind.

Whatever you do, don't get lured into making up numbers just to get your funding. Aside from being unethical and jeopardizing your credibility within the organization, it will doom your program before it even starts. Be smart.

Tying Social Media to the P&L

If we were only addressing the issue of social media measurement, we could simply pick any number of social media–specific metrics—such as the changes in the number of followers or fans, the number of brand mentions during a given period, and sentiment mix—and leave it at that. We could monitor changes in each purely social media metric and report on engagement, conversations, and reach:

- Twenty-three hundred people accessed our website through Facebook.

- Six thousand heard about our latest promotion through Twitter.

- Our latest video was downloaded 25,000 times from YouTube.

What do these numbers really tell us? In terms of ROI, or as performance relates to the P&L, absolutely nothing. Remember, what we are trying to do in this chapter is outline how to tie the company's initial *investment* in its social media program to a *gain* that can be measured in terms of ROI.

In other words, we are trying to show that our social media program supports business objectives and actually helps drive business growth.

As a matter of accounting and business measurement, the number of people following the company's Twitter account or the number of comments on the company blog do not—on their own—impact the P&L. The trick here lies first in understanding that measuring nonfinancial outcomes isn't enough. Financial outcomes are where ROI measurement needs to take place (see Figure 15.8).

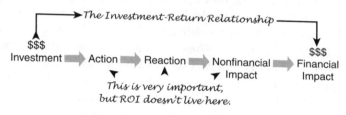

Figure 15.8 The investment-return relationship.

Everything hinges on conversions: The company converts funds to resources. These resources convert their funding into activities on the social web. These activities are converted into interactions between the brand and users of social networks and each other. These interactions are converted into bandwidth. This bandwidth is converted into nonfinancial outcomes: followers, mentions, sentiment, clicks, downloads, recommendations, replies, participation in chats, shares, likes, retweets, and so on. Changes in these nonfinancial outcomes can be interpreted as the manifestation of shifts in familiarity, alignment, preference, and finally purchasing habits. At the end of the line, nonfinancial outcomes are converted into financial outcomes.

Tying a social media program to the P&L is simply a matter of understanding the relationship between each milestone along this conversion path and measuring them properly. "Simply" in theory. In *practice*, though, it's not difficult to measure; it's difficult to prove. The best you can hope for is correlation. In other words, I may understand the relationship between 10,000 net new followers per month on

Twitter, 8,000 net new customers per month, and $2,000,000 in net new sales revenue per month; I may be able to put them side by side on a report, but can I empirically prove that adding 10,000 net new followers on Twitter last month resulted in 8,000 net new customers? No. Likewise, can I empirically prove that these 8,000 net new customers generated $2,000,000 in sales *because* of their involvement with the brand on Twitter? No. (And I should hope not.)

However, I can show that every one of the 8,000 net new customers acquired this month are also Twitter followers, and if I really dig deep, I can also show that the additional $2,000,000 in net sales revenue did in fact originate from these 8,000 customers.

One way to occasionally but accurately test the effectiveness of a social program on the bottom-line is to track sales derived directly from promotional codes and links provided exclusively through social web channels.

Here is how that would work: Say your company has a retail website that allows people to buy your products online. You could publish special discount codes on social media channels of your choice and track them at the point of sale. Say the discount code for Twitter and Facebook is "DiscountXYZ." All you would have to do is capture how many times the discount code was used in an e-transaction, and you would be able to know exactly how much sales revenue you generated from that particular set of updates via your social media program. Another way to do this is to create special landing pages for unique promotions and embed the hyperlink into your Twitter and Facebook promotions. Every time someone makes a purchase from that particular page, you capture that data as well.

With this type of tactic, you can capture not only sales volumes, but a wealth of valuable data as well, from varying degrees of conversions (Tweets to clicks, visits to purchases, and so on) to who among your customers is likely to respond to promotions from you on social web channels. You could also track deltas/changes between response rates at different times of the day and on different days of the week. You could compare responses between products and product categories. (Perhaps your Twitter followers and Facebook fans are more comfortable buying computers online than toothpaste, for example.)

This is all fine and good, but direct promotions most likely won't constitute the bulk of your conversion funnel. This is the easy stuff. These metrics don't require a whole lot of analysis and interpretation. All you have to do is follow the clicks and the discount codes, and the numbers tell the story on their own.

The rest requires a little more analysis and reasoning and deeper insights into what makes your customers tick.

The trick, then, isn't to tie net new revenue to the P&L. It also isn't to tie deltas/changes in frequency, reach, and yield—see Chapter 16, "F.R.Y. (Frequency,

Reach, and Yield) and Social Media"—into that net new revenue figure, although that will help. The trick, the real work, is this: tying nonfinancial outcomes to financial ones (cost reductions and net new revenue).

Tying Nonfinancial Outcomes to Social Media Performance

Let's first consider where you stand today in terms of business measurement and the role media "value" plays in it.

It's difficult to accurately calculate the ROI of your latest advertising campaign, of your latest PR push, or of your tradeshow expenditures. And by this I don't mean accepting arcane dollar values such as its estimated media value. I mean the *actual* financial impact of an ad in a national publication, of a billboard next to the auditorium, or of a spot during a nationally televised sporting event. The ad, billboard, or TV spot cost $X, and it generated $Y in revenue.

You have an idea. You can track deltas/changes in sales during a time after the launch of the ad, right? If you graph it, it looks a lot like what's shown in Figure 15.9.

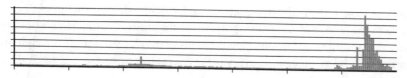

Figure 15.9   Sample graph of changes in sales.

Let's say this graph represents sales volume along a timeline. Obviously, there are two significant events here, represented by spikes in sales volume. The first is small. The second is large.

Now let's add a little bit more information about your business development activity during the same timeframe (see Figure 15.10).

Figure 15.10   Sample graph of changes in sales with activities marked.

You can see correlations between the start of specific activity (in this case, radio spots) and increases in sales volume. You can't empirically prove that the radio spots were the cause of the deltas/changes in sales volume...not yet anyway. You don't have enough information to make a good case for the ad's impact on sales yet. All you have are several pieces of a much larger puzzle. How might you prove that the ad was responsible for the change in transactional behavior? Bear in mind that the same question can be applied to a social media program, campaign, or activity.

In this particular example, a good place to start would be with what you know: The first two tests were in Greenville, South Carolina, and Chicago, Illinois. Nowhere else. What you might want to do is determine what percentage of the sales volume you saw during either spike was concentrated in the Greenville and Chicago markets. If you can show a link between not only the timing of the ads but their impact on the areas they targeted, you might have enough evidence to take your findings to your boss. If, however, these spikes in sales occurred all over the United States and you can find no clear evidence that either the Greenville or the Chicago market was significantly impacted by the ads, then you need to look for another cause. The apparent correlation between the ads and the increase in sales may have been a coincidence. Start digging: What else could have caused the increase in sales if not the ads?

Now let's look at the really big spike on the far right—the one that might be attributable to the launch of the radio spots across the entire country. How would you prove that the ad were responsible for the jump in sales volume? If through no other means, by extinguishing every other alternative cause (see Figure 15.11).

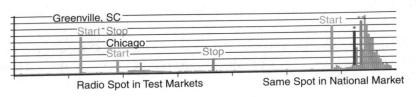

Figure 15.11   Sample graph of changes in sales with spikes marked.

So we start digging, and digging, and digging. And what we find is that other events of note happened while the radio spot was airing across the country. See that blue line with the single asterisk on top? Yes, the one just before the singular little spike in sales volume. Guess what? It was a favorable review of the product aired on a popular national television program. For a week afterward, sales of the product soared and then fell back to pre-review levels. Hmmm. What could that mean? Was that bizarre spike in sales volume merely a quirk in responses to the radio spot, or could it be that the product review produced a short but powerful spike in sales?

Now look at the orange line to its right—the one with two asterisks on top. The event it marks on the calendar is a drop in price for the product, from $199.99 to $149.99. Look at what happens immediately after the price change: another huge spike in sales volume, this one sustained over several weeks.

Now let's look at this timeline again and see what questions we have answered. As it turns out, the radio spots in test markets were proven to have been the main cause of the increase in sales volume. The increase in sales for the markets in which the radio spots were aired accounts for 95% of the volume. From here, we can do our ROI math:

$$ROI = (gain\ from\ radio\ spot - cost\ of\ radio\ spot) \div cost\ of\ radio\ spot$$

Now, let's look at the far right of the graph. We have identified three possible causes for the increase in sales volume. I think it's safe to say that the radio spot on its own cannot be proven to have caused the entire change in sales volume. The positive review and the drop in unit price also contributed to the overall spike in sales volume. If you are responsible for the radio campaign, how, then, can you measure the ROI of your spot once it airs in the national market?

The joke here would be, "very carefully."

The truth is that you probably cannot calculate it precisely. With a combination of factors, you may be better off batching the cost of all three events (as applicable) and letting the accountants figure it out. Another way to look at it would be to measure how sales were trending between the start of the national campaign and the first interruption (the positive review) and then model those numbers against the previous market tests to get an idea for where sales seemed to be going before the interruptions. That would at least give you a baseline to work from. It is not exactly a precise measurement, but rather a reasonable estimation based on solid performance data obtained in test markets. You could then lay that data over your actual sales volume data and extract sales volume in excess of what your model projects. This would give you the best possible approximation of what impact your ad, on its own, had on sales volume. The degree to which you will have to approximate depends on the quality of your data. The more precise the data, the more precise the measurement.

The next step would be to look at the difference between your model and total sales volume for the period that seems to have been influenced by the positive review (a three-to-four-day spike in sales) and attribute what you have left to the review. If it was the result of a PR push, share your numbers with the members of the PR team and let them know they have their own ROI report to present.

Next, do the same thing with the unit price change: Subtract your model's numbers from the total sales volume for that time period and share that data with the members of the product management team. Let them know that their decision to drop the price point of the product may be responsible for X% of the company's sales volume, starting from the moment the price drop was announced. They will also have their own report to put together. Because the process of determining ROI is media-agnostic, every step of this process can be applied to social media activity.

Here are the two points you should get out of this exercise:

- **Connecting the dots between your company's activities, nonfinancial impact, and financial outcomes often amounts to detective work—** You can't just piece sales and circumstantial data together and paint a convenient picture. You have to both prove and attempt to disprove cause-and-effect and correlation. It isn't as easy as plugging a bunch of numbers and metrics into an ROI calculator or bogus equation. It takes hard work. Diligence. It takes smarts. You have to be as thorough as a research scientist. Most of the time, the best you can hope for is a pre-ponderance of evidence that supports your theory, combined with the absence of data to disprove it. Interpretation and reasoning go a long way.

- **Ethics matter—**Looking for easy answers, not backing up your analysis with thorough research and an exhaustive hunt for other possible causes to an effect are ill-advised.

In our example, how would the overall business have been impacted had the project manager tasked with analyzing ROI for his radio ad campaign chosen to ignore other possible reasons behind the increase in sales volume? How might the value of the PR and product management team's activities been viewed by the C-Suite had a faulty ROI analysis praising the radio campaign been received as anecdotal fact? How might budgets and resources been assigned in the next performance period?

Don't cut corners. Don't go for the easy win. And share your success with those who played a part in it.

Though our radio example illustrates how easily business measurement can be applied to activity across a breadth of media, the advantage that social media has over traditional channels in terms of measurement is that the social web offers both a wealth and velocity of data that simply don't exist with traditional media.

So how does this process actually work for social media? Let's take a look at it one step at a time.

Step 1: Establish a Baseline

This could be for the start of a program, the start of a campaign, or the start of a measurement period. This baseline will apply to every bit of data you plan on measuring—from sales volume and net transactions to the number of times your brand name is uttered on the Web. Everything you will be measuring must begin with its own baseline. What you are essentially creating is a trending model for where you have been lately (see Figure 15.12). You were trending at 8% YoY growth? Great. That's your baseline. Your company name only gets mentioned three times per day across the Internet? That's your baseline for that.

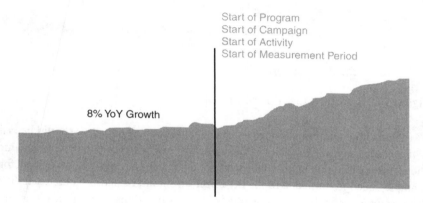

Figure 15.12   Step 1: Establish a baseline.

Step 2: Create Activity Timelines

This can be a group exercise. In the best of worlds, the social media program manager shouldn't have to keep track of what PR is doing on any given day or what the marketing department is doing with the 17 advertising agencies it works with across three continents. Things can get pretty complicated pretty fast. The point is that however you do it, whatever way works best for you, find a way to create a thorough set of activity timelines that plots everything the company does and is involved with that might impact your program's impact on nonfinancial outcomes (see Figure 15.13).

We saw in our radio campaign example how the timing of both the positive review on the popular TV show and the change in product price interfered with the campaign's results. Had these two events been plotted on an activity timeline accessible by the radio campaign manager, he could have identified them right away as likely culprits. Getting in the habit of creating and maintaining activity timelines helps everyone in the entire organization get a better view of how their efforts might overlap, helps speed up analysis, and can help prevent errors caused by false assumptions.

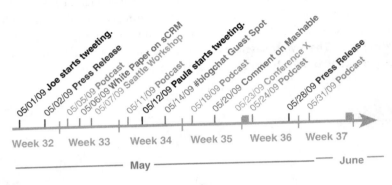

Figure 15.13   Step 2: Create activity timelines.

Two quick little additional notes: First, although every department should be tasked with maintaining its own piece of the activity timeline (or calendar), the timeline should reside in a public hub (a SharePoint Server might not be a bad option, for example). Second, someone in the organization should be acting as the custodian of this resource, preferably someone involved with operations, communications, or project management.

Step 3: Monitor the Volume of Mentions

This is not something you can do with traditional media, so this piece of the puzzle deserves its own step. Chances are, as we discussed in Part III, "Social Media Program Management," you are already monitoring conversations. All you need to do here is measure certain aspects of them (see Figure 15.14).

First things first: Measure the volume of mentions around your company or brand. That essentially means measuring how many times your company's name is mentioned across the Web. Most monitoring tools nowadays will give you a detailed breakdown of mention volume by channel, which is to say that you can see where—from blogs to news sites to social networks—your name seems to come up the most (or not at all). Analyzing changes not only in the overall volume of mentions but also from channel to channel over time can help.

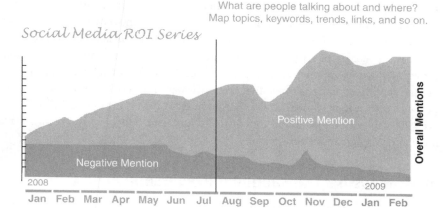

Figure 15.14 Step 3: Monitor volume of mentions.

Second, measure the mix of sentiment from these mentions: How many times was your company mentioned in a positive context last month? How many times was the context of the mention negative? You are hopefully already gathering information on what people like and don't like and addressing those insights appropriately. Measurement allows you to gauge whether the changes you have made are having the desired effect or not.

Typically, the greater the ratio of positive sentiment to negative sentiment (far more positive than negative mentions) means people want to do business with you. In the opposite case, people might think twice before doing business with you again. In terms of tying nonfinancial data to financial outcomes, it's easy to see that an increase in positive sentiment could be an indicator of a shift in preference for your brand or product and—due to the word-of-mouth value of increased positive mentions across social networks—a business driver as well. In other words, watch deltas/changes in mentions and sentiment carefully because they may be the closest thing you have to a crystal ball in the social web.

Automated sentiment analysis isn't very reliable. Some monitoring tools tout that they are powered by solid automated sentiment algorithms, but in my experience, the reliability of these sentiment engines is sometimes overstated. A good rule of thumb is to double-check their reliability by letting human beings decide whether mentions are positive or negative.

I can hear the groans already. But if you don't go through sentiment analysis data manually, you run the risk of it not being any good. You know how most polls tell you that they are within a 3% margin of error? That's a good standard to keep in mind. A 3% margin of error in sentiment analysis isn't too bad. Put whatever monitoring tool you use to the test for a few months. If after your trial period, your human sentiment analysts prove that the tool's margin of error is 3% or less, you're in the clear. If it looks more like the margin of error hovers around 25%, 40%, or even 70%, then either get a new tool or make sure your budget accounts for a sentiment analysis person on your team.

Step 4: Measure Transactional Precursors

That is to say, measure *pretransactional* metrics (also known as nonfinancial metrics). For a complete list, see Chapter 14, "Creating a Measurement Practice for Social Media Programs." They are basically all of the nonfinancial outcomes that may indicate changes in behavior triggered by your activities (see Figure 15.15).

Figure 15.15   Step 4: Measure transactional precursors.

Mentions and sentiment actually fall into this category, but I like to give them their own step. Everything else falls here: web analytics, fans and followers, shares, likes, recommendations, requests for catalogs, RSS subscriptions, content downloads, email signups, registrations for contests, and so on.

Figures 15.16 and 15.17 show some examples.

Figure 15.16   Graph of store traffic.

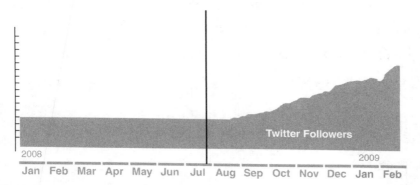

Figure 15.17   Graph of Twitter followers.

Step 5: Look at Transactional Data

This means sales volume. If you can measure it, it also means changes in the number of net transacting customers. You might also want to look at the net number of transactions/receipts.

Why that last one? Sometimes you will find that although the total sales volume has increased by X%, the net number of transactions has increased by Y%. What the difference might indicate is a shift in yield (the average dollar amount of transactions). This type of discrepancy between total sales volume and the number of net transactions could signal (if the percentage of change in net transactions is significantly greater than the percentage change in sales volume) that new customers have begun buying small items from you. If the relationship is reversed (the percentage of change in the sales volume is greater than the percentage of change in net number of transactions), what you may be looking at is an increase in yield for existing customers. In other words, your loyal customers are suddenly spending more money per transaction than before.

We measured nonfinancial metrics in steps 3 and 4. In this step, we measure transactional and financial data (see Figure 15.18).

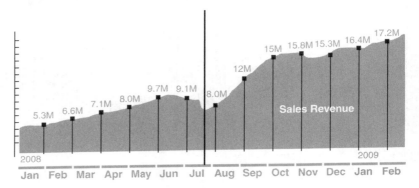

Figure 15.18   Step 5: Look at transactional data.

Figures 15.19 and 15.20 show some examples.

Now comes the fun part.

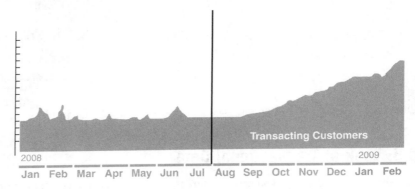

Figure 15.19   Example of transacting customers.

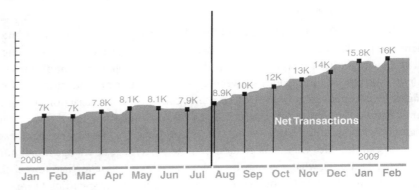

Figure 15.20   Example of net transactions.

Step 6: Overlay All Your Data (Steps 1–5) onto a Single Timeline

This includes your baselines, all your activities, your social data, web data, loyalty metrics, all nontransactional data, all of your transactional and financial outcome data, and whatever else seems relevant—such as your competitors' product releases or important events that might interrupt or impact your activities. This could be anything from hurricanes, earthquakes, and outbreaks of bird flu, to the introduction of new technologies.

What you essentially want to do in this step is line everything up along a common timeline to establish a chronological sequence of events between all of these elements (see Figure 15.21).

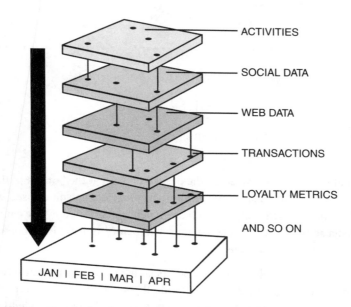

ACTIVITIES

SOCIAL DATA

WEB DATA

TRANSACTIONS

LOYALTY METRICS

AND SO ON

JAN I FEB I MAR I APR

Figure 15.21   Step 6: Overlay your data onto a timeline.

Step 7: Look for Patterns

Now that everything is lined up in chronological order, look for patterns. You are not yet looking to establish correlations or cause-and-effect—only patterns (see Figure 15.22).

This example shows three distinct types of patterns you can expect to encounter at this stage of the analysis. The first is illustrated by the data set at the top of the graph showing a steady increase of activity even before the start of the social media program. As you can see, the impact of the social media program on this data set is difficult to determine. It appears to be trending at about the same rate of growth since the start of the program or measuring period. We will leave that metric alone for now, as there isn't much we can infer from it.

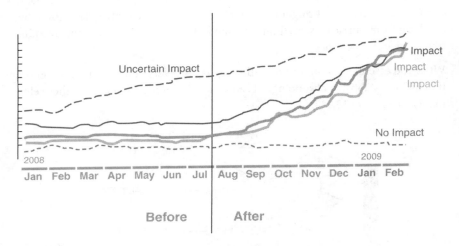

Figure 15.22   Step 7: Look for patterns.

The second pattern is illustrated by the dashed data set at the bottom of the graph, and indicates a lack of effect from social media program. As you can see, whatever metric this line represents appears to be completely unaffected by the company's social media activities. It was seeing flat growth before and still is. (Hopefully, this line does not represent revenue.)

At some point in the analysis process, the social media program team should look into reasons why this particular metric (and others like it) were not impacted by the social media program. This type of disconnect could yield valuable insights into hurdles standing between activity along social media channels and activity outside of these channels.

For example, what if this line indicated brick-and-mortar sales of a particular product, yet by all accounts, the social media program indicated a significant increase in foot traffic to brick-and-mortar retail locations? This would suggest that the social media program was successful in bringing customers to retail stores, but something happened inside the stores that interrupted the conversion process. Perhaps the product was not available, or the price was not what customers expected it to be, or the packaging turned customers off from the product. Perhaps long lines at the cash register or unpleasant customer service turned customers away.

From a more generic perspective, this type of disconnect could also be illustrated by an increase in Twitter followers, Facebook "likes," and other social media metrics without a corresponding increase in sales. This tells you that the social media program, assuming that it had an ROI objective, is falling short when it comes to converting engagement into actual business.

A flat line always constitutes a red flag. Investigate every instance in which a relevant business metric is not impacted by a social media program. Learn why your program had no impact there. You will probably uncover a crucial bit of insight that could make a significant difference in your business performance in the coming months and could help make your program more effective.

The third pattern, one that seems to illustrate some kind of impact from the social media activity, is illustrated by the three data sets at the center of the graph. What we see here is that an increase in activity occurred shortly after the start of the program or measurement period. At first glance, there *appears* to be a connection between the start of the company's activities and whatever these lines represent. This is the type of pattern we are looking for.

Step 8: Prove and Disprove Relationships

Now that you have identified patterns of change (deltas), it's time to prove (as much as you can) that your activities are responsible for these changes and, if so, to what degree (see Figure 15.23).

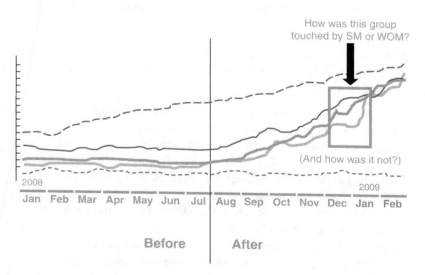

Figure 15.23   Step 8: Prove and disprove relationships.

Use the process we used in our radio campaign example earlier to look for every possible trigger for a change in behavior. Let's start at the end and work our way back:

1. Connect the metrics that fall into the "possible impact" category to your social media activity for the same time period. How are they connected? Can you show a correlation, for example, between a Facebook campaign that helped introduce a new product, a subsequent increase in volume of conversations relating to the product, a matching proportion of visits to product pages and microsites, and an increase in sales for that product? Connect the dots. Use your timeline. Bring together the metrics and activities that seem to be connected to one another. Work your way backward from the transaction data.

2. When you think you can reasonably begin to connect the dots and link outcomes back to specific activities, when your conversion narrative begins to emerge from the fog of analysis, play devil's advocate and seek to disprove your work. Look for inconvenient triggers—those that may have contributed to the increases you want to assign to your social media activity but actually exist outside of your program. This could be a positive review of the product by *The New York Times*, or a price drop, or a special sales promotion. One of your competitor's competing products might have just suffered a setback, propping yours up as the best alternative for a few weeks. Leave no stone unturned. Find a way to invalidate your theory that social media was responsible for the increase in business.

Don't assign credit for a business win to your social media program if it isn't deserved. The point here is to prove your program's value without a shadow of a doubt.

Better yet, ask someone else to do this for you—someone with a neutral perspective and a good understanding of social business, who can conduct a social media program or campaign audit. Let this person do his part and then meet to discuss each other's findings once he is done. See what he has turned up and, together, weigh all the options. If it turns out that your social media program was only partially responsible for a business success, define that part. Quantify it. Find common ground. Together, make sense of the data and do your best to establish a proper conversion narrative that focuses on what activities seem to be triggering deltas/changes (or not) as well as begins and ends with hard financial data: from *investment* to *gain* to *return*, by way of social media activity in these particular areas.

We revisit some of these diagrams and concepts at the end of Chapter 17, "Social Media Analysis and Reporting," so don't worry if you don't grasp it all right away.

Calculating the ROI of a social media program can be a complex process, but it is generally a straightforward one. First, a social media program management team must acknowledge that only financial outcomes are relevant to an ROI calculation. Nonfinancial outcomes like number of followers, web visitors, or share of conversation do not apply. Second, financial outcomes and costs associated with the program or an activity must be combined through the ROI equation to calculate its actual return on investment. Third, the relationship between budgets and activities, then activities and outcomes, and finally nonfinancial outcomes and financial outcomes must be established and mapped out first through a process of analysis and then a process of elimination. This third element of the process is crucial in understanding the mechanics by which the program actually yielded results and the extent to which it did, but it also serves to validate (or invalidate) the social media activity's role in the business outcome.

The types of insights a management team can draw from this kind of exercise range from determining a program's exact financial value to an organization to understanding what aspects of the program work and which ones do not. As a bonus, thoroughly analyzing the connection (and occasionally the lack of connection) between activities and outcomes can help a social media program's management team determine precisely what elements of the program are working and which ones are missing the mark. ROI thus finds its value not only as a business measurement equation and program validation tool, but also as a diagnostic tool within the program itself. The more comfortable you become with the process of calculating the ROI of social media activity, the better equipped you will be to build a solid social media program for your organization.

16

F.R.Y. (Frequency, Reach, and Yield) and Social Media

For years, I searched in vain for a way to add a little more sophistication to the "Do this, and you'll sell more stuff" conversation. I already knew, both instinctively and from experience, that good products combined with good marketing and customer-focused business practices drove business forward. I just hadn't found a formula to help frame the mechanism by which this worked. Whenever I met with a roomful of executives, the Sales VPs in the room weren't buying into the argument that the revenue their departments generated was merely the outcome of good design and friendly customer service. "I agree with everything you said in there," one of them told me after a meeting once, "but my people aren't just order-takers."

He was right.

He and I talked some more, and I asked him how he rewarded his teams of sales-people. He explained that they were assigned goals and targets, and that each target came with its own reward. On the low end of the scale, they got to keep their jobs. On the high end, they made increasingly large bonuses. Having spent some time in sales myself, I understood this. But still, as we talked about various strategies to drive sales and how other departments (such as Marketing) played a part in the process, I ran into the same no-man's land of *selling more stuff*. It was frustrating.

The Importance of Finding the Right Words in the Language of Business

For the most part, although both aim to drive business, Sales departments and Marketing departments don't really work together all that well. Their strategies and metrics are completely different, as are their world views. Until I figured out the solution, I could talk to a roomful of marketing professionals and be heard. I could also talk to a roomful of sales professionals and be heard. But with both in a room, things became a little more complicated. What I said either resonated with one group or the other, but rarely both. Something was missing.

"There's no secret to it," the Sales VP told me. "It's a numbers game. My people know how it works: You want to sell more? Just talk to more people. Pick up that phonebook and dial all day long. Go knock on more doors. That's how it works."

That wasn't the answer I was after. As right as he may be, this was the sales end of the "outcome" spectrum, which almost invalidated what I knew about brand man-agement: that a good product pretty much sells itself.

I don't know about you, but I have never received a sales call from Apple. Steve Jobs has never sent me a coupon in the mail. But I've seen lines of people wrapped around entire city blocks, in the rain, waiting be the first to get their hands on the company's latest release.

I realized that my search for clarity wasn't going anywhere. I was looking at it the wrong way, bouncing back and forth between world views: the Marketing religion versus the Sales religion. This was dogma. What I was after wouldn't be found there.

And to be honest, I have to admit that I wasn't even sure what I was looking for. I just knew that "sell more stuff" was somehow too vague. Something was missing. Something that would allow me to devise specific strategies and tactics that both Marketing and Sales could get behind together to drive specific outcomes.

It wasn't until 2007 that I finally found what I was looking for, and I stumbled upon it completely by accident. I was working with Microsoft at the time, and my job within the software giant's distribution channel was to help drive business in the SMB (small-to-medium-sized business) space.

The distributor I was working for had a sales-driven culture, and the modus operandi there was once again "just sell more stuff." I was frustrated, and so was Microsoft. So the company came up with a solution.

To this day, I still don't know where F.R.Y. came from. Whether someone at Microsoft came up with it, it came to them through back channels, or it was found in some obscure business book only academics read—I don't know. All I know is that it was what I had been looking for. With its F.R.Y. scheme, Microsoft essentially forced its distribution partners to rethink how they drove business by splitting up "sales" into three separate types of transaction drivers:

- **F** stands for *frequency*, which is another term for "buy rate."

- **R** stands for *reach*, which speaks to the conversion funnel ending in net new customers.

- **Y** stands for *yield*, which is an expression of the "average $ value of a transaction."

Instead of simply pushing out marketing programs and asking salespeople to push harder and harder as each month came to a close, F.R.Y. methodology challenged us to completely change the way we approached business development. What we learned through the process was that sales could be impacted in three very specific ways: You could convince people already buying from you to do so more often, you could convince more people to buy from you, and you could convince people who were already buying from you, without doing business more often, to spend a little more than they already were per transaction.

This was so simple, I marveled that during all my years managing sales and marketing programs, I had never come across it. Yet F.R.Y. was the missing link between Marketing and Sales, between strategy and execution, between business objectives and performance measurement.

What F.R.Y. does is this: It provides a language that Marketing, Customer Service, Business Development, and Sales can all understand. It unites them under a common purpose and creates a new level of *specificity* in regard to their business objectives.

Before F.R.Y., the general idea was that if you wanted to sell more brown shoes, you created a marketing program to promote brown shoes. You made ads showing how cool people looked in brown shoes, how happy they were to be wearing brown shoes, and how beautiful and successful brown shoes made them. You reminded people that brown shoes were very fashionable this season. You gave people great reasons to buy your brown shoes instead of everyone else's brown shoes. You sent people incentives and reminders in the mail. You rented billboards and reached out to influential bloggers and made sure everyone who did a search for keywords such as "shoes" and "brown" on Google got to see an ad pop up that would lead them back to your website, which itself prominently featured brown shoes. Then you crossed your fingers and hoped for the best. Sometimes it worked; sometimes it didn't, and that was that.

F.R.Y. aims to raise the bar by focusing on specific types of consumers and specific purchasing triggers, rather than just awareness, desire, and preference.

Which proposal sounds better to an executive team trying to wrap their minds around the value of a strong, integrated social media program?

> **A.** "You guys need a social media program. It's the greatest thing to hit business since email! Your competitors are starting to use it, so you should, too, or they'll eat your lunch. There are hundreds of millions of people using Facebook, Twitter, and YouTube. What we should do is this: Start communities on all the popular social networks. Start a blog. Start engaging. We'll monitor conversations and boost engagement! It'll be good for business, you'll see."
>
> **B.** "Aside from building positive brand equity on social networks and using them as enhanced communications channels for customer service, business intelligence, PR, marketing, online reputation management, market research, and even sales, why don't we also focus on three basic business drivers that could impact your bottom line: a) increasing frequency of transactions, b) increasing reach (which is to say, acquiring net new transacting customers), c) increasing yield (average spend per transaction)?
>
> "Those are three distinctive ways we can drive revenue, and we can use a social media program to drive all three separately."

I like the second one better, and most executives do as well. Talking about business objectives and framing them clearly always helps. The conversation quickly shifts to strategies and tactics instead of immediately jumping to "So what do people do on Facebook and Twitter again?"

Bring *frequency* into the conversation, and "buy from us" immediately becomes "buy from us *more often*." This isn't just messaging anymore. It isn't just marketing and sales as usual. If you truly want to see customers change their purchasing habits, if you want to have them accelerate their buy rate, then you have to come up with a reason for them to do it. It forces you to take a closer look at your business. It forces you to shift your focus from messaging and outbound marketing to thinking tactically about your business itself: If one of the ways we can get more revenue in the door is to increase our customers' buy rate (shorten the sales cycle, in other words), what can we do to make that happen?

If you are entertaining special promotions, loyalty cards, or frequent-flyer programs, you are on the right track. Now you're *thinking*. You are asking yourself how your business practices can influence consumer behavior through more than just marketing campaigns and a push from your sales department. You are beginning to think not only holistically about how all the pieces of your organization fit together (as opposed to letting them operate as silos), but also tactically. You are starting to understand the process by which an investment in a program or activity results in specific outcomes. You aren't selling anymore; you are triggering specific behaviors.

The same reasoning applies to *reach*. This is the simplest of the three to understand and usually the one that companies are already pursuing. If a thousand transacting customers are good for business, then two thousand are twice as good. This is basic customer acquisition, which is nothing new. Reaching more people means potentially selling more stuff. (I never said any of this was complicated.) What is important to note here is simply this: that *reach* is just one of several strategies in our business development toolkit. Now we also have *frequency* and *yield*: Getting current customers who on average spend, say $20 every time they transact with you to start spending $25 instead.

Let's look at all this in greater detail and see how social media fits into it.

Financial vs. Nonfinancial Aspects of Frequency

When I talk about frequency, I am referring to two very different types of "rates." On the one hand, we have *frequency of transactions*, which is what we just talked about—buy rate, the sales cycle, how often someone transacts with your company. This is their transactional frequency. This could be once per quarter, once per month, once per week, or once per year.

On the other hand, we have *frequency of interactions*, which we come back to later in this section.

Quick question: Do you know who among your transacting customers falls into each of these three categories? In other words, if I asked you to organize all your customers by transactional frequency (which ones do business with you weekly, monthly, quarterly, or annually), could you do it?

If the answer is no, you might want to look into it. Not just because it is difficult to influence buy rate if you don't know who among your customers to target with the right message, but more importantly because if you cannot establish this type of baseline, you will not be able to measure changes in your customers' buy rate. And here is the tragic side of this: In this scenario, even if you were able to influence your customers to increase their buy rate—in other words, even if your *frequency* strategy worked—you would not know it. All you would see is more sales. All you would be able to report is, "We sold more stuff."

Not knowing where those sales came from, what influenced them, and that they came from existing customers you managed to convince to buy from you more often would be tragic. How would you know that the resources you assigned to that specific task were a better investment than other elements of your program? How would you be able to build on its success?

Being able to measure this is crucial. Find a way.

 Tip

If you cannot measure frequency at the point of sale or if your company doesn't use CRM, then poll your customers. Ask them directly.

How does a company convince customers to increase their transactional frequency? Well, it depends on the company. Before we discuss ways of doing this that involve social media, let's look at a few successful ways some companies and entire industries have managed to shorten sales cycles all around us.

Let's start with milk. What do you think the popular "Got Milk?" campaign targets? Frequency, reach, or yield? The answer isn't cut and dry: Like most campaigns, it targets all three.

Let's say you work in the dairy industry, and you are looking to increase sales. How do you "sell more stuff"? In this scenario, you would do it by increasing the rate with which your product is consumed. Here is why: You know that 10 million people in your market drink milk on average two to three times per week. Because you know this, you know their gallon bottle of milk lasts two weeks. If they shop for groceries once per week, they therefore only buy milk every other time they shop. By increasing the rate in which this group consumes milk, you increase the rate with which they run out, and therefore, the rate with which they must replace their empty bottle.

Ironically, *frequency* in this case can also double as *yield* because some households may increase their product volume from a half-gallon per trip to the store to a full gallon, or even from one gallon to two gallons because they find themselves drinking so much more milk per week.

This is the basic frequency element of the "Got Milk?" campaign: You didn't just "sell more stuff" through some arcane combination of marketing, media buying, and sales. You sold more stuff specifically by convincing a portion of existing customers to consume more of your product, forcing them to buy it more often.

The same principles can work for most industries, but there are exceptions. A monthly or weekly service charged at fixed intervals, for example, doesn't have the ability to increase frequency. It has to rely on reach and yield. But far be it from me to suggest that no business model can come up with a way to bring about a successful frequency strategy. Let me tell you why.

The very day I signed on to write this book, I was in New York, speaking at a conference. During my presentation, I offered spray versus stick deodorants as an example of a category that included products both subject to a *reach* strategy and immune to it. My argument was this: Spray deodorants could be marketed as "full body sprays." Therefore, consumers could be convinced to spray more than just their armpits with the stuff every morning, and thus use more of it per application. Moreover, because the sprays were now treated as a fragrance, these same consumers might start using them more often throughout the day. The result: Cans of spray deodorant would run out faster, forcing consumers to buy new ones more often. The same could not be done with deodorant sticks. In other words, spray deodorants offered a certain elasticity of frequency while the purchasing frequency of deodorant sticks was inelastic.

I was wrong.

After my presentation, a clever young man walked up to me, introduced himself, and with a grin stretching from ear to ear, proceeded to tell me why my argument didn't add up. He quickly reminded me of what happens when a deodorant sticks reaches the end of its life cycle: The deodorant itself runs out. What's left is the plastic piece its base was attached to. He raised his right arm, brought an imaginary stick of deodorant to his armpit, and mimed the gesture. "My deodorant stick just died. You know what I'm doing right now?"

I smiled with him. "Scraping your armpit with plastic?"

"Exactly," he replied. "I'm scraping my armpit with plastic." He brought his arms back down and grinned. "Why do we do that?"

"Because the deodorant runs out," I answered.

"Why do we wait until it runs out, and then scrape our armpits with plastic for three or four days after that?"

I wasn't sure. It did seem pretty absurd, putting it like that. "Because...we aren't going to make a special trip to the store just for deodorant?"

He beamed with excitement. "Exactly! Because we wait until the deodorant has run out to think about buying a new stick, and then we scrape our armpits with plastic until it's time to go to the store again. We don't think about doing it *before* it runs out." He marked a pause. "Now, what would happen if a deodorant company created a campaign aimed at stopping us from scraping our armpits with plastic?"

The entire campaign flashed in front of me and I laughed. "That would be pretty funny. It's clever." And then I got it. He was right. His idea was genius.

Here is how this type of campaign affects frequency: Let's say that a typical consumer buys a stick of deodorant once per month. That's a frequency of 12 purchases per year, or a sales cycle of 30 days, depending on how you want to look at it. Now imagine that your deodorant company green-lights the "Don't Scrape Your Armpits with Plastic" campaign, and amplifies it by leveraging your social media program. Let's also say that the company decides to insert a small tab at the top of the piece of plastic beneath the deodorant that can be clearly seen when the deodorant stick is about a week away from being spent, and that this tab simply says "replace me." What would be the impact on consumer behavior? That's right: A good chunk would stop scraping their armpits with plastic. They would buy their next stick of deodorant days *before* it ran out instead of days *after* it ran out.

Let's say the impact of this were three days. That's it: just three days. Consumers would go from buying their deodorant every 30 days to every 27 days. Not a big deal, right? Except it is: Three days per month multiplied by 12 months ads up to 36 days. Over the course of a year—*a fiscal year*, that is—the company would see a shift in its frequency of transactions for that group from 12 annual purchases to 13 annual purchases. Without acquiring any new customers, without convincing anyone to buy other products from that brand, without even increasing market share, a company with this type of model could with one swift stroke increase net annual sales by almost 10%. This is the power of an effective frequency strategy, and these types of wins don't happen by accident. They are deliberately engineered.

Aside from illustrating how important incorporating frequency strategies are to a business, the story also serves the purpose of reminding us all that even product categories and industries that may consider themselves immune to frequency strategies can find ways to apply frequency strategies to their revenue model. Blending frequency and social media comes down to simply looking at frequency as a means to achieve a business objective: Can I use social media to influence my customers to buy from me more often? Can I, through my interactions with them on social networks, make them want to use my product faster? Can I, through the right mix of exposure and repetition, convince them to want to use more often?

This isn't social media strategy. It is business strategy amplified by a fully integrated social media component. The real strategy has one focus and one focus only: Shorten the sales cycle. As clever as your social media team may be, remember that social media in and of itself will not improve your business or fix your problems. In order to get the most out of your social media investment, the program always needs to be driven by specific objectives. Without clear objectives and a thorough understanding of how to influence customer behaviors, social media alone cannot help your business move forward.

Earlier in the chapter, we mentioned that frequency could refer to transactions or interactions. As we just saw, the former refers to the frequency with which a customer purchases something from a company, whereas the latter refers to the frequency with which a customer interacts with a company. Let's turn our attention to the latter before moving on because it is important to our social media program's impact on customer behavior.

The question of frequency of interactions can be summed up as follows: All things remaining equal, without a clever slogan or campaign to trigger a change, can you influence Jane to transact with you more often by simply interacting with her more often?

I don't intend to answer the question for you. I am merely suggesting that you ask yourself that question and go find out. Here's how to do it: First, try to determine how many interactions, on average, it takes for you to remind someone to transact with you. If you have not been using social media yet, look at your channels of interaction now: outbound call centers, email, print advertising, TV, radio, mailers, POP, and so on. If you don't know, ask your advertising agency and your marketing managers. They should know this. If they don't, ask them to find out.

You can look at this data in one of two ways:

- Groups of customers who transact with you after x amount of interactions.

- Groups of customers whose buy rates are weekly, monthly, and so on. (You'll need to determine how many interactions you have with them on average during these time periods.)

Either of these groups can become your test group. Go with what feels more comfortable. The question you want to answer is this: Assuming my interactions are positive, will more frequent interactions shorten the sales cycle? Imagine that you are a chain of coffee shops and that some of your customers drop by two to three times per week for a coffee drink. You would like for them to increase their frequency of transaction from every two days to every day. Without changing anything about the way you do business with them, without coming up with promotions or incentives, would saying hello to them on Twitter or Facebook or leaving comments on their blogs more often trigger in them a desire to do business with you on days when the thought didn't occur to them on its own?

Simply by being in the periphery of their consciousness more than you already are, could you influence their habits? If the answer is yes, could you determine how many more interactions in the same time period might trigger an additional transaction? The answer is yes. I have seen some companies turn this type of experimentation into a science. For certain groups of customers, they can tell you precisely that three interactions in a week result in one transaction, and five interactions in a week will result in two.

Posting relevant content across social networks is a catalyst for such interactions. In the case of the coffee shop, what would be the impact of such content popping up on its customers' social media channels of choice several times per day? What if its community manager also interacted with its network on a daily basis? Increasing the frequency of interactions between your company and your customers is simply this: increasing your bandwidth and increasing mind-share.

The alternative (not seeking an increase in interactions by ignoring social media channels) means less opportunities to remind customers that they *like* coffee, that they *crave* coffee, and that their favorite coffee shop is just a few minutes down the road roasting a new batch of beans right now.

We have already discussed in earlier chapters how the social web allows companies to simultaneously scale and deepen their reach. Frequency can help drive both. If every interaction is a catalyst for memory, for need, for desire, for validation of preference, even, then it isn't a stretch to assume that more interactions, that is to say more *frequent* interactions—assuming they are positive—will have some degree of impact on purchasing behaviors.

In terms of the mechanism behind frequency of transactions, think of it this way: If frequency of transactions is the desired outcome, frequency of interactions can be one of its principal drivers. Having a well-designed and managed social media program can facilitate this process. A measurement practice that encompasses the link between frequency of interactions and frequency of transactions can be invaluable to an organization. This combination of metrics is one that you should absolutely focus on.

Financial vs. Nonfinancial Aspects of Reach

The second element of the F.R.Y. methodology is *reach*, and it, too, can be divided into financial and nonfinancial aspects.

Of the three elements of F.R.Y., *reach* is the most obvious and the most commonly pursued. Still, it's worth mentioning that *reach*, as it applies to nonfinancial outcomes is simply how many people you can touch. How many people might, at some point, see one of your ads, see your product on the street, or participate in a discussion about it within a social setting. This is the traditional and nonfinancial side of reach—the one measured in impressions and touches and a variety of other media-based measurements.

Reach, as it applies to ROI and financial outcomes, is simply the ratio of net *transacting* customers to noncustomers who have been touched either by your marketing or word-of-mouth. Effective reach is characterized by a 100% conversion rate. In other words, 100% of the people who come into contact with your brand become regular transacting customers. Because a 100% conversion rate is rare, reach can always be improved. There are always new customers to acquire. Even if your business is already at capacity with no want to grow, it doesn't mean it couldn't do more business with more net transacting customers if it wanted to.

Note that I didn't say "net customers." I placed an emphasis on net *transacting* customers. There is a difference between the two: Many companies count *nontransacting customers* as customers. That is a dangerous practice. If someone used to be a customer but hasn't done business with you in a while, guess what? He isn't a customer anymore. He is an ex-customer. Just because he is in your database and mailing list doesn't mean he is *transacting* with you. The first order of business when it comes to reach, if you keep a list of people who have at some point in their lives transacted with you, is to split up that list into categories, the two overarching ones being transacting customers and nontransacting customers. The rule of thumb is if your transacting customers typically transact from you once per month, anyone who hasn't transacted with you in three times that amount of time is no longer a transacting customer. She has fallen off and now belongs in the "nontransacting customer" column.

How you organize your transacting customer column is up to you. Some organizations look primarily at total dollar amount. In other words, customer hierarchy is defined by the amount of money customers spend with them. Others also look at transactional frequency, where customers are organized into categories based on how often they transact: every day, every week, once a month, or once per quarter. There is no wrong way to do it. If you can create a variety of models with which to batch your customers, the benefit is clear: You can identify which customers might be more susceptible to frequency and yield campaigns.

Once you have separated your customer database into these two macro columns, count how many *transacting* customers you have. You may have thought that you had 15,000 customers because that is what your database and mailing list told you. As it turns out, you may only have 6,534 transacting customers. The rest are just names on a list. This can be quite a shock to an organization, so be ready if you haven't done this in a few years.

That number, the sum of *transacting* customers, is your benchmark moving forward. The object of your reach strategy as it pertains to ROI, because it aims to drive net new revenue for the company through your social media program, is to grow that number. All things remaining the same, for every net new transacting customer you acquire and add to that first column, your net revenue will go up.

This is where I normally start talking about acquisition costs, beginning with a simple question: Do you know your cost of acquiring every next customer? Why is this important? How much you are spending to acquire every single customer gives you some notion of how effective (or ineffective) your current reach strategy is. That is to say, how effective are you at converting what your ad agency, public relations firm, and other marketing advisors would call "impressions" into actual business?

Let me illustrate: Say you are currently spending $300,000 per month on marketing programs and campaigns aimed at increasing your number of net new customers. Between the billboards, the print ads, the radio spots, the TV commercials, the coupons, the emails, and the point of purchase displays, your marketing department estimates that you are reaching 1,000,000 people per month. In terms of straight media reach, that's a bargain. It is only costing you three cents per person you touch. In terms of impressions, that could be less than one cent per person. Outstanding, right?

Not necessarily.

Out of those 1,000,000 people your message has reached, how many were already loyal transacting customers? Remove them from that 1,000,000 and adjust your costs accordingly. They can't be net *new* transacting customers: They're already in the "transacting customer" column. Now look at how many net new transacting customers you are actually gaining every month. 100? 1,000? Whatever that number is, compare it to that adjusted 1,000,000 number. That gives you your conversion rate.

Let's give our example some life:

- How many potential net new customers reached: 1,000,000 − 6,534 = 993,466.
- The entire campaign costs $300,000 per month.
- The cost of reaching each potential customer is about three cents.
- Let's say that the campaign generates 300 net new customers per month.
- Let's also say that the average total amount of transactions per customer per month is $500.

Here's what we end up with:

- The campaign's conversion rate is less than 1%.
- In spite of the cost of reaching potential customers or other metrics such as CPI (cost per impression), the true cost of acquiring a customer is $1,000. This is a far cry from the *pennies on the dollar* figure the marketing department originally claimed.

There is a lesson in this: Knowing the difference between relevant and irrelevant metrics will help you see the true strengths and weaknesses of a program.

The actual cost of acquiring a customer is far more important to your business and to your measurement practice than other media metrics that measure impressions and estimated values of media reach. If you don't already know, find out what every net new customer actually costs to acquire. This will help put CPI and other agency metrics in perspective before signing off on budgets and hoping for the best.

Now, let me put your mind at ease: At first glance, it would seem that $1,000 to acquire each customer seems high, given that he will only spend $500 per month. Well, not really. Assuming he won't bolt after his first transaction, you will recover your investment quickly: $1,000 per net new transacting customer could yield $6,000 in net new revenue per year. In terms of net ROI, that's $5,000 per customer just for the first year, with no new acquisition costs in years 2, 3, and beyond. (More reason to hold on to customers once you've acquired them.)

Now that we have been through this little exercise, let's look at the example again: 2,993,466 people reached every month, and only 300 net new transacting customers. That's only 300 conversions out of almost 1,000,000 people. I couldn't sleep at night if my campaign or program, even while producing a net financial gain (and therefore positive ROI) were that lousy. The question that would keep me up at night would be this: How do we either reduce the cost of each acquisition or increase the conversion rate? Could social media help? The answer is, of course, yes. Consider the following:

- **How social media can help lower the cost of customer acquisitions—** In terms of reach and scale, social media channels can be considerably cheaper than traditional media channels. Although an impression, in our example, may only cost about one cent, amplifying our company's presence by being active on digital social networks could, by increasing its exposure, reduce that cost exponentially.

  Compare the cost of an impression via TV to the same via radio. Compare print and billboards. Compare CPI by channel and medium. Now consider the cost of reaching 1,000,000 on Facebook or YouTube, not through ads but through mere presence and participation. If you aren't in the mood to do the math just now, fine, just visualize it.

  Now add another element to the mix: Traditional media channels are mostly vertical. The scale of the channel is limited to the breadth of its distribution. Social channels (digital and not) are both vertical and lateral. This means that every individual you reach in a social media channel isn't a dead end. Instead, each person you touch via social media can, if she wants, redistribute your content, your ad, your message to her own network of peers and friends. Although you may only aim to reach 60,000 fans and followers with one bit of content, you may end up reaching 200,000 through their ability to bookmark, share, retweet, or otherwise rebroadcast your message laterally. You can see how this mechanism can have a considerable impact on your overall *cost per impression* (and by default *cost per acquisition*) equation. Social media activity, through a well-designed and managed program, can allow you to multiply your reach by both volume and frequency, while reducing your overall CPI.

- **How social media can help increase conversion rates**—Consider the nature of social media. On the one hand, it is completely opt-in. Users of Facebook, Twitter, YouTube, and other networks choose what accounts to follow and interact with. If I like Ford, I follow Ford on Twitter and "like" its accounts on Facebook. I opt into its feed. From the get-go, in terms of effectiveness of reach, I am not a random potential customer. I am a potential customer who has expressed an interest in that brand and what it has to say. In other words, I have demonstrated a propensity to be influenced by that brand. On the other hand, much of what people see, read, and hear from brands on social networks doesn't just come directly from the company at all. A fair amount of it reaches them by way of their peers and friends—laterally rather than vertically. Ask yourself what has a better chance of having an impact on a shopper's preference and purchasing habits: a commercial message from a company or a commercial message from a company recommended by two or three trusted friends?

In the first item of the preceding list, we talked about efficiency in terms of breadth: reaching more people more easily. The second item addresses the flip side of that coin: depth. That is to say, the degree to which the message or value of a brand or product will influence the person interacting with it.

In truth, many of the forces at work with reach overlap each other. Increasing reach increases both volume and frequency. Messages that may have reached an individual directly from a company are reinforced and validated every time one of her peers rebroadcasts it. Social media channels are simultaneously echo and amplification chambers. Repetition within online communities results in both scale *and* validation. The effect of outbound reach through both vertical and lateral forces has a compounding effect on attention, bandwidth, preference, and ultimately behavior.

Within the world of F.R.Y., the relationship between financial and nonfinancial aspects of reach can be expressed by a simple conversion ratio: Out of x people "reached," how many have we converted to *transacting* customers? Seen from the perspective of the social media program as a whole, the question becomes, "How can you tie your social media activities to net new followers and fans and then attach these numbers to net *new* transacting customers?"

The Financial Value of Yield

Now we come to *yield*, which essentially deals with getting customers to spend more money per transaction. Look at yield this way: If you could not acquire any new customers (everyone in the world already buys from you), and there is no way for you to increase their frequency of transactions (customers have no way of transacting with you more often), then how would you generate new revenue? Simple: By changing *what*, or rather *how much*, your customers are buying from you each time they make a purchase. It is for this reason that of the three F.R.Y. metrics, yield is by far the most difficult to influence.

Let me give you two examples:

1. A TV cable company has three service offerings: Basic service, Premium service, and an "All Access" plan. In addition, it offers hundreds of pay-per-view selections involving movies, sports, and concerts. Increasing yield would look like this:

   - Converting a Basic plan customer to Premium plan.

   - Converting a Premium plan customer to the "All Access" plan.

   - Incentivizing a customer who normally purchases $2.99 pay-per-view programs to try purchasing $4.99 programs.

2. A restaurant notices that 25 out of its 40 Saturday evening regulars never buy dessert with their meal. Their average bill, excluding tip, usually ranges from $50 to $54. Adding a $10 dessert to their bill every Saturday would bring their bill to $60. Twenty-five customers × $10 amounts to $250 in net new revenue every Saturday if the restaurant operator can change their behavior. This, multiplied by 54 Saturdays, adds up to over $13,000 in net new revenue for the restaurant per year, just by increasing the yield of 25 customers' weekly transactions. The same thing could be done with wine, a salad, coffee, or an extra side. The principle is the same.

In most brick-and-mortar retail-type businesses, a yield strategy manifests itself around the cash register, where small items of every kind beg to be added to the shopping list just before the checkout. As you make your way to the cash register, you find yourself surrounded by packs of gum, chocolate bars, batteries, tabloid magazines, and anything you might be tempted to add to your overall purchase.

What stores are trying to impact by cramming their checkout areas with so many small, low-cost items is simply to increase the yield of each transaction.

Now the question is, can a social media program increase yield? The answer, as always, is, *of course.*

The process begins outside of your social media program, with an analysis of your business transactions. In order to measure changes in yield, you must be able to track the dollar value of each transaction. What you are looking for specifically is an increase in revenue that outpaces an increase in the number of net transactions. Here is how this might look:

- Q1: 100 transactions for a total of $100 in total revenue.

- Q2: 100 transactions for a total of $150 in total revenue.

What you see here is an increase in yield: The number of transactions remained the same, but the average value of each transaction has grown from $1 to $1.50. In its most basic form, this is what you are looking for.

In the real world, the net number of transactions will likely fluctuate, but the principle remains the same: Divide total revenue by the net number of transactions between one measurement period and the next, and you will be able to calculate changes in yield.

The next step in the process is to understand what new types of purchases are affecting your yield. Look at your sales receipts and look for patterns. Are you suddenly selling more $4.99 pay-per-view programs? Are you selling more apple pie on Saturdays? Identify the new winners in your product line. This is going to be important. In Chapter 15, "ROI and Other Social Media Outcomes," we talked about proving and disproving relationships between activities and outcomes. Here, we have an opportunity to do just that.

Ideally, your social media program or campaign, as it pertains to your yield strategy, may have focused on specific products. If you were the cable company, you may have used social media channels to promote $4.99 pay-per-view programs by increasing awareness for them and up-selling their value. If, upon analysis of an increase in yield, you find that sales of $4.99 pay-per-view programs remained flat, then you know that your social media activity relating to that particular push was ineffective. You may find, however, that 100% of the increase in yield came from Basic cable to Premium cable upgrades. Start there and work your way backward to activities: Where did you push for package upgrades? Narrow it down to the channels you used to impact customer behavior. All that is left to do is determine the impact that each medium has on these types of changes. A simple way of doing this is to incorporate channel-specific promotional codes into an upgrade campaign and see how many of each turn up with the new transactions. Here is how it works:

- TV: Use upgrade promo code UPGRADE01TV.

- Print: Use upgrade promo code UPGRADE02PT.

- Social media: Use upgrade promo code UPGRADE03SM.

As customers upgrade from Basic to Premium, collect the promo codes and see what the ratio is at the end of the measurement period. If UPGRADE01TV constitutes 70% of the promo codes used in this process, then you know that 70% of your increase in yield was the result of your TV advertising. If 15% of the upgrades came with the social media promo code, then you know where you stand.

If ROI is part of your measurement methodology, the next step is to calculate the value of the 15% upgrades acquired through social media channels. Say this number amounts to $250,000 in additional yield over the course of the next 12 months and that your program (or this particular element of your program) costs the organization $35,000 per year. Using the ROI equation outlined in Chapter 15 , you can demonstrate positive ROI for your social media activity even if social media channels only accounted for 15% of the overall increase in yield.

To dive deeper into this type of analysis, you can seed channels with far more specific promo codes, each specific to a particular publication, TV network, or social media channel. This can help you further analyze the value of one channel against another. You could determine if your activities on Facebook are more effective than your activities on Twitter, for example. Don't let broad industry numbers fool you: Find out which platforms and channels work best for you. Test them yourself.

F.R.Y. methodology simply helps organizations focus on core objectives and metrics. It is by no means the end-all, be-all of social media program planning and measurement, but it is a great place to start. Organizations that use F.R.Y. as the core of their social media measurement methodology (and business development planning) will have a definite advantage over organizations that do not. Test it in your own business, adapt it to your model, and see where it takes you.

17

Social Media Program Analysis and Reporting

Because every social media program is a collaborative effort from start to finish, the same degree of collaboration we have seen in the management of the program also applies to the analysis of its data, activities, and outcomes.

Shattering the Vacuum: The Need for Collaborative Analysis

Think back to your program's initial objectives and how many different departments they touched: public relations, marketing, sales, and customer service, for starters. These objectives were not *social media* objectives. They were *business* objectives. Your social media program, if developed properly, was not geared toward feeding buzzwords such as "engagement" and "conversations" with idle chatter on social media channels. Neither was its purpose to acquire followers on Twitter and "Likes" on Facebook or to increase the number of retweets. Your social media program was established in support of your business's existing functions and driven by specific objectives. Some of these may have been the following:

Facilitate market research.

Gain real-time insights into consumer preferences and perceptions.

Improve crisis monitoring and response.

Increase the reach of marketing efforts.

Increase the stickiness (effectiveness) of marketing efforts.

Reduce customer service costs.

Improve customer service outcomes.

Amplify a campaign's impact.

Increase sales through Frequency, Reach, and Yield methodologies.

Humanize your brand.

Improve your image in a particular market or industry.

Help reverse an event's negative impact to the brand.

Penetrate new, more technologically savvy markets.

Modernize communications channels.

Improve customer relations to help increase customer loyalty.

Because these objectives touch on specific elements of the business—PR, sales, customer service, marketing, market research, advertising, brand management, digital crisis management, and corporate communications—each department's manager may feel a natural urge to try and own his small part of the program, data, outcomes, and analysis. This is to be expected but resist the urge to completely separate the analysis of the program's activities and outcome in this way.

Consider the functional overlap typical of an operationally integrated social media program: Community managers assisting digital customer service representatives, bloggers working side-by-side with the public relations department, their crisis management team, the marketing department working closely with advertising and digital agencies, and product managers working with the sales department and community managers. None of what happens in and around a social media program exists in a departmental vacuum. If the program is being collaboratively managed, the analysis of its successes and shortcomings must also be a collaborative endeavor.

To illustrate this point, let's imagine that we are looking back at an awareness campaign for a new product that encompassed a number of social media program components: Corporate bloggers created and published content about the product, answered questions in the Comments section of their blogs, and met with consumers and journalists at industry events. Community managers seeded social media channels with links to all of the content and press published about the product and managed conversations about its release and features. The PR team monitored conversations for negative mentions and alerted community managers at the first sign of trouble they had not already spotted. Customer service representatives answered technical questions. Sales managers worked with marketing to gauge interest. With all of this overlap and combination of activity across departments, the analysis of this campaign has to be, at its core, a team effort. If it is not, the analysis of the program's outcomes will fail to encompass the full scope of its impact on the organization.

Reporting on numbers scrubbed of context will rob decision makers of precious insights they need to make good decisions. The cumulative impact that the program's data may have on sales, brand management, consumer perceptions, reputation management, and scores of other interconnected aspects of the organization's areas of focus, needs to be considered as a complete package during both the analysis and reporting processes relating to all social media activity.

Also bear in mind that numbers alone cannot tell the full story of the program's outcomes. It is easy to forget that the more removed from an activity a decision maker is—in other words, the more layers exist between a decision maker and the data's point of collection—the more the decision maker tends to lack the context with which to make sense of that data. Technology and automation cannot help here. Ultimately, the intellectualization of data that results in extracting from it valuable insights must be guided first by a high degree of familiarity with the source of the data and then by an understanding of the context from which the data derives its relevance—and ultimately by the validation of its significance by the very people who found the data important in the first place. Because of this, the analysis of a social media program's activities and outcomes must always be a collaborative exercise.

Best Practices in Data Reporting for Social Media

Unlike analysis, reporting does not always have to be a group exercise. Whether the data's analysis takes place before the initial reporting or results from discussions that follow a report does not matter. The reporting itself is fairly straightforward: It needs to be efficient, timely, clear, and to the point. As simple as this may sound, it often takes time to develop a strong reporting mechanism. All elements of the program with reporting responsibilities must learn how to best convey their information to the individual they are reporting to. This means developing an understanding for what type of reporting they are most comfortable with, what information matters and what information does not, the degree of detail expected from each report, the preferred medium, and scores of other details that change from individual to individual. If anything, reporting is a process of continuous improvement in which every report and every interaction between individuals teaches them how to communicate with each other more efficiently. Over time, if approached with this frame of mind, even the most complex reporting procedures can become as natural as breathing.

This focus on efficiency in the reporting process is particularly important to a social media program because of its potential operational complexity: With so many different disciplines, departments, and management layers touching on the program, the reporting process can sometimes seem a little daunting. Don't let all of the moving parts get in the way. Remember to always keep things as simple as possible. Find the path of least resistance. Start with the basics: Create a structure for your reporting and make it as simple as possible. In Chapter 8, "Laying the Operational Groundwork for Effective Social Media Management," we talked about vertical management structures and horizontal collaboration structures. These same structures can help us bring order and efficiency to our reporting process.

Lateral Reporting

Lateral reporting is the type of reporting that allows independent elements of a social media program to come to each other's assistance, share data, and forward information to one another when needed. The purpose of this type of reporting is twofold.

The first category of lateral reporting is a daily process of information sharing across departments and different elements of the social media program. Much like a daily briefing, it ensures that every element of the social media program has visibility to the other elements' activities and observations. This type of lateral reporting focuses mostly on planning and coordination across program tiers.

For example, if a community manager wants to establish a weekly chat on one platform that focuses on a particular product or theme, that information should be shared with the rest of the social media program's execution tier. If a blogger is planning a week-long series of posts that will focus on a particular aspect of the business, this information must be shared as well.

Another aspect of this first category of lateral reporting deals with sharing observations and analysis: Say that the PR department has been monitoring shifts in the volume of mentions of a particular product as well as sentiment in regard to it and notices changes in the trending of either. It may want to keep the rest of the program informed as to their daily, weekly, and even monthly impact on these fluctuations. For example, it may want to indicate to the customer service department that its work seems to be driving an increase in positive sentiment and to the community management team that *its* activities seem to be steadily driving up the volume of mentions.

Likewise, the PR department's analysis of conversations in the space may find that the marketing department's strong-handed approach in social media channels is having a detrimental effect on the public's perception of the company. This may prompt the marketing department to take a closer look at its activity in social media channels and consider an adjustment in tactics. As a group, preferably under the supervision of the social media program manager, the marketing department might come up with a solution to this problem—perhaps reducing its volume of unsolicited marketing messages on Twitter and Facebook, for example, or taking a closer look at the timing of these messages.

The second category of lateral reporting moves beyond the realm of daily briefings and steps into real-time collaboration. This mode of reporting focuses on a situation (or potential situation) in the "now." An example of this would be a community manager, upon noticing a sudden surge in negative comments on the company's Facebook wall, alerting other elements of the program. The "report" alerting them to the situation would prompt them to immediately begin actively monitoring it on their end, analyze it as a group, and possibly lend a helping hand.

Social media program managers, when developing their programs, must keep an eye out for fluid modes of lateral reporting to facilitate collaboration in their day-to-day operations. If the various elements of the program don't have visibility to every planned activity and noteworthy observation managed by their peers, if they are not aware of each other's goals and objectives, if they are not briefed regularly on the success and shortcomings of each other's points of focus, the program will consist of little more than a series of disjointed efforts with little hope of generating a long-term positive impact on the organization.

The purpose of lateral reporting is to ensure that all of the elements of each tier of the program have visibility to what the others are planning to do, what their observations are, and how they can all help one another accomplish their objectives. This process is in many ways similar to the type of collaboration that often exists between law enforcement agencies who share intelligence, coordinate activity in key investigations, and collaborate on busts, stings, and arrests. Lateral reporting is mostly an operational requirement of effective collaboration. Half of it should focus on planning and resource allocation. The other half should focus on the coordination of activities in real time.

Without a smooth lateral reporting mechanism that allows each element to sound the alarm when something goes wrong, the rest of the program's elements will not be able to react to a crisis in time to address it before it becomes a trending topic across key media channels. Speed is of the essence in times of crisis, especially in the age of the social consumer. A social media program cannot rely solely on lateral reporting mechanisms that consist of daily briefings and activity reports. Create a real-time crisis management lateral reporting process as well. It may come in handy sooner than you think.

Vertical Reporting

Vertical reporting focuses on sharing data, information, and analysis upward to management and serves two key purposes: The first is to equip decision makers with the information they need to make the best possible decisions in regard to future courses of action, and the second is to validate the program's value to the organization. No surprises there.

Before we go any further with vertical reporting processes, you need to focus first on clearly understanding what type of data, analysis, and presentation each individual being reported to wants to see. Do not guess. Ask. Sit down with every person and ask them ahead of time what type of data they want to see, what type of data they don't want to see, how it should be presented, what the intervals should be, and so on. Leave nothing to chance. After every report, ask again if there was anything else they wanted to know. Always seek to improve your reporting mechanism. There is always room for improvement in this area.

The most important function of vertical reporting is providing decision makers with the information they need to make sound business decisions. Even outside of social media, information is gold. In the military world, the term used when trying to describe the optimal outcome of good reporting is "seeing the field." The better a general "sees the field," the better his chance of winning the day. Reporting plays an essential role in this process because the more removed a general is from a battle, the more he requires fast, accurate, insightful information not otherwise available to him.

Strangely enough, vertical reporting, even within the scope of a social media program, finds its roots in ancient warfare and has not changed all that much in the last few centuries. The basic tenets of reporting are still today what they have always been: People on the field report what they see, successive middle layers above them filter and distill the information, and by the time it reaches a decision maker, the information has been verified, clarified, and analyzed by people whose job it is to do so. With an efficient reporting mechanism, decisions as to what to do next—continue on the current course, wait and see, or make a change—can be made in mere moments.

Keep in mind that the higher up the chain of command you report to, the more details, context, timing, and urgency surrounding a report can erode. Also remember that the more senior the executive, the more her time may be limited. When it comes to packaging information for this type of reporting, specificity, clarity, and brevity go a long way toward making your reports effective and actionable. Crafting a 12-paragraph email explaining a situation may not be an ideal reporting method, for example. Instead, devise a system that ensures that your information is succinct, easily verifiable, and pertinent to a decision maker's daily concerns. Rule of thumb: If it cannot all fit on an index card, you have probably not distilled the report enough. For day-to-day operational reporting, stick to the basics:

I am...

I see...

I hear...

The context is...

The potential impact is...

The window of opportunity is...

What has been done already is...

The current status is...

This should be followed, if need be, by a request for further instructions, authorization, and so on.

An example of this type of reporting would look like this:

To: Jane Roberts, VP Brand Management, mobile devices

To: Sam Johnson, VP Social Business

From: John Smith, Community Manager, mobile devices

Over the last few days, I have noticed a rapid and unusual increase in negative mentions in regard to our new XYZ smart phone. See attached graph showing the volume of mentions and change in ratio of positive-negative sentiment over the last 72 hours.

The focus of the negativity stems from press reports Monday implying quality control issues affecting reception and the reliability of the phone. The activity we are monitoring may both reflect and contribute to uncertainty in the product that could result in a weak release and sluggish sales in Q1. We need to restore confidence in the product before this takes root. The window of opportunity for action is immediate.

My team has already begun responding to the negative chatter, and we are working with PR, product management, and marketing to create content that will restore the public's faith in the product. Currently, our efforts seem to have stopped the increase in negative mentions, but uncertainty remains high. My team would like 20 minutes of your time to discuss options and review the material we have already begun working on.

Keep this type of reporting short and to the point. No matter what the subject is, clarity and purpose combined with brevity are your best assets when reaching out to upper management echelons. If your supervisor needs more information, he will ask for it.

When it comes to *validation* reporting—the kind that usually happens monthly and quarterly—brevity is not as critical to the effectiveness of your report as it is for day-to-day operational reporting. For validation reporting, focus once more on what matters most to the executives. If you have not yet asked them, do so. In instances where an executive is not being clear about what he wants you to report on (it happens), ask yourself what would matter to you if you were in his shoes. For example, will a VP Sales be interested in net new Twitter followers or the net new transacting customers acquired via Twitter during the closing quarter? Will a PR director be interested in the increase in unique website visits attributed to content published on the company's Facebook wall or in the 17% increase in positive sentiment captured across the social web since the catastrophic product recall the company endured last month?

Go back to the objectives that drove your program's activities and connect the dots: What outcomes benefit what departments? What elements of the program fall under the authority of specific managers whom you are reporting to? Focus on what matters. Do not fall into the common trap many social media program managers fall into, which is reporting mostly on "social media" metrics. Hint: Very few people in the organization, especially at the executive level, care about how many followers, fans, likes, and retweets a social media program is generating from one month to the next. How do 100,000 new Twitter followers help the business? How do 50,000 views of a video posted to YouTube really justify the program's cost? What is the material value of 10,000 mentions of the company's name across the social web? As long as you keep your focus on the program's business objectives, your report will be on the right track. Lose sight of these objects and default instead to digital media metrics, and your report will be a waste of everyone's time.

The thought process behind the creation of a validation report is fairly easy to convey: If one of the objectives were to facilitate market research, start there. How did you determine, early in the program, how you would measure and quantify results for this objective? Did you set a particular set of targets? If so, measure your current status and present it opposite those initial targets. If one of the secondary objectives were to reduce the monthly cost of market research by $35,000 and you reduced market research costs by $20,000, report on that. Show how you did it. Explain why you fell short of your target and what remains to be done to reach it during the next measurement period. If another secondary goal were to begin conducting real-time market research across five different social media channels and you accomplished this goal, report it. Show numbers. List the types of insights you have already collected, measured, and analyzed. Report on the positive impact this project has already had on the organization in terms of cost savings, increased potential, and opportunities gained.

If one of the objectives was the amplification of a marketing campaign's impact on consumers, report on that. Here, *reach* matters, so this is an instance in which demonstrating an increase in activity and connections on Facebook, Twitter, YouTube, and other platforms is actually relevant. If you can show that your social media activity around the campaign generated an increase in visits to a web page, an increase in positive conversations about the campaign, the product, or the organization, an increase in foot traffic to retail stores, and even an increase in sales, then report on this as well. Connect the dots: State the objectives and targets, outline the activities, quantify the outcomes, and connect them to your objectives and targets.

A social media program manager who only reports on "social media numbers" is just being lazy. Always keep your eye on the business objectives that your social media program is there to support:

- Gaining real-time insights into consumer preferences and perceptions
- Improving the organization's crisis monitoring and response process
- Increasing the reach of marketing efforts
- Increasing the impact of marketing efforts
- Reducing customer service costs
- Improving customer service outcomes
- Amplifying a campaign's impact

- Increasing sales through frequency, reach, and yield (F.R.Y.) methodologies

- Humanizing or otherwise improving the organization's image in the eyes of consumers

- Helping reverse an event's negative impact to the brand (such as a PR faux-pas, an ecological catastrophe, or an interruption of service)

- Improving customer relations to help increase customer loyalty

If you must report on typical social media metrics such as net new followers, views, likes, subscriptions, mentions, comments, visits, shares, and retweets, do so in context. Explain why these numbers are relevant to a business objective. Make every number count. Reporting for reporting's sake has little value. Ultimately, if data is not meaningful to the executives or peers you are sharing it with, why are you including it in your report? Trim off the fat by cutting out data that serves little or no purpose.

One last note about effective reporting: Whenever possible, use graphics in conjunction with raw numbers. Helping decision makers visualize data can help them interpret both its scope and its importance. Use pie charts and bar graphs to illustrate connected data sets and "share of" data. Graph net gains and losses. Assign colors to negative and positive mentions so that changes in sentiment over time leave nothing to the imagination. Do not underestimate the power of bringing your data to life by making your reports visually insightful.

Figure 17.1 provides four simple examples of the types of basic visualizations commonly used to convey context in social media reports. Starting clockwise from the top left, we have a pie chart showing the relative volume of mentions of a particular keyword by channel; a matrix of overall volume of mentions and ratios of positive-to-negative sentiment for those mentions between January and May; changes in monthly reach by channel between February and May, expressed in followers, likes, and blog subscribers; and a basic sentiment analysis snapshot for four topics relevant to the organization.

Note how the example in Figure 17.2 shifts from a purely social media perspective to focus on data specific to a customer service department's analysis of a recent Twitter integration. The implied scenario: Our customer service department shifted 20% of its resources to Twitter in an attempt to lower call center costs and increase ticket resolution rates. The graphic occupying the top half of the diagram tracks the increase of positive outcomes between February and May, showing significant improvement in complaint resolutions. The bottom graphic shows a dramatic shift in customers' use of inbound channels between February and May. Note the decreased use of the telephone and the increased use of Twitter and blogs.

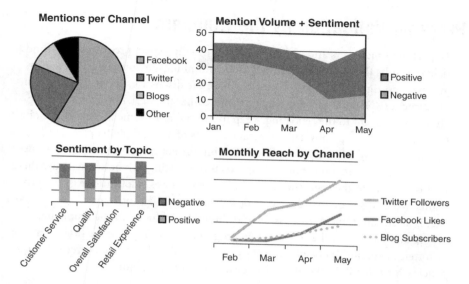

Figure 17.1   Basic data visualization for validation reporting.

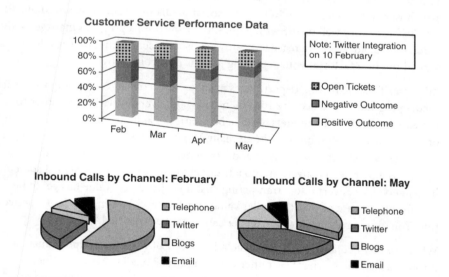

Figure 17.2   Customer service data visualization samples.

Presenting your numbers alongside graphics like these will make your reports much easier for upper echelons to digest. Never underestimate the power of a few good graphs to help data tell its story.

Program Validation by the Numbers

Department managers and senior executives usually expect programs they fund to deliver results that justify their initial (and continuing) investment in these programs—and rightly so. This is typically where the discussion about the return on investment (ROI) of a social media program comes up. ROI, however, may not always be relevant to the reporting. Keep in mind that in some instances, the objectives and targets originally set for certain aspects of a social media program had nothing to do with financial outcomes. During the course of your reporting, you may find yourself in a position to help executives distinguish between areas where ROI is relevant to the reporting and where it isn't. For example, if one of the program's objectives were to reduce cost or increase revenue (both financial outcomes), ROI is a relevant topic of discussion and should be included in the reporting. Where an objective of the social media program was to improve the brand's image or soften the public's perception of the organization's politically incorrect hiring policies, however, ROI may be an irrelevant topic of discussion.

Learn to differentiate between financial and nonfinancial impact in your reporting and be clear when discussing which activities were intended to deliver ROI and which were not: "What is the ROI of the social media program in regard to our PR efforts?" may very well be the wrong question. How does a program manager assign a dollar value to a 17% increase in positive consumer sentiment? He can't. ROI should not be a factor in your reporting for this particular activity.

Likewise, if the marketing department's principal objective in co-funding the social media program was to acquire 100,000 net new followers on Twitter in order to increase its reach, can a monetary value be arbitrarily assigned to each follower in order to satisfy an ROI question? Not really. What is the dollar value of a follower? $1? $3.75? $27.99? Your guess is as good as mine. The reality is that until that follower has either been converted into a transacting customer or has helped someone in his network convert into a transacting customer, his dollar value has yet to be actualized. Because of this, the dollar value of a Twitter follower, Facebook connection, YouTube subscriber, or blog reader can never be estimated.

What *can* be calculated, however, is the relative *cost* of reaching an individual through social media channels rather than traditional media channels. When reporting on reach and impressions whose outcomes cannot be directly tied to sales, the proper unit of measure to focus on is *cost* per impression, not the *value* of a follower, contact, blog post, tweet, or Facebook update. Reporting is not a guessing game. Report on what you know, not on what you *think* you know.

In instances where ROI is not the objective, be sure that you understand how to effectively measure the success of a particular activity. For example, if one of the program's objectives is to help set the record straight in regard to the company's alleged use of child labor in some of its manufacturing facilities, be sure to always begin your report with a benchmarking brief that outlines where the company was at the start of the measurement period:

> At the start of Q1, our Facebook wall was receiving, on average, 150 comments per day in regard to our alleged child labor policies. Our company was mentioned 850 times per day, on average, across all digital channels in regard to this topic. Sentiment for our company in the context of this story was 89% negative, 3% neutral, and 8% positive. General sentiment for the brand was 73% negative, 7% neutral, and 20% positive.

> Our activities during this period included... (fill in the blanks).

> At the close of Q1, our Facebook wall was receiving, on average, 12 comments per day in regard to our child labor policies, most of which were inquisitive, not negative. Our company is currently mentioned less than 30 times per day, on average, across all digital channels in regard to this topic. Sentiment for our company in the context of this story is now 60% positive, indicating a significant a turnaround in public perception. General sentiment for the brand is now 68% positive, 12% neutral, and 20% negative, again showing a return toward a positive perception of the brand. (Accompany this with graphs and visual aids to drive the point home.)

This is how validation by numbers drives vertical reporting for social media programs.

When validating a social media program focused on a number of ROI-focused objectives, your analysis becomes much narrower and less strategic as it targets financial metrics. That said, think about the cumulative impact of your program on a breadth of financial outcomes. In the following example, assume that the entire program cost was $100,000 for the previous quarter. Your job is now to validate the program's effectiveness to an organization's executive team eager to be briefed on the ROI of the program it funded at your request. Here are your four principal objectives tied to some expectation of a positive financial impact:

> **ROI objective #1**—Reduce head count costs in customer service department by shifting 20% of service tickets from the organization's call center to Twitter.

> **ROI objective #2**—Acquire 1,000 new transacting customers through activity on social media channels.

> **ROI objective #3**—Increase frequency (buy rate) from existing customers through social media activity.

> **ROI objective #4**—Increase yield of transactions (average transaction amount) from existing customers using social media channels.

Your report should include data that shows how the objectives were met or if they weren't. For example:

For objective #1—Shifting 20% of the customer service department's tickets to Twitter—the program resulted in a reduction in headcount while improving response times and outcomes. The net cost savings of this aspect of the program was $75,000 with no adverse effect to the quality of service.

For objective #2—The 1,000 target was not met. Social media activity only generated 400 new transacting customers, not 1,000. Their cumulative transactions, however, yielded a net $200,000 in net new sales revenue.

For objective #3—Increasing buy rate from a portion of existing customers by using social media channels—the program yielded a net 9% increase in sales volume for that group, resulting in $135,000 in net new sales revenue.

For objective #4—Increasing the yield of transactions from a portion of existing customers—the program resulted in a net 4% increase in sales revenue for that group, generating in $89,000 for the quarter.

Adding up the positive impact of these four specific activities of the program, we can see that it generated a cumulative gain of $499,000 for that quarter: More specifically, $75,000 in cost savings and $424,000 in net new revenue. From this data, the ROI of the program for that quarter can be easily calculated.

Now imagine if an executive team expecting this type of reporting in regard to the ROI of the social media program received instead a report that focused almost exclusively on net new followers, mentions, retweets, Facebook "shares," digital impressions, web traffic, and other media metrics. Would their expectations be met? Probably not. Always remember to connect your reporting to business outcomes relating to specific objectives.

Remember that the value of a program or activity cannot always be expressed in monetary terms. Good press, positive public perception, and focus on the type of topics that are beneficial—not detrimental—to an organization all contribute to its success in the end. Everyone understands that. Proof of success and evidence of value can sometimes be subjective. Use common sense. Do not let ROI dominate every conversation dealing with social media program validation. Prove your program's value to the organization every day by demonstrating its positive impact in a multitude of ways but learn early on to divide your reporting between financial outcomes and nonfinancial outcomes.

Looking at Performance Data as Actionable Intelligence

Data exists first and foremost to allow analysts and decision makers to *derive* insight from it and *act* upon it, not simply nod at it in quiet acquiescence. Do not regard the reporting of information about your social media program as the end of the process. Your validation report—whether delivered as a slide deck, oral presentation, or a written document—is meant to be a catalyst for further discussions regarding the direction and management of your social media program. Your report should thus prompt a number of questions, the most important of which are the following:

What are we doing well?

What are we not doing well?

Where can we improve?

How can we improve?

What did we miss?

What should we start working on next?

The data and insights contained in a report should help easily answer the first two questions: *What are we doing well* and *what are we not doing well?* In the example used in the previous section of this chapter, we saw that a number of the program's objectives were met: from shifting 20% of customer service tickets to digital platforms and reducing operating costs, to increasing transaction yields to the tune of $95,000 for the previous quarter. One area that, in spite of a positive impact on sales, fell short of its target was the conversion of followers and fans into transacting customers: The target was 1,000 conversions for the quarter. The program only delivered 40% of this number. In this instance, either the target was too high or the execution was lacking. This is an area we might consider, in the scope of our analysis, to be one in which the organization is not doing well.

Where can we improve? is the type of question that can generally be answered with a single word: everywhere. If a 20% shift in customer service tickets from a call center to digital channels were good, a 21% shift will be better. Although 400 conversions that yielded $200,000 in net new sales for the quarter was a good start, 800 conversions yielding $400,000 in net new sales for the quarter will be a worthwhile improvement. Although a 9% increase in sales volume driven by an acceleration in *buy rate* was a great success, a 10% increase next quarter will be even better. Opportunities for improvement can be found anywhere. Properly analyzing and then prioritizing these types of opportunities should always follow the reporting process.

How can we improve? is the logical follow-up to the *Where can we improve?* question. It isn't enough to simply turn up the heat on an element of the social media program. "Get me more followers" or "go get me some more conversions" simply isn't realistic for a social media program if you are looking for real results. In devising ways for a social media program's elements to grow in their efficiency, consider round-table discussions with the entire social media program team. If round-table discussions are not possible because of geography or the complexity of the team's schedules, include these types of questions in the program's daily briefings. Turn these questions into problems the entire team can work on.

Asking the team how it might improve conversion rates from social media contact to transacting customer will begin a dialogue that will eventually yield potential solutions: Could the community manager insert subtle reminders of upcoming special sales or new distribution channels into some of her discussions? Should a "buy now" tab be added to the organization's Facebook wall? Should customer reviews be moved to a more visible place on the product manager's blog? Perhaps all of these ideas might work equally well. As a social media program manager, don't assume that you have to come up with all the answers. Put the question to your staff members and let them work on the problem as a team. They know their jobs well and have good instincts as to what will work (and what will not work) in the space. Use their expertise to your advantage.

In the same spirit, always put the question *What did we miss?* to the members of your team. They may already see something you don't, and if they haven't yet, they will. When in doubt, turn to your data. Look at your business and media metrics since the start of your program or a specific activity and see where your program is having an impact versus where it appears not to be having an impact.

In Figure 17.3, we see five different metrics being observed simultaneously. (You may remember this example from Chapter 15, "ROI and Other Social Media Outcomes.") The uppermost metric shows steady upward trending *before* the activity and *since* the social media activity started. At first glance, the impact of the activity on this metric seems uncertain, so we will leave it be. The middle three metrics indicate a change in trending since the start of the program or activity, and the bottom metric shows absolutely no reaction from the program or activity.

The first step in the analysis process is to look at the metrics that seem to have been impacted by the program or activity. Establish how this data set was touched by the social media program or activity. You must show a link between your social media program and each data set in order to move forward with your analysis. Once this step is complete, reverse your analysis by asking how this data set might have been impacted by activity *outside* the scope of your social media program. The objective here is to determine whether or not another activity or event may be responsible (even in part) for the change in this metric's trending rather than your program (see Figure 17.4).

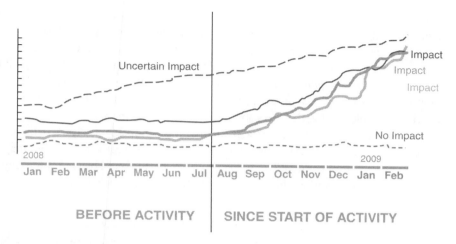

Figure 17.3   Drawing program insights from business data.

Imagine, for example, that this triple data set relates to sales of a particular product, volume of mentions relating to this particular product, and positive reviews for the product. Judging by Figure 17.3, one might infer that the social media program drove positive awareness for the product and caused sales to increase. The timeline overlay shows that as soon as the program began, all three metrics shifted upward.

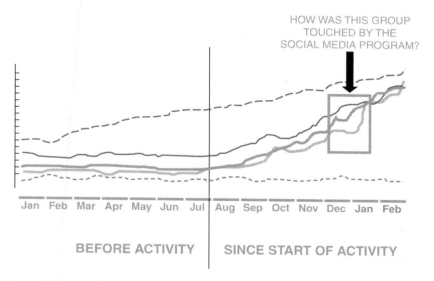

Figure 17.4   Proving and disproving a connection with social activity.

If we failed to take into account other possible reasons for this uptick, we might deduce that the social media program was responsible for the change. What if something else had caused the change? By asking what else could have impacted these numbers, we look for things we might have missed. In our example, this could be the announcement of a price drop for the product in the month of July. This, more than the social media program, could have led to the high volume of positive mentions (people sharing the news about the price drop with their network) and the subsequent lift in sales. The social media program's impact on sales may therefore have contributed to the changes in trending for these specific metrics but may have not been its root cause. *What did we miss?* can be answered by simply looking at our data and questioning our assumptions. Always look for what you missed. Never assume anything.

This type of data analysis can also answer the *What did we miss?* question in another way: by taking a look at how some metrics were absolutely not impacted by the social media program. In Figure 17.5, we see how the bottom metric seems to be disconnected from social media activity. The question we seek to answer is *why?*

Find out what this data set represents: Is it a sales figure? Is it foot traffic to retail stores, visits to a web page, mentions on Facebook, recommendations, or retweets? Once you know what it represents, dig into your business processes to understand why this metric was not touched by your activity.

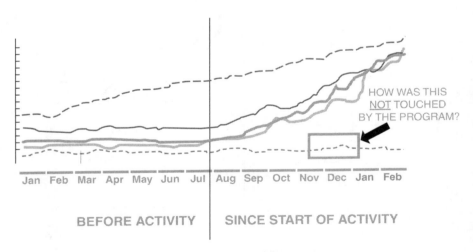

Figure 17.5 Understanding why a data set was not impacted by social activity.

What if this data represented brick-and-mortar retail sales? By combining other sales data for the same time period, you might learn that online sales of the product increased and that foot traffic at retail outlets also increased, but that sales at these physical retail outlets were flat. Normally, good sales online and an increase in foot traffic to brick-and-mortar stores should lead us to expect that brick-and-mortar retail sales should be good as well. The fact that they aren't should raise a red flag. This type of analysis might help us identify a problem where we didn't expect a problem to exist. Perhaps something about the retail experience is off. Could it be an inventory problem? Could it be long lines at the cash register? Could it be something else? What did you miss?

This example demonstrates the extent to which the reporting and analysis of a social media program's performance edges beyond the narrow scope of social media metrics. When a social media program supports the organization as a whole rather than being relegated to serving as a "social" digital conduit for marketing content, the wealth of insights it can generate can positively impact every facet of the business.

This fact is best illustrated by the final question on our list: *What should we start working on next?* I cannot answer that question for you, but I can tell you that the answer is not "more Twitter followers" or "better content strategy." The answer to that question may not have anything to do with social media at all. It may rest with your retail sales team or lie with the need to build new features and compatibility into an upcoming product. It may focus on new distribution channels for information, marketing content, and even sales. It may deal with simpler collaborative processes within your organization and more transparent communications with your customers. Beyond all of this, "what is next" may be as simple as realizing that your activity on social media channels should focus less on acquiring new customers and more on retaining them, less on taking aim at the low-hanging fruit and more on inspiring and earning true loyalty from your customers, less on short-term marketing thinking and more on cementing long-term relationships with your best customers.

What your data's reporting and analysis *should* show is that social media is first and foremost social and that the more truly human your program is, the more positive its impact will be on the organization as a whole and the environment within which it breathes, lives, and grows.

Afterword

Designing, building, managing, and measuring social media programs is hard work. It takes time, diligence, focus, and a lot of patience. Don't be intimidated by all the do's and don'ts, all the moving parts, and the challenge that comes with connecting all the dots. Break the process down. Keep things simple. Start with what matters and fill in the blanks as your program begins to shape up. You don't have to build it all in one go. I cannot emphasize this enough: Take your time. Move at your own pace. Ease into every step of your program's evolution. Slow is good. Just like building relationships doesn't happen overnight, building the processes through which these relationships will be built will not happen overnight either.

Remember that this book is merely a guide, written with one thought in mind: to provide you with just enough information and structure to help you create a framework for your social media program. Use what works and find a way around what doesn't. Experiment. Test. Build on what you learn and fill the empty spaces with what you know. Measure success and adapt as needed. That is ultimately how this works. You decide where to go and how to get there.

I want to leave you with a few last little bits of advice:

- No two social media programs are the same, so don't worry too much about basing your program on what other companies have already put together. Borrow as needed but be sure to create your program's structure based on *your* organization's needs and capabilities. Focus on supporting *your* business objectives. Infuse your social media activity with *your* business culture. Don't worry a whole lot about what everyone else is doing or how fast they are doing it. Build your own program from the ground up. The more custom your program, the greater its chances of success.

- Don't let technology, the jargon, and the ebb and flow of digital channels obscure the simplicity of being a *social business*. When you look beyond the platforms and software, the tweets, videos, and geo-location check-ins, the Facebook updates, blog posts, podcasts, and product recommendations, all you will see are the same social interactions you would encounter at a party, at a dinner, at the water cooler: People sharing photos of their loved ones, videos of their trips, blog posts about their hobbies, tweets about anything that pops into their minds. A conversation might be prompted by anything—from a political debate to a great song they just discovered, from a pertinent news story to their favorite book or movie, from the birth of a child or landing a new job to how delicious their meal was at a restaurant they just tried for the first time. As complicated as social media may sometimes seem to business managers, the truth is that it is as simple and human as a handshake, a friendly smile, and the conversation that ensues. Just be there, listen, and participate. The rest will fall into place.

- Don't put the cart ahead of the horse. Because "social" is something you *are*, not something you *do*, most organizations cannot succeed in the social space by changing what they *do* and not who they *are*. A director of social media can only do so much. Being social speaks at least as much to your company's DNA as it does to its business practices. If you don't really care about your customers, social media won't magically transform you into someone who does. If you care about your customers, your activities in the social media space will reflect that. Keep in mind that effective change management can be as important to the development of a strong social media program as any tool, training, or strategy your social media team will ever put together.

- Do not think of social media channels solely as marketing channels. Although they can be used for marketing purposes with terrific effect, your organization's social media program should not be managed by your marketing department any more than your phones should be managed by your sales department. Think about how "social" plugs into your entire company, not just your marketing efforts. Make your social media efforts fit into every department. If you only remember one insight from this book, let it be that.

- Listen at least twice as much as you speak. Everywhere I look, I see companies spending a good deal of their time (and budgets) focusing on producing content, blog posts, social media press releases, tweets, updates, and events, and looking to "content strategy" to make sure it all fits smoothly together. That is great, but what works even better is to make sure to put more effort into your *listening* strategy. Listen to your customers. Listen to your competitors' customers. Find out what makes them tick, what they like and don't like, what they want and don't want. Learn from them how to be the best at what you do.

- People are more important than technology. Hire people who care about other people. If you hire and promote people who don't care that much about delighting customers and being a part of their lives, it doesn't matter how much Twitter and Facebook you add to your company's communications or how many awesome monitoring dashboards you buy: Your social media program will never go anywhere. Start with your people, not your tools. *They* are what makes social either work or fail.

- One of the most difficult aspects of social media program management is the seeming divide that exists between the social nature of interactions that take place on social networks and the business objectives they aim to support. Think of the role that social interactions play in the development of your business in the same way you regard the role of a handshake. Don't make it all about your business. Don't just talk about what you do. Give your customers something to talk about, but let them lead the conversation at least as much. Get to know them through these channels the same way you would if they came by your office every day.

- In spite of the social nature of your interactions with consumers, stay focused on your business objectives. This will give your social media both purpose and direction. Broadly speaking, focus your activities on developing customers by creating first awareness, then preference, then loyalty, and finally facilitating evangelism. The interactions themselves can be about anything, but their direction and their *purpose* always tie back to the reason why your social media program exists in the first place.

- Work with external partners as needed but be careful what elements of your program you choose to outsource. Market research can be outsourced. Monitoring can be outsourced. Page design and content planning can be outsourced. The advertising and marketing aspects of your social media activity, even, can be outsourced. One thing that cannot be outsourced, though, is the management of your relationship with your customers. Relationships, trust, respect, and attention, those cannot be hired out. You own your customers' trust. You own that handshake. Only you own the promise of what your interactions in social channels represent. Don't forget that.

- Read industry blogs. Attend conferences. Interact with other social media program directors. Make the development and management of your social media program a daily learning process. As you find yourself spending more and more time in this evolving space, you will realize that the community of dedicated professionals that constitutes its core is always eager to share knowledge and insights with anyone with a question or a problem to solve. You don't have to figure any of this out alone. We are all here to help and eager to do so.

Finally, remember to have fun. If you aren't having fun on the social web (and more importantly, if your customers aren't enjoying their interactions with you), you are probably doing something wrong. Build a program that allows you to be attentive, friendly, and helpful. If you can remember to do that, the rest will sort itself out. Just relax. It's only social media after all: listening and talking. We have been doing it for thousands of years—only now, we do it a little faster, a little better, and in a lot more ways than ever before.

Now go build something great.

Index

A

access to market research, 133
accuracy in market research, 133-134
acquiring new customers
  acquisition costs, 249-252
  overview, 19
activity timelines, 227-228
adoption of social media, 59
  centralized social media management
    model, 67-68
  decentralized social media management
    models, 68-70
  focused adoption, 60
  genesis model, 62
  operational adoption, 60-61
  operational integration, 61-62
  pirate ship model, 62-64
  skunkworks program, 64-66
  test adoption, 59
advertising, 143-144
agency partners, 94

analysis, 196-197
  acting on performance data, 271-275
  program validation, 268-270
angry customers
  conflict resolution, 168-171
  listening to, 171-172
anti-defamation guidelines, 90-91
auditing company via search engines, 129
auto-DMs, 142

B

bad customer service, impact of, 158-159
baselines, establishing, 227
basic collaborative dynamics, 105
best practices for social media program
  management, 179-183
blogs
  disclosure laws, 120
  Wal-marting Across America, 122
bottom-up buy-in, obtaining, 42-47

brand communications, 113
  confidentiality, 122-124
  data protection, 122-124
  disclosure, 119-122
  social media's impact on, 114-119
  transparency, 119-122
brand management. *See* digital brand
  management
Brogan, Chris, 62
budget allocation, 208
bullying, 92-93
BullyOnline.org, 93
business goals, aligning social media with
  business intelligence, 24
  customer support, 20-22
  explained, 13-14, 258
  human resources, 22-23
  integrating social media into
    organization, 52-53
  measurable business objectives, 194
  not-for-profit organizations
    human resources, 25-26
    member loyalty, 26-27
    member support, 25
    outcomes, 24-25
    public relations, 26
  public relations, 23-24
  sales, 18-20
  strategy versus tactics, 15
  targets
    goals versus targets, 15
    setting, 17-18
  tying social media program to business
    objectives, 16-17
  value of social media to organization, 14
business intelligence, value of social media
  to, 24
business justification and ROI, 207-210
buy-in, obtaining, 42-47

C

campaign management, 176-179
  campaign cycles over time, 184-185
  campaigns and long-term growth,
    185-186
  characters, 177-178
  content, 177
  creativity, 179
  data, 178
  plateaus, 186-188
  social equity and long-term growth,
    185-186
  typical campaign cycle, 183-184
centralized social media management
  model, 67-68
CEOs, discussing value of social media
  with, 42-43
certifications, internal, 81-82
change management, 48. *See also* myths
  about social media
characters in marketing campaigns, 177-178
choosing social media measurement
  software, 30-31
CitizenGulf.org, 25
clarity of vision, establishing
  answering common questions, 43-46
  obtaining buy-in, 42-47
collaboration
  basic collaborative dynamics, 105
  basic response dynamics, 106-107
  collaborative analysis, 258-259
  collaborative technology, 105-106
  cross-functional collaboration, 100-103
  enabling, 103-105
  internal collaboration, 181
  management collaboration, 98
  open response dynamics, 107-108
  tools, 104

communications. *See also* listening; reporting
  brand communications, 113
    confidentiality, 122-124
    data protection, 122-124
    disclosure, 119-122
    social media's impact on, 114-119
    transparency, 119-122
  corporate communications, 146-151
  decentralization, 118
  between departments, 181-182
  explaining value of social media, 42-47
  feedback, 148-150
  history of, 114
  internal collaboration, 181
  PR, 146-151
  social, 7
  team briefings, 180-181
  trust, 118-119
  videoconferencing, 181
community management, 137-139
concierge service (digital), 166-168
confidentiality and nondisclosure (NDA) guidelines, 91
confidentiality in brand communications, 122-124
conflict resolution, 168-171
content in marketing campaigns, 177
contractors, social media guidelines for, 94
corporate communications, 146-151
counting transacting customers, 249
creativity, 179
crisis management, 152-156
CRM (customer relationship management), 103-111
cross-functional collaboration, 100-103
customer relationship management (CRM), 103-111

customer service
  angry customers, listening to, 171-172
  CRM (customer relationship management), 103-111
  digital concierge service, 166-168
  digital conflict resolution, 168-171
  impact of bad customer service, 158-159
  importance of, 157-160
  monitoring-and-response mechanism, 162-163
  as a product, 157-158
  responding to online mentions
    research mentions, 166
    status updates, 165
    validation and observation mentions, 164-165
  Superhero Principle, 160-162
  value of social media to, 20-22
customers
  acquiring new customers, 19
  acquisition costs, 249-252
  angry customers
    conflict resolution, 168-171
    listening to with social media, 171-172
  customer service. *See* customer service
  transacting customers, counting, 249
cyber-bullying, 92-93

D

data
  campaign management, 178
  data protection, 122-124
  data reporting, 260
    acting on performance data, 271-275
    lateral reporting, 260-262
    vertical reporting, 262-267
  data visualization, 266-267
  overlaying onto single timeline, 233

decentralization of communications, 118

decentralized social media management models, 68-70

defamation

anti-defamation guidelines, 90-91

defined, 90

Dell, 19, 38

digital brand management

advertising, 143-144

community management, 137-139

corporate communications, 146-151

crisis management, 152-156

digital departments, 145-146

explained, 135-137

marketing, 140-143

online reputation management, 151-152

PR, 146-151

product management, 144-145

transitioning to, 156

digital citizenship contract, 92-93

digital concierge service, 166-168

digital conflict resolution, 168-171

digital departments, 145-146

digital support. *See* customer service

direct authority, establishing, 98-100

disclosure in brand communications, 119-122

discount codes, 19-20

disproving relationships, 235-237

disputes, mediating, 138

Domino's, 134

E

Edelman PR, 122

employees

digital citizenship contract, 92-93

hiring. *See* hiring

social media bill of rights, 85-86

social media guidelines. *See* social media guidelines

employment disclosure guidelines, 89-90

enabling collaboration, 103-105

engagement, 108

ethics, 226

Eurostar, 154

event visibility, 108

explaining value of social media, 42-47

external representatives, social media guidelines for, 94

external social media usage guidelines, 87-88

F

Federal Trade Commission (FTC), 120

feedback, 148-150

financial aspects

of frequency, 243-248

of reach, 248-253

of yield, 253-255

financial outcomes

examples, 211

role of nonfinancial impact relative to financial impact, 211-215

focused adoption, 60

Ford, 23, 137-138

frequency

explained, 242-243

financial versus nonfinancial aspects, 243-248

frequency strategies, 36-37

Frequency, Reach, and Yield. *See* F.R.Y. (Frequency, Reach, and Yield)

F.R.Y. (Frequency, Reach, and Yield)

explained, 35-40, 239-243

frequency

explained, 242-243

financial versus nonfinancial aspects, 243-248

frequency strategies, 36-37

reach
> *explained,* 243
> *financial versus nonfinancial aspects,*
>   248-253
> *increasing,* 38-39
> yield
> *financial value of,* 253-255
> *increasing,* 39-40, 254-255
FTC (Federal Trade Commission), 120
function mapping, 110-111

G

Gale, Porter, 39
genesis model, 62
goals. *See* business goals, aligning social
  media with
Got Milk? campaign, 244
Greenpeace, 25, 139
guidelines
> for agency partners, contractors, and
>   external representatives, 94
> anti-defamation guidelines, 90-91
> employee digital citizenship contract,
>   92-93
> employee social media bill of rights,
>   85-86
> employment disclosure guidelines, 89-90
> external social media usage guidelines,
>   87-88
> goals of, 83-85
> internal social media usage guidelines,
>   86-87
> need for, 78-80
> official versus personal communications
>   guidelines, 91-92
> social media confidentiality and
>   nondisclosure (NDA) guidelines, 91
> training resources, 93-94

H

hiring, 71-72
> internal certifications, 81-82
> social media directors, 72-76
> social media policies, guidelines, and
>   training, 78-80
> tactical social media roles, 76-78
history of communications, 114
HR. *See* human resources
human nature and social media, 4-6
human resources, 78-80
> not-for-profit organizations, 25-26
> value of social media to, 22-23

I

importance of social media to
  businesses, 7-9
increasing yield, 254-255
inevitable socialization of business, 4-6
integrating social media into organization,
  52-53
> centralized social media management
>   model, 67-68
> decentralized social media management
>   models, 68-70
> genesis model, 62
> phases of social media adoption
>   *focused adoption, 60*
>   *operational adoption, 60-61*
>   *operational integration, 61-62*
>   *test adoption, 59*
> pirate ship model, 62-64
> skunkworks program, 64-66
internal certifications, 81-82
internal collaboration, 181
internal social media usage guidelines, 86-87
interviewing
> social media directors, 72-76
> tactical social media roles, 76-78
investment-return relationship, 221

J-K

key performance indicator (KPI), 32-35

keyword monitoring, 176

KPI (key performance indicator), 32-35

L

lateral collaborative networks, 100-103

lateral engagement, 9-11

lateral reporting, 260-262

leadership

    management. *See* management

    organizational structure, 96-100

        creating org charts, 97-98

        identifying roles, 96

        illustrating direct authority, 98-100

        management collaboration, 98

libel, 90

LinkedIn, 22-23

Liquid Highway, 165

listening, 196

    building a listening and monitoring practice, 128-130

    importance of, 127-128

    market research options, 133-134

    real-time situational awareness, 130-132

    spotting trends, 130

listing

    items you can measure, 198-199

    items you must measure, 200-202

long-term growth

    and marketing campaigns, 185-186

    and social equity, 186

loss, 220-223

lowering acquisition costs, 249-252

loyalty, creating, 26-27

M

macro measurement, 200-201

management. *See also* organizational structure

    campaign management

        characters, 177-178

        content, 177

        creativity, 179

        data, 178

    centralized social media management model, 67-68

    crisis management, 152-156

    decentralized social media management models, 68-70

    digital brand management

        advertising, 143-144

        community management, 137-139

        corporate communications, 146-151

        digital departments, 145-146

        explained, 135-137

        marketing, 140-143

        PR, 146-151

        transitioning to, 156

    management collaboration, 98

    online reputation management, 151-152

    product management, 144-145

    social media program management, 173

        best practices, 179-183

        campaign management, 176-179

        importance of, 188

        marketing campaigns. See marketing

        measurement practice, 176

        monitoring, 176

        outsourced management, 174-175

market research options, 133-134

marketing

    digital brand management, 140-143

    F.R.Y. (Frequency, Reach, and Yield). *See* F.R.Y. (Frequency, Reach, and Yield) market research options, 133-134

marketing campaigns, 183-188

    campaign cycles over time, 184-185

    campaigns and long-term growth, 185-186

    plateaus, 186-188

    social equity and long-term growth, 185-186

    typical campaign cycle, 183-184

    reach, increasing, 19

material connections, disclosure of, 122

measurable business objectives, tying social media programs to, 194

measurement practice, 29

    analysis, 196-197

    best measurement tools, 202

    cautions, 195

    considering in context, 195

    focusing on what works, 203-204

    F.R.Y. (Frequency, Reach, and Yield). *See* F.R.Y. (Frequency, Reach, and Yield)

    items you can measure, 198-199

    items you must measure, 200-202

    key performance indicator (KPI), 32-35

    macro measurement, 200-201

    measurable business objectives, tying social media programs to, 194

    measurements, tying to business objectives, 196, 203

    micro measurement, 200

    monitoring, 196

    objectivity, 203

    reporting, 197

    social media measurement software, 30-31

    social media program management, 176

    tools, methodologies, and purpose, 30

    transactional precursors, measuring, 230-231

    velocity and specificity, 204-206

mediating disputes, 138

member loyalty, 26-27

member support, 25

mentions, monitoring volume of, 228-230

metrics. *See* measurement practice

micro measurement, 197

monitoring, 196

    building a listening and monitoring practice, 128-130

    outsourced monitoring, 176

    sentiment, 151-152

    social media program management, 176

    volume of mentions, 228-230

monitoring-and-response mechanism, 162-163

Monty, Scott, 23, 137

Mustafa, Isaiah, 143-144

myths about social media

    anyone can do the job, 50

    I will have to change the way I work, 51

    social media is a fad, 50-51

    social media is a waste of time, 49

    social media is complicated, 49-50

N

negative mentions

    conflict resolution, 168-171

    listening to with social media, 171-172

Nestlé, 25, 139

network triggers, 108-109

neutrality of employees, importance to measurement practice, 203

nondisclosure (NDA) guidelines, 91

nonfinancial aspects

    of frequency, 243-248

    of reach, 248-253

nonfinancial outcomes

    examples, 210-211

    role of nonfinancial impact relative to financial impact, 211-215

tying to social media performance,
223-237

   creating activity timelines, 227-228

   establishing baseline, 227

   looking for patterns, 233-235

   measuring transactional data, 231-232

   *measuring transactional
precursors, 230-231*

   *monitoring volume of mentions,
228-230*

   *overlaying data onto single
timeline, 233*

   *proving and disproving relationships,
235-237*

nonprofits. *See* not-for-profit organizations

not-for-profit organizations

   human resources, 25-26

   member loyalty, 26-27

   member support, 25

   outcomes, 24-25

   public relations, 26

O

objectives. *See* business goals, aligning social
media with

objectivity in measurement practice, 203

observation mentions, responding
to, 164-165

official communications guidelines, 91-92

Old Spice, 143-144

online bullying, 92-93

online forums, representing organization in,
137-138

online mentions

   negative mentions

      conflict resolution, 168-171

      listening to with social media, 171-172

   responding to

      research mentions, 166

      status updates, 165

      *validation and observation mentions,
164-165*

      window-breakers, 166

online reputation management, 151-152

open response dynamics, 107-108

operational adoption, 60-61

operational integration, 61-62

opportunity cost, 209

organizational charts, 97-98, 180

organizational structure

   CRM (customer relationship
management), 103-111

   cross-functional collaboration, 100-103

   leadership and reporting, 96-100

      creating org charts, 97-98

      identifying roles, 96

      illustrating direct authority, 98-100

      management collaboration, 98

outcomes, 24-25

outsourced monitoring, 176

outsourced social media program
management, 174-175

overlaying data onto single timeline, 233

P

P&L (profit and loss), tying social media
to, 220-223

patterns, finding, 233-235

PepsiCo, 144-145

performance measurement. *See*
measurement practice

personal communications guidelines, 91-92

phases of social media adoption, 59

   focused adoption, 60

   operational adoption, 60-61

   operational integration, 61-62

   test adoption, 59

pirate ship model, 62-64

planning
    collaboration, 103-111
    CRM (customer relationship management), 103-111
    cross-functional collaboration, 100-103
    leadership and reporting, 96-100
        creating org charts, 97-98
        identifying roles, 96
        illustrating direct authority, 98-100
        management collaboration, 98
    for social media integration, 58
    technical requirements
        basic collaborative dynamics, 105
        basic response dynamics, 106-107
        collaboration enablement, 103-105
        collaborative technology, 105-106
        engagement, 108
        event visibility, 108
        function mapping, 110-111
        network triggers, 108-109
        open response dynamics, 107-108
        prompts, 108
        share of response, 111
plateaus and marketing campaigns, 186-188
PR, 146-151
product management, 144-145
profit and loss. *See* P&L (profit and loss), tying social media to
prompts, 108
proving relationships, 235-237
public relations
    not-for-profit organizations, 26
    value of social media to, 23-24
purpose of performance measurement, 30

Q-R

qualifications for social media directors, 73-74
reach
    explained, 147, 243
    financial versus nonfinancial aspects, 248-253
    increasing, 19, 38-39
real-time situational awareness, 130-132
relationships, proving and disproving, 235-237
reporting, 197, 260
    lateral reporting, 260-262
    performance data as actionable intelligence, 271-275
    program validation, 268-270
    validation reporting, 264-267
    vertical reporting, 262-267
reputation management, 151-152
research mentions, responding to, 166
responding to online mentions. *See* online mentions
response dynamics, 106-108
return on investment. *See* ROI (return on investment)
ROI (return on investment)
    and business justification, 207-210
    equation for, 215-218
    explained, 215-220
    opportunity cost, 209
    ROI-focused objectives, 269-270
    rules for, 218-220
    tying social media performance to nonfinancial outcomes, 223-237
        creating activity timelines, 227-228
        establishing baseline, 227
        looking for patterns, 233-235
        measuring transactional data, 231-232
        measuring transactional precursors, 230-231
        monitoring volume of mentions, 228-230
        overlaying data onto single timeline, 233
        proving and disproving relationships, 235-237
    tying social media to P&L, 220-223
roles, identifying, 96

S

sales, value of social media to, 18-20

SCRM (social CRM), 103-111

search engines, 129

searching

    impact of searches on digital brand management, 147-148

    online content for business intelligence, 128-130

security, 122-124

sentiment, monitoring, 151-152

share of response, 111

skunkworks program, 64-66

slander, 90

Smith, Kevin, 159

social communications, 7

social companies, building, 3-4

    importance of social media to businesses, 7-9

    inevitable socialization of business, 4-6

    lateral versus vertical forces, 9-11

    social media versus social communications, 7

social CRM (customer relationship management), 103-111

social equity and long-term growth, 185-186

social media activity management dashboard, 103, 106

social media adoption, 59

    centralized social media management model, 67-68

    decentralized social media management models, 68-70

    focused adoption, 60

    genesis model, 62

    operational adoption, 60-61

    operational integration, 61-62

    pirate ship model, 62-64

    skunkworks program, 64-66

    test adoption, 59

social media confidentiality and nondisclosure (NDA) guidelines, 91

social media directors, hiring, 72-76

social media guidelines

    for agency partners, contractors, and external representatives, 94

    anti-defamation guidelines, 90-91

    employee digital citizenship contract, 92-93

    employee social media bill of rights, 85-86

    employment disclosure guidelines, 89-90

    external social media usage guidelines, 87-88

    goals of, 83-85

    internal social media usage guidelines, 86-87

    need for, 78-80

    official versus personal communications guidelines, 91-92

    social media confidentiality and nondisclosure (NDA) guidelines, 91

    training resources, 93-94

social media program management, 173

    best practices, 179-183

    campaign management, 176-179

    importance of, 188

    marketing campaigns, 183-188

        campaign cycles over time, 184-185

        campaigns and long-term growth, 185-186

        plateaus, 186-188

        social equity and long-term growth, 185-186

        typical campaign cycle, 183-184

    measurement practice, 176

    monitoring, 176

    outsourced management, 174-175

social media program validation, 268-270

social media roles
  hiring for, 71-72
    internal certifications, 81-82
    social media directors, 72-76
    social media policies, guidelines, and training, 78-80
  tactical social media roles, 76-78
Social Mention, 151
software, social media measurement software, 30-31
Southwest Airlines, 159
special offers, 19-20
specificity in measurement practice, 204-206
spotting trends, 130
status updates, responding to, 165
strategy versus tactics, 15
Stream Graphs, 151
success in social media, timetable for, 3-4
Superhero Principle, 160-162

T

tactical social media roles, hiring for, 76-78
tactics versus strategy, 15
targets
  versus goals, 15
  setting, 17-18
team briefings, 180-181
technical requirements, 103-111
  basic collaborative dynamics, 105
  basic response dynamics, 106-107
  collaboration enablement, 103-105
  collaborative technology, 105-106
  engagement, 108
  event visibility, 108
  function mapping, 110-111
  network triggers, 108-109
  open response dynamics, 107-108
  prompts, 108
  share of response, 111
test adoption, 59

timelines
  activity timelines, 227-228
  overlaying data onto single timeline, 233
tools, performance measurement tools, 30
top-down buy-in, obtaining, 42-47
training
  overview, 78-80
  training resources, 93-94
transacting customers, counting, 249
transactional data, measuring, 231-232
transactional precursors, measuring, 230-231
transparency, 119-122
Transport Security Administration (TSA), 132
trends, spotting, 130
Tropicana, 144-145
trust, 118-119
TSA (Transport Security Administration), 132
Tweet Cloud, 151
tying social media program to business objectives, 16-17

U-V

validation mentions, responding to, 164-165
validation of social media program, 268-270
validation reporting, 264-267
value of social media to organization, 14
velocity
  in market research, 133
  in measurement practice, 204-206
vertical engagement, 9-11
vertical reporting, 262-267
videoconferencing, 181
Virgin America, 39
volume of mentions, monitoring, 228-230

W-X-Y-Z

Wal-Mart, 122

Wal-marting Across America blog, 122

Wieden+Kennedy, 143-144

window-breakers, responding to, 166

WOMMA (Word of Mouth Marketing Association), 121

Word of Mouth Marketing Association (WOMMA), 121

word-of-mouth, 10-11

yield

    financial value of, 253-255

    increasing, 39-40, 254-255

Zappos, 159

SOCIAL LOCATION MARKETING

Outshining Your Competitors on Foursquare, Gowalla, Yelp & Other Location Sharing Sites

SIMON SALT

SOCIAL MEDIA ROI

Managing and Measuring Social Media Efforts in Your Organization

OLIVIER BLANCHARD

BLOGGING TO DRIVE BUSINESS

Create and Maintain Valuable Customer Connections

ERIC BUTOW & REBECCA BOLLWITT

FACEBOOK MARKETING

THIRD EDITION

Designing Your Next Marketing Campaign

JUSTIN R. LEVY

que

Biz-Tech Series

Straightforward Strategies and Tactics for Business Today

The **Que Biz-Tech series** is designed for the legions of executives and marketers out there trying to come to grips with emerging technologies that can make or break their business. These books help the reader know what's important, what isn't, and provide deep inside know-how for entering the brave new world of business technology, covering topics such as mobile marketing, microblogging, and iPhone and iPad app marketing.

- Straightforward strategies and tactics for companies who are either using or will be using a new technology/product or way of thinking/ doing business

- Written by well-known industry experts in their respective fields— and designed to be an open platform for the author to teach a topic in the way he or she believes the audience will learn best

- Covers new technologies that companies must embrace to remain competitive in the marketplace and shows them how to maximize those technologies for profit

- Written with the marketing and business user in mind—these books meld solid technical know-how with corporate-savvy advice for improving the bottom line

Visit **quepublishing.com/biztech** to learn more about the **Que Biz-Tech series**

FREE Online Edition

Your purchase of **Social Media ROI** includes access to a free online edition for 45 days through the Safari Books Online subscription service. Nearly every Que book is available online through Safari Books Online, along with over 5,000 other technical books and videos from publishers such as Addison-Wesley Professional, Cisco Press, Exam Cram, IBM Press, O'Reilly, Prentice Hall, and Sams.

SAFARI BOOKS ONLINE allows you to search for a specific answer, cut and paste code, download chapters, and stay current with emerging technologies.

Activate your FREE Online Edition at
www.informit.com/safarifree

STEP 1: Enter the coupon code: RDPRSZG.

STEP 2: New Safari users, complete the brief registration form. Safari subscribers, just login.

If you have difficulty registering on Safari or accessing the online edition, please e-mail customer-service@safaribooksonline.com